D1380666

Global Justice, Natural Resources, and Climate Change

Global Justice, Natural Resources, and Climate Change

Megan Blomfield

OXFORD
UNIVERSITY PRESS

OXFORD
UNIVERSITY PRESS

Great Clarendon Street, Oxford, OX2 6DP,
United Kingdom

Oxford University Press is a department of the University of Oxford.
It furthers the University's objective of excellence in research, scholarship,
and education by publishing worldwide. Oxford is a registered trade mark of
Oxford University Press in the UK and in certain other countries

© Megan Blomfield 2019

The moral rights of the author have been asserted

Impression: 1

All rights reserved. No part of this publication may be reproduced, stored in
a retrieval system, or transmitted, in any form or by any means, without the
prior permission in writing of Oxford University Press, or as expressly permitted
by law, by licence or under terms agreed with the appropriate reprographics
rights organization. Enquiries concerning reproduction outside the scope of the
above should be sent to the Rights Department, Oxford University Press, at the
address above

You must not circulate this work in any other form
and you must impose this same condition on any acquirer

Published in the United States of America by Oxford University Press
198 Madison Avenue, New York, NY 10016, United States of America

British Library Cataloguing in Publication Data

Data available

Library of Congress Control Number: 2018961779

ISBN 978–0–19–879173–7

Printed and bound by
CPI Group (UK) Ltd, Croydon, CR0 4YY

Links to third party websites are provided by Oxford in good faith and
for information only. Oxford disclaims any responsibility for the materials
contained in any third party website referenced in this work.

Acknowledgements

I have been working on this text for a long time and have received a lot of help along the way. Firstly, from my PhD supervisor Chris Bertram, who guided me throughout my doctoral research with just the right mix of criticism and reassurance. I don't think I would have found my focus without Chris's guidance. He remains a valued colleague and friend and I am lucky to have him as a mentor. Then, my external examiner Simon Caney, without whose encouragement I doubt I would have pursued this as a book project. I am very grateful that Simon took the time to convince me this was worth attempting. Many others were exceptionally generous with their time and attention in giving feedback on written material, including Chris Armstrong, Tudor Baetu, Brian Berkey, Joanna Burch-Brown, Dan Butt, Stephanie Collins, Tim Fowler, Steve Gardiner, Bob Goodin, Tim Hayward, Lisa Herzog, Clare Heyward, Alex Levitov, Aaron Maltais, Alejandra Mancilla, Catriona McKinnon, Margaret Moore, Anne Newman, Cara Nine, Ed Page, Giles Pearson, Will Perry, Richard Pettigrew, Alan Ryan, Debra Satz, Emma Saunders-Hastings, Fabian Schuppert, Henry Shue, Patrick Taylor-Smith, Karim Thébault, Kyle Whyte, Han van Wietmarschen, and several anonymous reviewers for the *Journal of Political Philosophy*, *Res Publica*, and Oxford University Press.

This work is partly the product of my doctoral research at the University of Bristol, funded by a University of Bristol Postgraduate Research Scholarship, and postdoctoral work at the Stanford Center for Ethics in Society, funded by a McCoy Family Fellowship. I am very thankful and extremely privileged to have received this support.

An earlier version of Chapter Two is published as 'Global common resources and the just distribution of emission shares' (*Journal of Political Philosophy* 21 (3) (2013), 283–304). This material is reproduced with permission from Wiley-Blackwell. The version appearing in this work has been updated to include more recent literature on the topic and has been streamlined, particularly in the section concerning option one for the equal per capita view. Chapter Nine draws extensively on my paper 'Historical use of the climate sink' (*Res Publica* 22 (1) (2016), 67–81). This material is reproduced with permission from Springer under the Creative Commons Attribution License. Chapter Ten uses material from 'Climate change and the moral significance of historical injustice in natural resource governance' (in *The Ethics of Climate Governance*, ed. Catriona McKinnon and Aaron Maltais (Rowman & Littlefield International: 2015)). This material is reproduced with permission from Rowman & Littlefield International Limited.

Some of this material was presented at Ideals and Reality in Social Ethics 2013; MANCEPT Workshops in Political Theory 2013; the ECPR Joint Sessions of Workshops 2014; the Stanford Political Theory Workshop 2014; the University of Washington Rabinowitz Symposium 2015; and the University of Reading Climate, Territory & Natural Resources workshop 2017. I would like to thank the organizers and participants for the valuable feedback that I received at these events.

This book would have been much harder to write without the friendship and support of my fellow researchers and colleagues. There are too many people to list here, and many of them have already been mentioned above, but I would like to express my gratitude to Joanie Berry, Alexander Bird, Havi Carel, Anthony Everett, Josie Gill, Eve Hendrick, Jess Kaplan, Rosanna Keefe, Kerry McKenzie, John McTague, Samir Okasha, Tom Richardson, Tom Sperlinger, Giulia Terzian, and Dagmar Wilhelm, among others.

I am also indebted to my parents and sister, for being a constant source of support; and my remarkable friends, for providing much-needed distractions—particularly D, J, E, and R, who have lived with and sustained me during difficult periods of writing. And above all to B, for everything.

Contents

Part I
Climate Justice

1

Introduction: Global Justice and Climate Change

It is commonly recognized that in pursuit of climate justice, various conflicting claims over natural resources must be navigated. This has long been obvious in the case of fossil fuels and greenhouse gas sinks including the atmosphere, forests, and oceans; but it is also becoming increasingly apparent that many ways of responding to climate change could spur new competition over land and extractive resources. This makes climate change an instance of a broader, more enduring and—for many—all too familiar problem: the problem of human conflict over how the natural world should be cared for, protected, shared, and used.

The struggles over natural resources that arise in the context of climate change are many and varied. Consider, first, the swelling opposition to continued fossil fuel exploitation in places like Alberta, Canada. Thought to contain one of the largest reserves of oil in the world, the Alberta bitumen sands can only be exploited via extraction techniques that are highly polluting and that wreak destruction on the local environment, including the land and natural resources of indigenous communities.[1] Such extraction is also extremely energy intensive, with a high 'well-to-wheel' carbon footprint compared to conventional oil.[2] There have been ongoing disputes about the extraction of this resource and its intended transportation via the construction of new pipelines, some of which are planned to cross unceded First Nations territory.[3] These clashes have seen environmentalists from across the world siding with local indigenous communities to protest bitumen

---

[1] See Indigenous Environmental Network n.d.

[2] See Swart & Weaver 2012: 135; Brandt et al. 2013: 701.

[3] The Kinder Morgan pipeline, for example, is proposed to cross 518km of Secwepemc territory, which is unceded land in the sense that 'the proper title and rights holders are the Secwepemc people, according to both the Supreme Court of Canada and to the Indigenous laws of the territory' (Indigenous Network on Economies and Trade 2017: 3).

sands development.[4] The Canadian government, on the other hand, has used claims of national ownership and arguments about economic benefit to defend the exploitation of this resource (see Oliver 2012).

In Ecuador, a different approach was initially taken to the oil below Yasuní National Park. There are an estimated 846 million barrels of oil in this reserve, below an area of Ecuador that is known for its biodiversity and is home to the voluntarily isolated Tagaeri and Taromenane indigenous peoples. The government of Ecuador—claiming to have the support of 78 per cent of the population—offered to forgo the economic benefits of extraction if the rest of the world would provide 'compensation' of US$3.6bn.[5] This figure was supposed to represent half the loss of income to Ecuador from preserving Yasuní, with 'the balance being the contribution of the people of Ecuador to global goods' (UNDP 2013). Proponents of the Yasuní Initiative pointed to the significant benefits that would result from leaving the oil in the ground and preserving the rainforest, for example due to the millions of tons of CO_2 emissions that would be avoided. In 2013, the initiative was abandoned after failing to secure sufficient pledges of international funding (see Valencia 2013).

Forest preservation schemes can provoke conflict even when fossil fuels do not complicate the picture. Take, for example, the UN's REDD+ (Reducing Emissions from Deforestation and Forest Degradation) programme. This initiative 'creates a financial value for the carbon stored in forests', providing developing countries with incentives to conserve and reduce emissions from forested lands (see UN 2016). The scheme is promoted by the UN, seeks to encourage private sector investment, and possesses obvious appeal for some in forest-rich developing states. REDD+ has, however, also been opposed by many, notably including indigenous peoples and other local communities who worry about the impacts of the programme on forest-dwelling peoples. There are reasonable fears that the new financial value placed on forests, and the incentives thereby created, can result in the dispossession of forest peoples with insecure resource tenure, interference with traditional use and management of forests, and local groups being marginalized from decision-making concerning these resources as control over them is recentralized (see Cotula & Mayers 2009; Phelps et al. 2010). Many allegations of rights abuses have already been documented (Barletti & Larson 2017). Some indigenous environmentalists also object to REDD+ because it represents a further intrusion of commodity markets into the natural world (Indigenous Environmental Network 2015).

Large-scale renewable energy schemes may also fuel natural resource conflicts, insofar as they demand metals and minerals for the manufacture of their

---

[4] See, for example, Greenpeace 2016.
[5] Ecuador Yasuní ITT Initiative Fact Sheet (downloaded from UNDP 2013).

technologies (see Arrobas et al. 2017), or significant tracts of land for their implementation. Consider, for example, the problem of land-grabbing for biofuels in Africa. Biofuels (fuels made from plant material) are promoted as an important means of reducing emissions from transport, but large plantations are required for their manufacture. Whilst biofuel production is largely driven by mitigation targets adopted in wealthier states with a history of high per capita car and fuel use, many of the plantations are in poorer countries. Some hope that biofuel investment has the potential to reduce poverty here, but there is evidence to suggest that this will only be the case if there is prior security of land tenure. Where the interests of those who live on the land can be ignored by foreign investors or their own government, poorer groups can lose access to the land that they depend upon. In such cases, the spread of biofuel plantations 'can have major negative effects on local food security and on the economic, social and cultural dimensions of land use' (Cotula et al. 2008: 2). Biofuel production may also have harmful knock-on effects for global food prices by reducing the amount of land devoted to agriculture (HLPE 2013). Similar worries about the displacement of existing communities and destruction of valued natural resources have been raised about other methods of renewable energy production, such as hydroelectric dams.[6]

These are only a few examples of the conflicts over natural resources that are being generated, or exacerbated, by climate change. Dealing with climate change fairly will involve adjudicating between such claims. Growing awareness of these conflicts may help to explain why many academic philosophers have been returning to the question of the just allocation of natural resource rights.[7] As many are recognizing, our answers to this question promise to be informative regarding the problem of climate change.

In this work, I aim to deliver on this promise by examining the problem of climate change in the light of a new theory of justice for natural resources. This theory is novel in carving out a space between two common but oppositional views concerning natural resource justice: namely, natural resource sovereignty and distributive equality. Roughly speaking, the former view prioritizes state or national control over territorial resources and resists redistribution in pursuit of equality, whilst the latter defends equality of natural resources shares irrespective of state or national membership. In the middle section of this work, on Natural Resource Justice, I argue that natural resources are indeed appropriate objects of egalitarian justice, because all human beings have an equal original claim to them. However, this does not entail that

---

[6] See, for example, the protests surrounding the Belo Monte dam (Cultural Survival 2013).
[7] See, for example: Armstrong 2017; Blake & Risse 2007; Casal 2011; Fabre 2005; Hayward 2006; Kolers 2012; Mancilla 2016a; Mazor 2010; Miller 2012; Moore 2012; Nine 2013; Pogge 2011; Risse 2012, Part 2; Schuppert 2014; Steiner 2011b; and Wenar 2016.

individuals are entitled to substantively equal *shares* of the world's resources, but rather that any theory of natural resource rights must be justified from a perspective that respects the equal *standing* that every individual possesses as a co-claimant.

The principles of natural resource right justified from this perspective will, I argue, be ones designed to protect the ability of all human beings to satisfy their basic needs as members of self-determining political communities, where I take it that the genuine exercise of self-determination is not possible for communities that occupy a position of significant disadvantage in global wealth and power relations. These principles will underwrite a system of resource rights that endows each political community with a presumptive right of jurisdiction over the land and surface resources of a region, subject to various important restrictions. I term this a system of *limited territorial jurisdiction* over natural resources and conclude that this, rather than equal shares, is what natural resource egalitarianism really demands. The resulting view offers a more principled, though more qualified, defence for some of the key resource rights that proponents of natural resource sovereignty seek to protect, thereby defusing their objection to natural resource egalitarianism.

Having defended this theory of justice for natural resources, in the final section of this work I return to explore some of its implications regarding the problem of climate change. I use my conception of natural resource justice to address the question of where to set the ceiling on future greenhouse gas (GHG) emissions and how to share the resulting emissions budget, in the face of conflicting claims to fossil fuels, climate sinks, and land. I also defend an unorthodox understanding of historical accountability for the problem of climate change, based on its provenance in past injustices concerning various natural resources.

In what remains of this introductory chapter, I provide some necessary background for the discussion to follow. I start by explaining the physical phenomenon of climate change and the options for responding to it (§1.1). I then briefly introduce the debate about global justice and climate change, as it has appeared in one major branch of the philosophical literature concerning this topic (§1.2). After providing further characterization of, and motivation for, my own approach to climate justice (§1.3), I conclude with an outline of the chapters to follow (§1.4).

1.1 Climate change

In this section I explain the basic science of climate change, identify many of its expected impacts, and outline some potential responses. In presenting this information I will draw heavily on the reports of the Intergovernmental Panel on Climate Change (IPCC). The IPCC, acting under the auspices of the UN, is the international body charged with periodically collating and reviewing scientific research on climate change. It is widely considered to be the go-to authority on climate science and I will be relying on it as such. This choice is not without problems, as many believe the IPCC to be too conservative in its climate predictions.[8] The information provided by the IPCC reports will nevertheless suffice for the purposes of my arguments here.

1.1.1 *The science*

To explain the process of climate change, it helps to start by defining what scientists are referring to when they talk about the 'climate'. I will be using the narrow definition of climate given by the IPCC as 'the average weather . . . over a period of time ranging from months to thousands or millions of years'; where the average weather is given in terms of a statistical description of certain relevant variables, such as temperature and precipitation (IPCC 2013: 1450). Climate in this narrow sense is determined by the state of the climate system: 'a complex, interactive system consisting of the atmosphere, land surface, snow and ice, oceans and other bodies of water, and living things'. This system is powered by solar radiation and evolves over time, influenced by its own internal dynamics but also by *external forcings* (factors outside the climate system itself) such as volcanic eruptions and human activities (IPCC 2007a: 96).

The atmosphere is the component of the climate system consisting of 'The gaseous envelope surrounding the Earth' (IPCC 2013: 1448). Numerous gases compose the atmosphere: mostly nitrogen and oxygen, but also GHGs—the primary species of which are water vapour, carbon dioxide (CO_2), methane (CH_4), nitrous oxide (N_2O), and ozone (IPCC 2013: 1455). GHGs are added to the atmosphere via various natural processes (such as respiration and decay), and are removed from the atmosphere by mechanisms termed *sinks*. The main sink for CH_4, for example, is atmospheric reaction with the hydroxyl radical (IPCC 2013: 167). CO_2, on the other hand, is removed from the atmosphere by vegetation, soils, and the ocean (IPCC 2013: 544–5).

GHGs play a significant role in the climate system. When solar energy reaches the surface of the Earth, some of it is emitted outwards again in the form of infrared radiation. In the phenomenon known as the greenhouse effect, GHGs act like a sort of blanket to prevent some of this radiation from escaping, trapping heat in the lower atmosphere (IPCC 2007a: 115). The natural greenhouse effect—resulting from the natural presence of GHGs in the atmosphere—makes life as we know it possible, because without it the

---

[8] See, for example, Brysse et al. 2013.

average temperature at the surface of the Earth would be below freezing (IPCC 2007a: 115).

Climate change is said to occur when there is a change in the properties of the climate that persists over an extended period—'typically decades or longer' (IPCC 2013: 1450). *Anthropogenic* climate change takes place when such change in the climate results from anthropogenic external forcings on the climate system. Anthropogenic external forcings include land use change and other activities that alter the composition of the atmosphere. To list some major examples: burning fossil fuels releases GHGs into the atmosphere; deforestation reduces the amount of vegetation acting as a carbon sink, leading to increased concentrations of CO_2, and is usually accompanied by GHG emissions from the burning of biomass; and agriculture raises atmospheric concentrations of CH_4 and N_2O (IPCC 2007a: 2–3).

By increasing atmospheric concentrations of GHGs, these human activities enhance the greenhouse effect. This changes the Earth's energy budget, with significant consequences for the evolution of the climate system. That the climate system has warmed is 'unequivocal', with many of the changes observed since the 1950s 'unprecedented over decades to millennia' (IPCC 2013: 4). In three out of the four future climate policy scenarios considered by the IPCC in its 2013 report, global surface temperature for the end of the twenty-first century was found '*likely* to exceed 1.5°C relative to 1850 to 1900' and *more likely than not* to exceed 2°C (IPCC 2013: 20).[9]

As more heat is trapped in the lower atmosphere, large amounts of ice will melt (adding water to the ocean) and the ocean will heat up (leading it to expand). Sea level is already rising as a consequence and it is *virtually certain* that it will continue to do so during the twenty-first century and beyond—though the exact magnitude is difficult to predict (IPCC 2013: 1204–5). This heating of the ocean, combined with the fact that a warmer atmosphere holds more water, will lead to an increase of water vapour in the atmosphere. As a result, it is *virtually certain* that precipitation will increase globally and *likely* that it will become more intense. Atmospheric and oceanic circulation patterns are also *likely* to be impacted, with effects that are hard to predict (IPCC 2013: 1032–3).

The strength of different natural and anthropogenic drivers of climate change is assessed in terms of a metric called 'radiative forcing' (RF). Factors

---

[9] In order to provide projections of climate change, the IPCC has to make assumptions about future GHG emissions and other climate forcings. In the 2013 report, these hypothetical future scenarios are termed 'Representative Concentration Pathways' and are used to consider 'a range of 21st century climate policies' (IPCC 2013: 29). The following expressions are used to state the IPCC's evaluation of the likelihoods of certain outcomes: *virtually certain* (99–100% probability); *very likely* (90 to 100%); *likely* (66 to 100%); and *more likely than not* (>50–100%). Italics are used to indicate that these terms should be understood in a technical sense (IPCC 2013: 36).

with positive RF lead to an increase in global surface temperature whilst factors with negative RF lead to a decrease, and RF in watts per metre squared (Wm^{-2}) can be used as an index to compare the significance of different anthropogenic influences on the climate system. By 2011, for example, the principal GHGs emitted by human activities—CO_2, CH_4, halocarbons, and N_2O—were estimated to have RF values of 1.68, 0.97, 0.18, and 0.17 Wm^{-2} respectively (IPCC 2013: 13–14). This is what makes CO_2 the 'most important' anthropogenic GHG, with cumulative CO_2 emissions from human activities identified as being 'the single largest anthropogenic factor contributing to climate change' (IPCC 2007a: 2, 511).

1.1.2 The impacts

The impacts of climate change are already being observed (see, e.g., IPCC 2007b: Ch. 1). As atmospheric concentrations of GHGs increase, so will the likelihood of severe impacts such as sea level rise and coastal flooding, storm surges, extreme weather events, heatwaves, drought, and flooding. These impacts threaten knock-on effects including ecosystem and biodiversity loss, disruption to livelihoods, food insecurity, water scarcity, breakdown of infrastructure and critical services, injury, ill health, and death (IPCC 2014a: 13).

These risks affect vast numbers of people. Over the next century, for example, the IPCC concludes that climate change 'is *likely* to adversely affect hundreds of millions of people through increased coastal flooding, reductions in water supplies, increased malnutrition and increased health impacts' (IPCC 2007d: 65). The World Health Organization estimates that climate change is already causing over 150,000 deaths each year (WHO 2018).[10] Furthermore, climate-related risk is unevenly distributed and particularly high for already disadvantaged and marginalized individuals and communities—including those located within affluent countries (IPCC 2014a: 12). The reasons why certain individuals and communities are at greater risk than others are complex and will be discussed further in Chapter Ten, but some significant drivers of such risk include poverty, 'scarcity of livelihood options for the poor' and 'lack of . . . social support mechanisms' (IPCC 2012: 70).

1.1.3 The options

As explained in §1.1.2, if nothing is done to address climate change, it can be expected to have grave consequences for vast numbers of human beings. From

---

[10] Non-profit humanitarian organization DARA, on the other hand, estimated in 2012 that climate change was causing '400,000 deaths each year on average', largely due to hunger and an increase in communicable disease (DARA 2012: 17).

this, it seems impossible to avoid the conclusion that there is a strong moral imperative to take action on climate change.[11] I will discuss some significant positions that have been taken on the normative dimensions of this issue—and the questions of justice that it raises—in §1.2. First, however, I will outline the available means for responding to the problem. Whilst it is not difficult to conclude that something must be done about climate change, it is harder to say exactly what, and by whom. Knowing the options is a first step.

State cooperation on climate change is taking place under the auspices of the United Nations Framework Convention on Climate Change (UNFCCC). The UNFCCC has near universal membership: 196 countries have signed up to this convention and meet at a yearly conference of the parties (COP), where international strategies for dealing with climate change are discussed and decided upon. There are various options here, which are generally demarcated using two broad categories: mitigation, which covers actions designed to prevent or reduce the progress of climate change; and adaptation, which encompasses actions intended to counter the negative effects of the climate change that is not avoided.

Mitigation options are often discussed before adaptation, partly because the level of success regarding the former will largely determine how much—and what kind—of the latter will be needed in the future. It is clear, however, that a mix of both policies will have to be employed to successfully reduce the negative impacts of climate change. Without some mitigation, the effects of climate change will exceed the capacity of natural and human systems to adapt; whilst even immediate, extremely aggressive mitigation policies will not suffice to address the significant climate impacts that are already taking place, or have been locked in for the future.

Mitigation has two essential components: the reduction of global GHG emissions and the enhancement of global climate sinks. Emissions can be prevented by reducing energy use (via either a reduction in consumption or an increase in efficiency); switching to fossil fuels with a lower emissions profile; developing carbon capture and storage capability; replacing methods of energy production that utilize fossil fuels with carbon-neutral techniques (either renewable or nuclear); adjusting agricultural practices; and reducing the burning of biomass that accompanies deforestation. Climate sinks can be enhanced by preserving and maintaining existing forests, reforestation, afforestation, and utilization of land management techniques that improve soil carbon storage.[12]

---

[11] For several arguments to this effect, see Roser and Seidel 2017: Part 1.

[12] For more detail on how these broad techniques would be implemented in practice, see IPCC 2007c: 10.

Adaptation, on the other hand, refers to an adjustment in natural or human systems in response to actual or expected climate impacts, in a way that 'moderates harm or exploits beneficial opportunities'. Such adaptation can be anticipatory or reactive (IPCC 2007b: 869). Examples of anticipatory adaptations include the development of seasonal climate forecasting capability, the building of coastal protection infrastructure, crop and livelihood diversification, insurance, and water storage. Reactive adaptations include disaster responses and migration (IPCC 2007b: 721).

Another potential climate response that is receiving increasing amounts of attention is geoengineering. Roughly speaking, geoengineering involves an intentional, large-scale modification of the Earth system (with the aim, in the present context, of counteracting climate change). An oft-cited report by The Royal Society identifies a diverse array of geoengineering proposals, which can be classified into two main groups. The first type—Carbon Dioxide Removal—includes techniques such as engineered capture of CO_2 directly from the air and fertilization of the world's oceans to enhance CO_2 uptake (The Royal Society 2009: 9–21). The second—Solar Radiation Management (SRM)—refers to methods designed to increase the Earth's albedo (the fraction of solar radiation that it reflects) or divert incoming solar radiation. Suggested SRM techniques include planting more reflective crops, building large-scale reflective surfaces in the desert, whitening clouds, releasing aerosols into the stratosphere to reflect incoming sunlight, and even positioning sun shields in space (The Royal Society 2009: 23–36). I will not discuss geoengineering further in what follows. Elsewhere, I argue that when geoengineering techniques are designed to have global effects, research attempting to reduce uncertainty about the nature and regional distribution of those effects should be delayed until institutions that can ensure the fair global governance of such technologies have been established (Blomfield 2015b).[13]

Finally, where adaptation to climate change is not possible—or leaves individuals and collectives worse off than they ought to be—the question arises whether there are duties of compensation to be discharged and if so, by whom. This is a pressing concern. Scientists suggest that 'Many communities in highly vulnerable regions—such as the Arctic—are already facing limits in their capacity to adapt, and losses that are difficult to compensate for' (Dow et al. 2013: 307). Impacts that seem to demand some efforts at compensation or rectification include death and injury, displacement, and destruction of or damage to resources.

---

[13] In brief, this is because such research—*if* it can succeed in predicting the likely regional distribution of geoengineering impacts—threatens to identify the winners and losers of different deployment options. This could undermine the establishment of fair and effective global governance by revealing divergent national interests with respect to different regulatory schemes.

1.2 Global justice and climate change

An obligation to tackle climate change can be defended from the perspective of many different and competing ethical theories. Such defences might invoke a duty not to harm, or a duty to protect others from harm; an obligation to help the least well off, the vulnerable, or those in need; an obligation to promote or maximize the goods of human autonomy, well-being, capabilities, or flourishing; or a non-anthropocentric duty to care for the natural world or the creatures that inhabit it.

Many theorists have also deemed climate change an issue of global justice. In this section, I introduce the background literature on global justice from which some of this discussion emerges. I then outline several approaches that have been taken to understand climate change as a problem of global justice and identify some methodological issues that arise in this field. With this groundwork laid out, I will be able to characterize my own approach to climate justice in the subsequent section.

1.2.1 *The global justice debate*

In the field that I am schooled in, which some might term *Western political philosophy*,[14] much work on climate justice interestingly seems to emerge from a literature that had largely been focused on discussing whether any significant principles of justice apply at the global level at all.[15]

A major facet of this preceding debate concerns the *scope of application* for egalitarian principles of justice. Egalitarian principles of justice insist that certain distributive or social inequalities, between the individuals to which those principles apply, should be limited or eradicated. Egalitarian principles of *distributive* justice include those demanding that individuals be granted strictly equal shares of some good and more loosely egalitarian distributive rules such as John Rawls's difference principle (according to which departures from equal shares are permitted, but only if they improve the position of the least advantaged (see Rawls 1999a: 65–8)). Exactly what it is that individuals should have (more) equal shares of is a matter of some debate, with candidates including welfare, resources, natural resources, capabilities, and rights. Principles of *relational* egalitarianism, on the other hand, demand that individuals be secured with equal respect, power, status, or standing; or equality in social and political relationships.

Those debating the scope of egalitarian principles of justice argue about whether they apply at the global level (demanding some form of global

---

[14] See, for example, Mills 2015.   [15] For a survey of this literature, see Blake & Smith 2015.

distributive or relational equality), or only within separate political communities. The positions roughly characterizing the two sides of this disagreement can be termed 'global egalitarianism' and 'statism', respectively. I use statism as a label for a family of views characterized by two fundamental commitments: firstly, *relationism* about the grounds of egalitarian justice, according to which egalitarian principles of justice only apply to individuals that stand in certain 'practice-mediated relations' (Risse 2012: 7–8; see also Sangiovanni 2007: 5); and secondly, the *statist scope thesis*,[16] according to which the relevant practice-mediated relationship only holds between co-members of a state (or people), co-nationals, or those who share domestic institutions.[17] Examples of some of the practice-based relations that might be invoked by statists include common culture, shared subjection to coercion, socio-economic cooperation, or reciprocity. The terminology used here has the potential to be confusing, and it is important to clearly distinguish between relationism about the *grounds* of egalitarian justice and relational egalitarianism. The former is a view about *why*—and to whom—principles of egalitarianism apply, whilst the latter is a view about the *kind* of equality that principles of egalitarianism demand.

Given their core commitments, statists either hold that no principles of justice apply at the global level, or that any such principles are not egalitarian in nature. Often, statists accept global principles of a *sufficientarian* kind, where a sufficientarian principle of justice demands that everybody within its scope be provided with *enough* of something in particular, remaining silent on inequalities above this threshold. For example, though a statist might insist that egalitarian principles of justice only apply to co-nationals, they may well also hold that at the global level, justice demands that everyone be over the threshold defined by human rights satisfaction.

Global egalitarians defend the opposing view that there exist egalitarian principles of justice with global scope. This position may also be defended on grounds of relationism, often via analogy arguments that aim to show that a given practice-mediated relation used to defend the statist scope thesis (e.g. cooperation) is in fact instantiated globally. Alternatively, one might defend global egalitarianism by rejecting relationism in favour of *nonrelationism* about the grounds of egalitarian justice. Nonrelationists about the grounds of egalitarian justice take egalitarian principles to apply to all human beings in virtue of certain characteristics that they share (based on their common humanity, for example), independently of any practice-mediated relations in which they

---

[16] This term is from Caney 2008: 488.

[17] Exactly how to characterize the group to which egalitarian principles are claimed to apply is a matter of some disagreement. I use the term 'statist' to refer to all the views within this group—not only those that take states to be the pertinent entities for egalitarian justice.

may stand. Bearing in mind the distinction between relationism about the *grounds* of egalitarian justice, and relational *forms* of egalitarianism, one should note that a theorist might well appeal to nonrelationist grounds when attempting to defend principles of relational egalitarianism with global scope.

This debate can be illustrated by the disagreement between John Rawls (a statist) and Charles Beitz (a global egalitarian), concerning whether principles of egalitarian justice with global scope can be defended by means of contractualism (the significance of this example will become clear in Chapter Five, where I draw on both theorists to develop a contractualist theory of natural resource justice). Roughly speaking, contractualism is the view that the correct conception of justice is one that would be agreed to in an appropriate hypothetical contract between all those that will be subject to its principles. In *A Theory of Justice*, Rawls famously models this hypothetical agreement using a device called the original position. In the imagined situation of Rawls's original position, parties representing co-citizens seek agreement on principles of domestic justice to govern the 'basic structure' of their society. The parties seek this agreement from behind the 'veil of ignorance', which shields them from any knowledge of their individual circumstances, such as their social status, natural abilities, or conceptions of the good (Rawls 1999a: 7–11). These epistemic restrictions are designed to ensure that the parties will reason impartially—and thus that the principles agreed to will be fair. From this situation, Rawls argues, one principle agreed to would be the difference principle, according to which social and economic inequalities will only be permitted when they are 'to the greatest benefit of the least advantaged' in society (1999a: 266).

Rawls's defence of egalitarianism does not, however, extend to the global level. In his later book, *The Law of Peoples*, Rawls does accept that original position reasoning should be used to defend principles of global justice, but he here deploys what I will term an *international* original position (where the parties are representatives of societies), rather than a *cosmopolitan* original position (where the parties would be representatives of individuals) (Rawls 1999b: 32–3, 82–3). From this international original position, Rawls argues, parties representing separate peoples would only agree to relatively minimal principles of global justice, including respect for human rights and a sufficientarian duty of assistance (1999b: 37).

Beitz is one of several theorists to criticize Rawls for this disparity by arguing that the original position is correctly deployed in defence of global egalitarianism.[18] First, Beitz claims, even in an *international* original position, parties representing societies that are ignorant of the natural endowment of their

---

[18] See also B. Barry 1973: 128–33; Pogge 1989: §22.

own territory would agree to an egalitarian resource redistribution principle (RRP), designed to mitigate natural resource inequalities (1979: §3.2). But furthermore, Beitz argues, principles of global justice should really be considered from the perspective of a *cosmopolitan* original position, where the parties represent individuals ignorant of their nationality. Beitz imagines that the parties in this cosmopolitan original position will reason analogously to those in Rawls's domestic original position, entailing that the difference principle will again be accepted and thus have global scope (Beitz 1979: 151). Originally, Beitz defends his global egalitarianism by appeal to relationist grounds, arguing that the original position should be cosmopolitan due to the existence of relations of global cooperation (1979: 143–53). Later, he gives a nonrelationist defence instead, arguing that the original position should be cosmopolitan because all individuals are in possession of Rawls's two moral powers (Beitz 1983: 595). In response to defences of global egalitarianism along these lines, numerous statist theorists have argued on grounds of relationism that original position reasoning is not appropriate at the global level. These arguments will be discussed further in §5.3.1.

1.2.2 *Some approaches to climate justice*

Against this background, several approaches have been taken to understanding climate change as a problem of global justice, three of which are introduced in this section. The first explores climate change as a human rights issue; the second, as a problem of distributive justice; and the third, as a problem of natural resource justice. As will become clear, these approaches are not mutually exclusive. A single theorist may consistently accept principles of justice concerning human rights, natural resources, and the global distribution of certain goods; all of which might be fruitfully applied to the problem of climate change.

The human rights approach to climate justice starts from an assumption that global justice demands respect for certain rights that are universally held (possessed, that is, by all human beings); and argues that climate change is a problem of global justice because it consists in, or threatens to result in, widespread violation of such rights. These accounts focus on claim-rights, which are supposed to come with correlative duties of provision or non-interference. This allows theorists to argue that certain climate policies must be adopted if the duties correlative to human rights are to be discharged; and that certain of those who contribute to climate change, or fail to protect others from climate change, contravene this system of rights and duties.[19]

---

[19] See the collection of papers in Humphreys 2010. Bell (2013a) provides an overview of the human rights approach to climate change.

The set of rights in question could be minimal or expansive. Some focus mainly on the right not to be harmed, for example,[20] whilst others discuss the normative dimensions of climate change with respect to a wider set of human rights. Within the latter category, some attempt to avoid controversy by focusing only on basic human rights that they hope will be broadly accepted (to life, security, subsistence or health, say),[21] whilst others attempt defences of new, *climate-related* human rights. Steve Vanderheiden, for example, proposes a universal right to a stable climate (2008a: 246); whilst Henry Shue suggests that there is 'a universal right to a minimum share of emissions' (2014: 116)—a view that Vanderheiden also shares (2008a: 247).

The more conservative rights-based approaches to climate justice can potentially draw quite broad support given that even theorists who are otherwise sceptical about principles of global justice tend to accept that duties to respect at least certain *basic* human rights apply globally.[22] Depending on the nature of one's full theory of global justice one may or may not claim that once everybody's rights are satisfied, no further duties of justice exist at the global level. A human rights approach to global justice might, that is, be statist and sufficientarian in nature: holding that global inequalities persisting beyond the normative threshold represented by those rights do not matter from the perspective of justice. Alternatively, the human rights theorist might also accept additional, egalitarian principles of global justice. Caney is an example of such a theorist. A strong advocate of the human rights approach, Caney is also clear that he takes human rights to be 'only part of a complete political morality', albeit the most fundamental part (2010: 165). In accordance with this, Caney also adopts the second approach to climate justice: that which treats climate change as a *problem of global distributive justice* that may need to be governed by more egalitarian principles.

On this distributive justice approach, some take climate change to be a *counterexample* that undermines statist theories of global justice. Caney, for example, takes the problem of climate change both to undermine the statist scope thesis and to suggest that egalitarian principles could well apply at the global level (2008: 508–10).[23] This is because climate change is a 'paradigmatic case where principles of distributive justice apply', since (Caney 2008: 497):

---

[20] See Baer 2010; Brooks 2012; Broome 2012: Ch. 5; Cripps 2011b.

[21] Bell 2011a; Caney 2010.

[22] Statists Rawls (1999b: 65) and Miller (2007: Ch. 7), for example, accept basic human rights as a standard of global justice.

[23] Caney claims climate change provides reason to think that principles of distributive justice either apply to all those who stand in relations of causal interdependence, or apply to all individuals in virtue of their common humanity (2008: 497, 515, fn.15). Chris Armstrong similarly suggests that climate change poses a 'serious challenge' for 'minimalist' accounts of global justice (according to which every human being only needs to be secured with 'access to the conditions of a decent or minimally decent life') and lends plausibility to solutions of a global egalitarian nature (2012: 12, 194). Arash Abizadeh considers the problem of atmospheric pollution

there is a global process leading to the production of benefits (those who benefit from activities producing greenhouse gases) and burdens (dangerous climate change). Given such circumstances, principles of distributive justice are required to govern this process and to regulate the distribution of the opportunity to emit greenhouse gases and the distribution of the burdens of adaptation.

Furthermore, it seems that climate change, left unchecked, will give rise to a distribution of benefits and burdens that is prima facie unfair. Roughly speaking, those that have benefited from high emissions of GHGs are generally wealthy and less vulnerable to climate impacts, whilst low emitters tend to be the poor and most at risk. Many have concluded from this that climate change should be addressed using principles of global distributive justice.

Those who view climate change as problem of distributive justice often focus on the question of how to distribute a specific type of climate-related benefit or burden; the benefits and burdens in question often being the opportunity to emit GHGs and the financial costs of dealing with climate change, respectively. Those focusing on the benefit of GHG emission entitlements frequently discuss the choice between an equal per capita view and the 'grandfathering' approach (according to which emission entitlements should be distributed on the basis of previous levels).[24] Those taking the 'burden-sharing' approach,[25] on the other hand, commonly debate whether the costs of dealing with climate change should be allocated on the basis of causal responsibility (often referred to as the 'polluter pays principle'), ability to pay, or to those who have benefited from the emissions that cause climate change.[26]

Within discussions of the just distribution of GHG emissions, it is common to come across what I have termed the third approach to climate justice: that which considers climate change *as a problem of natural resource justice*. Natural resources have been a concern of political theorists since at least the seventeenth century, when writers such as Hugo Grotius and John Locke debated how the

to be informative about global justice (and its grounds), claiming it to support the idea that 'the relevant existence condition for justice is simply the existence of pervasive impact on life chances', regardless of whether individuals stand in relations of social coordination or cooperation (2007: 339). And Vanderheiden claims that 'insofar as a justice community develops around issues on which peoples are interdependent and so must find defensible means of allocating scarce goods, global climate change presents a case in which the various arguments against cosmopolitan justice cease to apply' (2008a: 104).

[24] This would mean that higher emitters could continue to emit more than others. There are few philosophical defences of grandfathering. Bovens (2011); Knight (2013); and Schuessler (2017) are exceptions, although all endorse a moderate form of grandfathering, to be balanced against other demands of justice. Sufficientarian and prioritarian principles for the distribution of GHG emissions have also been proposed (see, for example, Shue 1993; Meyer & Roser 2006).

[25] Paul Baer coins this phrase explicitly in order to contrast the burden-sharing approach with a (natural) resource-sharing approach (2002: 395–6).

[26] See, for example, Caney 2005c; Page 2011; Shue 1999. As Caney and Page note, hybrid accounts are also possible.

removal of resources from the commons could be justified.[27] Locke, for example, claimed (very roughly speaking) that individuals could appropriate from the commons through labouring on land and resources, 'at least where there is enough, and as good left in common for others' (1690: V.27). This restriction has become known as the 'enough and as good' proviso on appropriation and could be given a sufficientarian ('enough') or an egalitarian ('as good') interpretation. Some advocates of left-libertarianism (a view characterized by a core belief that natural resources 'belong to everyone in some egalitarian sense' (Vallentyne, Steiner & Otsuka 2005: 201)) have been inspired by Locke to defend the principle of equal division, according to which the world's resources—or their value—should be shared on an equal per capita basis (see Steiner 2009: 5–6). More equitable sharing of natural resources has also been defended by liberal egalitarians including Brian Barry (1989: 515–16) and Beitz (as outlined in §1.2.1).

Many theorists have appealed to a global principle of natural resource egalitarianism to argue that unequal GHG emissions should be deemed unjust, because they entail unequal consumption of global climate sink capacity (a natural resource).[28] Luc Bovens (2011), on the other hand, uses a Locke-inspired argument about natural resource rights to provide some defence of grandfathering. Arguments from natural resource justice have also been used in attempts to show that historical high emitters have incurred some form of climate debt, stemming from their use of natural resources beyond a fair share.[29] Another popular focus for those considering the problem of climate change from the perspective of natural resource justice has been duties of forest sink preservation (see Armstrong 2016; Page 2016; Schuppert 2016). The approach has also been used to consider duties to refrain from exploiting fossil fuel reserves (Armstrong 2017: Ch. 10); rights of relocation for those displaced by climate impacts (Risse 2009); and issues of intergenerational justice in the context of climate change.[30] The natural resources approach has the potential to be applied much more broadly than this, however,[31] as I will demonstrate in the final part of this work.

These are not the only approaches one can take to understanding climate change as a problem of global justice. One could also, for example, consider

---

[27] See the collection of extracts in Vallentyne & Steiner 2000.

[28] See, for example, Athanasiou & Baer 2002: 64, 74; Broome 2012: 69–70; Vanderheiden 2008a: 223ff.

[29] See, for example, Athanasiou & Baer 2002: 82; Halme 2007; Hayward 2007: 445; Kartha 2011: 508–9; Neumayer 2000; and Sinden 2010. These views will be discussed further in Chapter Nine.

[30] See, for example, the symposium on 'Intergenerational Justice and Natural Resources' in *Moral Philosophy and Politics*, where all the papers 'place (to varying degrees) their discussions within the context of climate change' (Meyer, Sanklecha & Zellentin 2015: 1).

[31] This potential is noted in a 2016 special issue of the journal *Res Publica* on 'Justice, Climate Change, and the Distribution of Natural Resources' (Vol. 22, Issue 1). See also Ayelet Banai's 2016 review article titled 'Sovereignty over natural resources and its implications for climate justice'.

climate change as a problem of procedural justice, assessing the fairness of the institutions and processes via which international collective action is decided;[32] as a problem of cultural injustice, for example towards indigenous peoples;[33] or as a problem of justice from the perspective of collective rights, such as the right to collective self-determination.[34]

1.2.3 Two methodological distinctions

Before continuing, there are two methodological distinctions pertinent to the climate justice literature that should be noted: integrationism versus isolationism; and ideal versus nonideal theory.

ISOLATIONISM VERSUS INTEGRATIONISM

Caney helpfully outlines two distinctions with which we can categorize theories of climate justice. Firstly, we can distinguish between 'atomist' or 'holist' positions *within* climate justice. These positions represent the two extremes along a scale of approaches: with holists seeking principles of justice that are informative about the whole set of responsibilities relating to climate change; atomists attempting to provide principles for *particular* climate responsibilities (e.g. to reduce emissions) in abstraction from all others; and other views potentially falling somewhere in between.

Secondly, one can distinguish between those who take an isolationist or an integrationist approach to climate justice with respect to global justice more broadly. Isolationists treat climate change as an issue that can or should be dealt with independently of other matters of global justice, whilst integrationists seek to situate their theory of climate justice within a broader account of what global justice requires (Caney 2012: 258–9).[35] We might further differentiate between full or partial forms of integrationism about climate justice: where the former is an attempt to draw normative conclusions about climate change by reference to what purports to be a comprehensive theory of global justice, but the latter draws on a more limited conception of the demands of justice at the global level.

Some claim that isolationist and atomist accounts should be considered complementary to holist and integrationist accounts (see Zellentin 2015a). Whether or not this is the case, when such accounts diverge in their assessments and recommendations concerning climate justice, theorists must defend their choice of methodology. Caney advocates an integrationist (and holist) approach to climate justice.[36] Those defending the alternative,

---

[32] See, for example, Eckersley 2012; Shue 1992; Wong 2016.
[33] See Figueroa 2011; Heyward 2014.   [34] See, for example, Nine 2010; Tsosie 2007a.
[35] See also Caney 2018.
[36] See also Caney 2009: 137. Other defences of integrationism include: Bell 2013b: 198–202; Shue 1992.

isolationist approach may claim that concerns of climate justice should be kept separate from other concerns of global justice on grounds of principle (see Posner & Weisbach 2010: Ch. 4). Alternatively, theorists may accept that integrationism is the superior approach in principle, but argue that we nevertheless have *pragmatic* reasons to take an isolationist approach to some questions of climate justice.

Axel Gosseries, for example, claims that a 'first-best' approach would consider climate change from the perspective of a general theory of egalitarian justice (2005: 306). For pragmatic reasons, however, he chooses to adopt isolationism in a paper discussing justice in climate mitigation, where he proposes that global egalitarians may usefully focus only on 'inequalities that are directly related with the climate change problem, or inequalities arising from the level of GHG-inducing activities and the impact of the greenhouse effect', independent of more general distributive concerns (Gosseries 2005: 283). Gosseries' pragmatic reasons for this isolationist move are twofold, relating to tractability and feasibility. Most importantly, he claims, such isolationism may help to clarify things 'before getting involved in a more complex "all-things-considered" enterprise'. But also, he assumes that integrationism will support 'politically more ambitious targets', and suggests that it is worth seeing how demanding a more minimal approach might be in the first instance (Gosseries 2005: 283).[37] For Gosseries, then, the method of isolationism—though admittedly *'second-best'*—has distinct merits of its own. Furthermore, it reveals that current efforts are falling short of what climate justice demands regardless of which methodological approach is taken (Gosseries 2005: 306).[38]

IDEAL VERSUS NONIDEAL THEORY

By talking in terms of first- and second-best approaches to climate justice, Gosseries gestures towards another important—though very contested—methodological distinction in political philosophy: that of ideal versus nonideal theory.

---

[37] In fact, Gosseries worries that pursuit of the more demanding climate policies supported by integrationism could backfire significantly, resulting in total failure to set up a climate regime (2005: 306).

[38] Gosseries uses different terminology to Caney, but appears to be latching on to the same distinction. Instead of talking in terms of integrationism versus isolationism, Gosseries contrasts a 'general' or 'all-things-considered' approach with a 'local justice' or 'problem-specific' one (2005: 282–3). Lukas Meyer and Dominic Roser, who take an atomist isolationist approach to the allocation of emission rights for reasons of tractability (Meyer & Roser 2006: 239) and 'political reality' (2010: 233), similarly accept that it would yet be 'desirable' to integrate this discussion 'with the background distribution of other goods' (2010: 247). Zellentin also cites the complexity of the climate change problem and concerns of feasibility to support an argument that isolationist (and atomist) approaches to climate justice have certain advantages, concluding that they should be developed *alongside* holist and integrationist proposals (2015a: 123). Elsewhere, Gosseries takes a somewhat different tack, arguing that their 'general theory of justice' *commands* global egalitarians to take an integrated, 'opportunistic' approach to climate justice; one that aims to promote global egalitarianism's 'general redistributive goal' (2014: 101).

As Laura Valentini points out in her article surveying the contemporary debate, this distinction can be given (at least) three interpretations. First, a theory of justice may be described as ideal if it is constructed on the assumption of full compliance with its principles, with nonideal theory addressing problems of non-, or partial, compliance. Second, the ideal/nonideal distinction may be used to differentiate between utopian and realistic theories of justice, respectively; to indicate, that is, how sensitive a theory is to feasibility constraints (including, presumably, feasible rates of compliance). And third, ideal theory may be understood as an attempt to define an end-state vision of perfectly just social arrangements, whilst nonideal theory offers an account of transition towards arrangements that are *more* just, at least, than what we have now (Valentini 2012: 654).

The claim that a given political philosopher is engaged in ideal theory sometimes constitutes an accusation rather than a mere observation. This terminology may be employed to charge political philosophers with an 'unwillingness to provide solutions to urgent problems' (Hamlin & Stemplowska 2012: 48); or to identify 'apparently useless, unrealistic, naïve, utopian—perhaps even ideological or dangerous—currents in contemporary political philosophy' (Stemplowska & Swift 2012: 373). Ideal theorists have been criticized for proposing accounts of justice that are out of touch with reality; for ignoring or obscuring some of the most significant injustices of our time; and for failing to make any recommendations that appear to be action guiding (see, for example, Mills 2005; Sen 2009).

The ideal theorist might perhaps reply that they are engaged in an academic exercise that does not need to make usable recommendations to be worthwhile, but lingering worries are bound to remain when the problems being theorized are of pressing moral concern. It might seem that ideal theorizing is particularly misplaced when discussing a problem of such urgency as climate change, where what we need *right now* are *feasible* recommendations that will help us *transition* to something better than our current circumstances of severe injustice (perhaps all that we can realistically hope for), in the knowledge that (at best) we will only have *partial* compliance with any such recommendations. One might also suspect that ideal theory will not have much to tell us about this problem since, in an ideal world, climate change presumably would not have progressed as far as it has in our own.

However, I follow Valentini in thinking that (2012: 662):

> there is no right answer to the question of whether a normative political theory should be 'ideal' or 'non-ideal' (meaning more-or-less realistic). What types of idealizations are appropriate, and what facts ought to be taken into account in the design of normative principles depends on the particular question the theory itself is meant to answer.

Furthermore, given that most political theories will be designed to address numerous more or less ideal questions, it seems that Zofia Stemplowska is likely to be correct in claiming that 'many, if not all, theories of justice... operate simultaneously at the ideal and nonideal level' (2008: 319). My own account will employ different idealizing assumptions depending on the questions under consideration, with the hope that the engagement in more ideal theory will be vindicated by the analysis of climate change that it enables me to provide and the recommendations that I am ultimately able to draw. Accordingly, across this work I will transition between more and less ideal forms of theorizing; most notably, between theorizing about a world already afflicted by the problem of climate change and theorizing about the kind of world that human beings should have strived to create.

1.3 My approach to climate justice

Having introduced numerous key pieces of terminology in the previous section, it is now possible to provide a more detailed characterization of my own approach to climate justice. I then outline some motivations for adopting this approach.

1.3.1 Characteristics

In this work, I consider climate change *as a problem of natural resource justice*. In doing so, I present an account of climate justice that is at the *holist* end of the atomism–holism spectrum (in that it considers the problem of climate change in broad aspect, rather than a restricted element of it) but only *partially integrated*. This account is only partially integrated because I reason about the normative dimensions of climate change by reference to a theory of justice for natural resources alone, rather than a fully comprehensive theory of global justice.

The middle section of this work is devoted to formulating the theory of natural resource justice that I will use to draw conclusions about climate change. I start by arguing that we should be *global egalitarians* concerning natural resources. I do this not by reference to any practice-mediated relations between human beings, but instead by appeal to the original relationship in which human beings stand with respect to the world's resources; a relationship that I argue is characterized by equal original claims. This is thus a *nonrelationist*, pre-political defence of natural resource egalitarianism at the global level. I then argue that since all individuals have an equal original claim to natural resources, principles of natural resource justice must be given an impartial defence; and that this defence can be provided through the method of *contractualism*, by considering what principles of justice would be agreed to in an appropriately designed hypothetical resource rights contract between all human beings. I model this contract using a global original position that is *cosmopolitan* in the sense that the parties, who are ignorant of their time and place of birth, represent individuals rather than societies. I term this method for defending principles of natural resource justice 'Contractualist Common Ownership'.

As noted in the introductory section of this chapter, the principles that I claim would be selected from this perspective are ones that serve to protect basic needs and support the self-determination of political communities. This conception of justice is very different in form to the principle of distributive equality that many natural resource egalitarians have defended. I argue that my account can nevertheless be viewed as the correct interpretation of global egalitarianism with respect to natural resources when egalitarianism is understood *relationally*—as a social and political ideal. In the final section of this work, I use this theory of natural resource justice to reflect on several normative questions that climate change raises, and the nature of climate change itself as a problem of global justice. In moving between questions relating to the most defensible principles of natural resource justice, and questions pertaining to climate change in a world where these principles have frequently been violated, I transition between *more and less ideal forms of theorizing*.

1.3.2 Motivation

As explained in §1.2.2, I am not alone in exploring climate change as a problem of natural resource justice—a number of theorists have adopted this approach. I do likewise for several reasons. First and foremost, because I think the natural resources approach is right about something very important: climate change is indeed a problem that raises many questions of natural resource justice, as illustrated by the examples at the start of this chapter. These examples help to demonstrate how climate change results from the overuse of particular natural resources and, by its very nature, acts on individuals and societies by disturbing the natural environment. Responses to climate change, such as forest preservation schemes and renewable energy facilities, also threaten to spur new conflicts over natural resources. In reasoning about climate justice, we are thus repeatedly presented with questions about how the natural world should be protected, shared, and used.

A theory of natural resource justice promises to be informative regarding these questions, and thereby promises to be informative regarding the problem of climate change. Furthermore, the discussion about climate change that may be generated from the perspective of natural resource justice is one that can be informed by many philosophies and worldviews, given that questions about how human beings should relate to the natural world—and to one another with respect to the natural world—are ones that all communities are confronted by. I hope, for this reason, that this work can be a small part of a broader conversation about climate justice and natural resources.

Another motivation for taking the natural resources approach to climate justice is that whilst many theorists appear to have recognized that this approach has promise, its full potential is yet to be realized. Two reasons for this are: first, that theorists have not always provided adequate support for the principles of natural resource right that they invoke in reasoning about climate change; and second, that the natural resources approach has largely been applied in a piecemeal—atomist-isolationist—manner, to single questions of climate justice considered in abstraction from other global concerns (such as how the global emissions budget should be shared, or whether responsibility for climate change can be assigned on the basis of historical emission rates). The length of this work enables me to avoid the first problem by offering a full defence of the theory of natural resource justice that I draw on. It also enables me to avoid the second problem, by taking advantage of one of the valuable features of the natural resources approach; namely, that it provides what Caney terms a 'Method of Integration' (2012: 259), by situating climate change within a broader theory of justice, rather than treating it as an isolated issue.

This method of integration is not a full one, because a theory of natural resource justice might itself be described as 'isolationist' in the sense that it does not provide a complete account of what justice demands at the global level. This partial form of integrationism will be defended more fully in §8.1, but for now can be motivated in brief by borrowing one of Gosseries' pragmatic reasons for isolationism: namely, that the focus on natural resources alone simplifies matters and leaves to one side the more complex task of integrating other global justice concerns (in particular, those concerning claims and rights over non-natural goods, over which there may be additional disagreements). And as I also argue in §8.1, the natural resources approach does at least enable one to take a relatively *holist* view of climate justice, because it can be applied to many of the important normative questions that climate change raises.

These questions can be roughly split into three categories, depending on whether they relate to the atmospheric target, mitigation, or unavoided impacts.[39] Questions in the first category relate to what atmospheric concentration of GHGs the current generation should avoid breaching. This can be

---

[39] Roughly the same three categories are identified by: Gardiner, who terms them the trajectory question, the allocation question, and the impacts question (2011b: 314); Baer, who terms them the target question, the allocation question, and the liability question (2011: 323); and Meyer and Roser, who talk in terms of the 'justifiable global quota', the mitigation burden, and the adaptation burden (2010: 230).

framed as a matter of how much the current generation should limit its consumption of climate sink capacity for the sake of preventing or limiting the disturbances to the natural environment outlined in §1.1.2. These climate sinks are natural resources: namely, the atmosphere, ocean, soils, and vegetation. Limits on their use also entail limits on the use of hydrocarbon deposits (from which we get the fossil fuels coal, oil, and natural gas).

Once these limits have been identified, questions in the mitigation category arise. Pertinent among these are questions of how the permissible use of climate sinks and fossil fuels should be shared globally. Mitigation also raises questions concerning rights over land and other natural resources that could be used as inputs or sites for renewable energy projects or sink-enhancement measures (such as afforestation). In Chapter Eight, I will demonstrate how a theory of natural resource justice can be used to address both questions of the atmospheric target and questions of mitigation.

Unfortunately, even extreme mitigation measures will not be sufficient to halt the negative climate impacts that are already taking place. Questions therefore also arise about the unavoided impacts of climate change. When these impacts threaten the natural resources on which human communities depend, there is a question of who should be held responsible for this, and who should bear the costs of adaptation, or rectification for loss and damage. When thinking about duties of compensation in the context of climate change, many have proposed that we conceptualize certain of such obligations as *climate debts*, stemming from historical overuse of the natural world.[40] As I will explain, a theory of natural resource justice again promises to be informative here, because it enables us to understand and identify some of these climate debts.

1.4 Structure of the work

In this chapter, I introduced the problem of climate change and identified three broad approaches that philosophers have taken to understanding climate change as a problem of global justice. This includes the natural resources approach, which I adopt in this work. In Chapter Two, I motivate the natural resources approach further, by examining the most prominent example of this approach in the climate justice literature—what I term the 'atmospheric commons argument' for equal per capita emission shares. This argument explicitly conceptualizes climate mitigation as a problem of natural resource justice, but whilst I agree with this framing, I point out some problems with

---

[40] Some instead talk in terms of ecological, natural, or carbon debts. See fn.29.

the argument itself. To address these problems, I conclude, we must examine the question of natural resource justice in more depth. This is the task that I take up in the middle section of the work, from Chapters Three to Seven, on Natural Resource Justice.

In Chapter Three I defend a view that I term 'Equal Original Claims' to natural resources and identify two rival accounts of how such claims should be understood: Equal Division and Common Ownership. In Chapter Four, I reject Equal Division. In Chapter Five, I formulate a contractualist understanding of Common Ownership, defend it from two key objections, and use it to defend a basic needs principle. In Chapter Six, I defend a principle of collective self-determination and argue that it will both justify and restrict a presumptive right of exclusive territorial jurisdiction over natural resources, for political communities understood in non-statist terms. In Chapter Seven, I summarize the resulting theory of natural resource justice and defend it from two further objections.

Chapters Eight to Ten—which form the third and final section of the book—turn back to the problem of climate change with this new theory of natural resource justice in hand. In Chapter Eight, I revisit the question of sharing the global emissions budget, drawing quite different conclusions to that of the atmospheric commons argument rejected in Chapter Two. In the following two chapters, I turn to the question of historical responsibility for climate change. I focus on the climate debt claim, according to which certain wealthy or industrialized states owe a debt of compensation to some of those suffering from the unavoided impacts of climate change; where the notion of a debt indicates that the obligation in question falls within the domain of rectificatory justice. In Chapter Nine I reject the Historical Emissions Debt view, according to which climate debts have arisen because some parties have historically emitted more than their fair share of greenhouse gases. In Chapter Ten I develop an alternative defence of the climate debt claim, via a broader discussion of how historical wrongdoing concerning natural resources appears to hold relevance for climate justice. On this defence, climate change is shown to be a new manifestation of an enduring form of injustice, which responses to climate change may serve to exacerbate if due care is not exercised. Chapter Eleven concludes.

2

Sharing the Global Emissions Budget

In this chapter I begin my engagement with the natural resources approach to climate justice by examining one of the most prominent examples of this approach in the literature. The example in question focuses on responsibilities to reduce greenhouse gas (GHG) emissions. This mitigation policy is usually taken to involve setting a limit on future emission of GHGs, with the resulting emissions budget to be shared between states or individuals by a quota system. This raises the question of what a just global distribution of the emissions budget would be.

I here discuss what has been termed the 'dominant view' regarding this distributive question (J. Barry 2008: ix; Caney 2012: 260). This is the view that emission quotas should be distributed to all human beings globally on an equal per capita basis, what I will refer to as 'the equal per capita emissions view' (EPC). There are several ways of cashing out EPC, with different understandings of what entity emission quotas should be allocated to (states or individuals, say), and which emissions and individuals should be included in the distribution (whether, for example, historical emissions should be included). My critique highlights a controversial commitment shared by all EPC theorists who defend the view using a certain form of argumentation, regardless of the species of EPC that they advocate.

EPC is a prevalent view amongst both theorists and campaigners. It is the second essential component of the Contraction and Convergence proposal, championed by the Global Commons Institute, according to which per capita emissions should converge to equality over a suitable length of time (A. Meyer 2000; gci.org.uk); it has been discussed by representatives to the United Nations Framework Convention on Climate Change (UNFCCC);[1] and some apply it historically to claim that those who have emitted more than an equal

---

[1] At the 2012 workshop on equitable access to sustainable development, for example, an EU representative spoke of 'a need for a gradual convergence of per capita emissions' (UNFCCC 2012: Item 38).

share of GHG emissions are now in possession of some form of climate debt.[2] I am interested in EPC not only because of its prominence, however, but also because it is frequently defended using arguments that incorporate a particular claim about natural resource rights.

I start by explaining how theorists have used claims about natural resource rights to defend EPC, outlining what I term the *atmospheric commons argument* (§2.1). Drawing on the assessment reports of the Intergovernmental Panel on Climate Change (IPCC) and Elinor Ostrom's work on common-pool resources, I show that these arguments invoke a misleading analysis of climate change as a global commons problem (§2.2). Accurate understanding of how climate change results from overuse of a global commons reveals proponents of this argument for EPC to be harbouring some controversial commitments (§2.3). I then discuss two options for EPC theorists who wish to maintain the view in the face of my critique and show that both necessitate deeper engagement with the question of how rights to the world's resources should be assigned (§2.4).

2.1 The atmospheric commons argument

Many defenders of EPC conceptualize climate change mitigation as a means to prevent overuse of a global commons, with the global commons in question said to be the atmosphere.[3] Equipped with this idea of an *atmospheric commons*, they defend equal per capita emissions using the following argument schema:[4]

---

[2] See Athanasiou & Baer 2002: 82; Baer 2002: 402; Kartha 2011: 508–9; Martinez-Alier and Naron 2004: 18; Matthews 2016; Neumayer 2000; and Sinden 2010: 343–5. This claim has also been made by Bolivian representatives at the UNFCCC (Navarro 2009). I discuss these views further in Chapter Nine.

[3] Anil Agarwal claims 'the atmosphere is a common property resource' (2002: 377). Paul Baer states 'the atmosphere is a global commons' (2002: 401). Brian Barry suggests that 'obviously, treating the atmosphere as a global commons to be divided up equally would itself constitute a just distribution of a scarce resource' (2005: 268). Broome compares the atmosphere to a 'tract of common land' (2012: 69). Michael Grubb states 'what has happened, and is happening, with the atmosphere is exactly the process enunciated by Garrett Hardin in his essay "The tragedy of the commons"' (1990: 77). Eric Neumayer talks of giving 'every human being an equal share of the global resource atmosphere' and 'equal sharing of the global commons' (2000: 185, 190). Steve Vanderheiden talks of 'the common global resource of the atmosphere', or the 'atmospheric commons' (2008a: 225, 228). The latter term is shared by Tom Athanasiou and Paul Baer (2002: 78). Similar ideas have been voiced at UNFCCC meetings. At the 2012 workshop on equitable access to sustainable development, a representative for China objected that developed countries had historically 'overoccupied most of the existing atmospheric space' (UNFCCC 2012: Item 29).

[4] This argument is given by Agarwal 2002: 376–7; Athanasiou & Baer 2002: 64; Baer 2002: 396–401; B. Barry 2005: 268; Brown 2002: 214; Grubb 1990: 77, 83; and Vanderheiden 2008a: 223ff.; and discussed by Baatz & Ott 2017: 166; Grubb et al. 1992: 312; Matthews 2016: 60; Moellendorf 2011; Müller 1999: 7–8; Posner & Sunstein 2009: 81; Posner & Weisbach 2010: 120; Raymond 2006: 656; Roberts & Parks 2007: 144; Roser & Seidel 2017: 153ff.; Sinden 2010: 319–21; and Singer 2010: 190.

(1) distributing emission quotas equates to distributing rights to the atmosphere;[5]

(2) the atmosphere is a global commons;

(3) rights to the atmosphere should be distributed to all human beings globally on an equal per capita basis;

(4) therefore, emission quotas should be distributed to all human beings globally on an equal per capita basis [from (1) and (3)].

It is in their defences of premise (3) that theorists tend to differ. Often (3) is taken to require little support, perhaps because the intuitiveness of this atmospheric commons argument is widely accepted—even by those who do not view it as decisive. Peter Singer, for example, thinks the idea that 'everyone has the same claim to part of the atmospheric sink as everyone else... seems self-evidently fair, at least as a starting point for discussion' (2010: 190).[6] Roughly speaking, the idea seems to be that all individuals are symmetrically situated with respect to this resource, and thus that a default position of equal claims (and rights) can be straightforwardly assumed.

Michael Grubb, for example, claims 'the moral principle is *simple*, namely that every human has an equal right to use the atmospheric resource' (1990: 83; emphasis added). Anil Agarwal seems either to likewise take (3) to be simple, or possibly to follow directly from (2), asserting that 'the atmosphere is a common property resource to which every human being has an equal right' (2002: 377). Tom Athanasiou and Paul Baer seem to think that (3) follows from (2) once it is accepted that: 'equity—defined specifically as equal rights to global common resources—must be affirmed as a *foundational* ethical and political principle' (Athanasiou & Baer 2002: 74; emphasis added).[7] John Broome supports (3) using what he terms a 'general rule of fairness': that 'when some good is to be divided among people who need or

[5] Vanderheiden instead talks of distributing 'atmospheric absorptive capacity' (2008a: 224); Broome, of distributing 'the ability of the atmosphere to absorb greenhouse gas' (2012: 69).

[6] Singer ultimately only favours EPC over prioritarian or utilitarian principles of distribution 'because of its simplicity, hence its suitability as a political compromise, and because it seems likely to increase global welfare' (2010: 194). See also Grubb et al. 1992: 318–20. James Garvey—although he acknowledges the main problem that I will identify with the atmospheric commons argument (2008: 162, fn.9)—suggests that 'the notion that everyone has equal access to the atmosphere' takes us 'at least a long way down the road to procedural fairness' (2008: 129). Even the California Public Utilities Commission has proposed that a key objective in distributing cap-and-trade GHG allowance revenues should be equitable allocation, 'consistent with the idea that the atmosphere is a commons to which all individuals have an equal claim' (2012: §5.2).

[7] Athanasiou and Baer also claim that a global climate accord will require us to 'find a fair way to divide up a finite "atmospheric space"' and '*there just isn't any way to conceive of such fairness except in per capita terms*'; and that 'from the point of view of both basic ethics and enlightenment philosophy, the case for equal per capita rights is an *obvious* one' (2002: 64, 86; both emphases added). See also Baer 2002: 401. Both Baer and Athanasiou later abandon EPC in favour of their Greenhouse Development Rights approach (see Baer et al. 2010).

want it, each person should receive a share that is proportional to the claim she has to the good'. Broome then claims it 'seems obvious' that nobody has a stronger claim to this natural resource than anyone else (2012: 69–70).

A more developed defence of the move from (2) to (3) is provided by Steve Vanderheiden, who invokes a restricted version of the resource redistribution principle (RRP) formulated by Charles Beitz. As explained in §1.2.1, the RRP is a principle according to which the world's natural resources should be redistributed in pursuit of more equitable shares (Beitz 1979: 138–9). Somewhat problematically—since (as I will explain in §5.1) it is not actually clear what form Beitz intended the RRP to take—Vanderheiden equates the RRP with the principle of equal division, according to which rights to the world's resources should be distributed on an *equal per capita* basis. Vanderheiden then restricts the scope of this principle so that it applies only to the 'common global resource of the planet's atmospheric absorptive capacity', and not to any resources that are 'physically located within national borders'. This is supposed to ensure that 'all territorial claims to a nation's other natural resources' are 'set aside'. When (2) is combined with this restricted interpretation of the RRP, (3) is thus taken to follow (Vanderheiden 2008a: 223–5).[8]

By offering principles for the just distribution of the atmosphere (or its absorptive capacity) alone, in abstraction from all other goods, these arguments take an extremely atomist-isolationist approach to climate mitigation; one divorced not only from broader matters of global distributive justice, but even from other topics within climate justice itself. An advocate of integrationism, Caney criticizes EPC for concentrating on 'greenhouse gas emissions in isolation from other goods and without putting matters into the relevant context', arguing that the question of the just distribution of emission quotas must be integrated into a wider theory that considers other important goods, differential needs, differential access to alternative energy sources, other duties to address climate change, and historical responsibility (Caney 2009: 133).[9] I provide a different critique, aiming to show that the atmospheric commons argument for EPC is built on a flawed foundation: namely, the conceptualization of the *atmosphere* as the global commons whose overuse has led to the problem of climate change. It will turn out, however, that once

---

[8] Vanderheiden's account is more complicated than this in two respects. Firstly, he defends what he terms a 'modified equal shares approach', which distinguishes between 'survival' and 'luxury' emissions and only seeks to equalise the latter (Vanderheiden 2008a: 226–8). In addition, Vanderheiden ultimately concludes that emission shares should be distributed in accordance with a version of Rawls's egalitarian difference principle (Vanderheiden 2008a: 224). This makes no difference to the problems that I raise for Vanderheiden's view, because the reasons I give for the failure of his argument for equality apply regardless of whether that equality is tempered in these ways.

[9] For similar criticism of EPC see Armstrong 2017: 77; Beckerman & Pasek 1995: 408–9; Bell 2013b: 198–202; and Caney 2012: 299.

this conceptualization is corrected, the atmospheric commons argument lends support to a view that is even more atomist than EPC.

2.2 Climate change and the global commons

Following Ostrom, I will refer to a commons as a 'common-pool resource', or CPR (see Ostrom 1990). A CPR is a natural or human-made resource system with two defining characteristics. The first is subtractability, or rivalness, such that 'what one person harvests from or deposits in a resource subtracts from the ability of others to do the same', making CPRs prone to overuse. The second is that it is costly (though not necessarily impossible) to exclude potential appropriators from accessing the resource, and thus also from enjoying any *improvements* made to the resource. This difficulty of exclusion means that each potential appropriator faces the temptation to freeride and gain benefits from the resource without contributing to its upkeep. These two characteristics give rise to a need for institutions of CPR governance that can 'deal with the threats of overuse and of free riding' (Dolšak & Ostrom 2003: 7–8). One thing such an institution might do is attempt to restrict CPR use by allocating quotas to appropriators.

When discussing CPRs, Ostrom points out, 'it is essential to distinguish between the *resource system* and the flow of *resource units* produced by the system, while still recognizing the dependence of the one on the other'. Resource systems can be thought of as 'stock variables that are capable, under favorable conditions, of producing a maximum quantity of a flow variable without harming the stock or the resource system itself'. Her examples include fishing grounds and groundwater basins. A resource unit is 'what individuals appropriate or use' from a resource system. Examples Ostrom gives here include fish and volumes of water (1990: 30).

A CPR can be open access or closed access, depending on whether limits are placed on who can appropriate from it (Ostrom 1990: 48). Such limits could be set socially, legally, or physically. I will take a *global* commons to be a CPR where *all* human beings are potential appropriators whom it is difficult to exclude from the resource. As for any CPR, failure to prevent overuse of a global CPR by limiting appropriation can eventually lead to problems of overcrowding, exhaustion of the resource system stock, and even destruction of the resource system itself—or its ability to continue producing resource units.

Which global CPR would climate mitigation protect from overuse? As explained, most defenders of EPC claim it is the atmosphere. They presumably suggest this due to the significant role that the atmosphere plays in the greenhouse effect (discussed in §1.1.1). To evaluate this suggestion, however, we should consider what resource units are relevant here. The object of distribution is GHG emission quotas, and the appropriators are individuals or collectives that emit GHGs. The emission quotas are not *appropriated* when agents emit GHGs, however, but rather *place limits* on appropriation. Likewise, the GHGs themselves are clearly not the resource units that individuals wish to appropriate, since these are released into the atmosphere.

Whenever agents engage in polluting activities, what they actually appropriate is *assimilative capacity* from a resource system; where this should be understood as the system's capacity to receive waste without being subject to overuse. What counts as overuse depends on the features of the resource system that one wishes to—or is obliged to—maintain. For example, one might say that the assimilative capacity of a water source is exceeded when it is no longer fit for human consumption; when it becomes unable to sustain the lives of certain organisms that inhabit it; when it is polluted so badly that it is no longer able to cleanse itself further; or when it loses some other significant feature.

When individuals emit GHGs, then, what they are appropriating from the global CPR in question is assimilative capacity. And it is true that one thing appropriated via GHG emissions is units of atmospheric assimilative capacity, from what can be understood as the global CPR of the atmosphere (a resource system from which it is difficult to exclude any human beings from appropriating these ultimately exhaustible resource units). However, it is not quite right to say that the atmosphere is *the* global CPR whose overuse leads to the problem of climate change. This is because the atmosphere is not the only, or the most significant, resource that assimilates anthropogenic GHG emissions. Whilst CH_4 and N_2O are mostly assimilated via destructive or reactive atmospheric processes (see IPCC 2007a: 142–3); in the case of CO_2, the atmosphere is not usually described as a sink at all. The atmosphere does appear to have *some* assimilative capacity for CO_2, in the sense that it is able to accommodate some increase in CO_2 concentration without being subject to overuse.[10] However, CO_2 is not *absorbed* or destroyed by the atmosphere. The main role played by the atmosphere in the carbon cycle is as a medium that simply contains CO_2 until it is removed and assimilated by the climate system's oceanic, vegetation, and soil sinks (IPCC 2013: 544–5).[11]

To omit these sinks would be a significant oversight given the importance of CO_2. CO_2 is emitted through many highly valued activities, but these

---

[10] The atmosphere acts as a pool for CO_2. The IPCC estimates that in pre-industrial times, atmospheric concentration of CO_2 was about 280ppm (parts per million) (IPCC 2013: 100). It has now exceeded 400ppm due to human activities (Earth System Research Laboratory 2018). To estimate how much CO_2 the atmosphere can assimilate, one must try to determine what level of concentration engenders consequences that human beings wish to, or are obliged to, avoid.
[11] Soil is also a minor sink for CH_4 (IPCC 2007a: 142).

emissions must be significantly curtailed since, as noted in §1.1.1, the IPCC considers CO_2 to be 'the single largest anthropogenic factor contributing to climate change'. Without climate sinks, the contribution of CO_2 would have been even greater. The IPCC claimed in 2007 that 'Were it not for the natural sinks taking up *nearly half* the human-produced CO_2 over the past 15 years, atmospheric concentrations would have grown even more dramatically' (IPCC 2007a: 511–12; emphasis added).

So, when defenders of EPC talk about the atmosphere as *the* global common resource whose overuse leads to climate change, they are misrepresenting matters somewhat. This means that the atmospheric commons argument goes awry at its very first premise: when individuals or collectives emit GHGs they do not only appropriate atmospheric assimilative capacity from the global common resource of the atmosphere; they appropriate what I will term *global climate sink capacity* from the global common resource of the *global climate sink*, which encompasses not only the atmosphere, but also the ocean, soils, and vegetation. It is only when the climate system's oceanic and terrestrial sinks are subjected to overuse that CO_2 starts to accumulate in the atmosphere, in turn exceeding *its* capacity to assimilate an increased concentration of GHGs without dangerous changes in the climate occurring.[12]

The global climate sink, like the atmosphere, possesses the two features that classify it as a global CPR. Firstly, it is difficult to exclude any human beings from accessing the global climate sink—individuals appropriate from it whenever they engage in activities that release GHGs. Secondly, any appropriation from the global climate sink subtracts from the ability of others to do the same (without dangerous climate impacts occurring)—this is the very source of the problem of climate change. The total extent of global climate sink capacity is determined by something like the UNFCCC's stated objective of preventing 'dangerous anthropogenic interference with the climate system' (UN 1992: Art. 2) and is the subject of scientific and ethical deliberation: scientific due to uncertainty about what effect any given quantity of GHG emissions will have on the climate; and ethical due to debate over what changes in the climate human beings have a duty to prevent.

2.3 Reassessing the atmospheric commons argument

Some might wonder whether my analysis points to anything beyond a terminological disagreement with proponents of the atmospheric commons

---

[12] I follow the IPCC in using the term 'terrestrial sinks' to refer to land-based (as opposed to oceanic) sinks. Overuse of oceanic sinks also results in another environmental problem of great significance: ocean acidification.

argument. This interpretation may be supported by Baer's comments in a later article, where he states that 'in the context of greenhouse pollution, the "atmospheric commons" is shorthand for the whole system of sinks (including oceanic and terrestrial) which remove or store GHGs' (2010: 259, fn.6). Similarly, Vanderheiden does admittedly at one point declare that absorbing GHGs is 'a function that is technically performed by terrestrial carbon sinks... which for parsimony are called here *atmospheric absorptive capacity*' (2008a: 79).[13] However, if defenders of EPC are indeed aware of climate sink processes and are using 'atmospheric commons' as shorthand, then their choice of language is unfortunate. The atmosphere and the global climate sink differ significantly, creating problems for the atmospheric commons argument.

Note firstly that whilst the atmosphere is a resource system that may be thought to transcend national boundaries, the same does not hold for the global climate sink, various important aspects of which—vegetation and soils, in particular—fall *within* state territories. According to the IPCC's estimates, these terrestrial sinks play a significant role in assimilating CO_2. The terrestrial and oceanic sinks are estimated to have assimilated over half of all human CO_2 emissions between 1750 and 2011: with the ocean reservoir accumulating approximately 155PgC (petagrams of carbon), the terrestrial sinks accumulating about 160PgC, and around 240PgC remaining in the atmosphere (IPCC 2013: 486–7). The next thing to note is that some people believe the territorial location of natural resources to have ultimate relevance in determining who possesses rights over them. This follows from what I will term the *principle of natural resource sovereignty*, according to which, roughly speaking, the natural resources within a territory belong to the people of that territory.

The principle of natural resource sovereignty receives support from both political theory and international law, with international declarations containing numerous statements of the principle of permanent sovereignty over natural resources. Both the International Covenant on Civil and Political Rights and the International Covenant on Economic, Social and Cultural Rights, for example, state in their first articles that 'All peoples may, for their own ends, freely dispose of their natural wealth and resources without prejudice to any obligations arising out of international economic co-operation, based upon the principle of mutual benefit, and international law' (UN 1966a, 1966b: Art. 1); later adding that 'Nothing in the present Covenant shall be

---

[13] There are two problems with this statement. Firstly, 'atmospheric absorptive capacity' is no more parsimonious than 'terrestrial carbon sinks'. And secondly, aside from this statement, Vanderheiden clearly understands 'atmospheric absorptive capacity' as a resource that is *not* physically located within state territories, with equal shares of it amounting to equal entitlements 'to use the common global resource of the *atmosphere*' (2008a: 224–5; emphasis added; see also 103–5). I therefore class Vanderheiden as an EPC theorist who misidentifies the relevant global commons, despite his claim to be using the atmospheric terminology as shorthand.

interpreted as impairing the *inherent* right of all peoples to enjoy and utilize *fully* and freely their natural wealth and resources' (UN 1966a: Art. 47; UN 1966b: Art. 25; emphases added). Though the precise meaning of permanent sovereignty is somewhat contested and evolving, it is at least widely accepted that any *legitimate* state has the right 'to possess, use and freely dispose of its natural resources' (Schrijver 1997: 391).

The principle of permanent sovereignty was developed as an element of efforts, in the 1950s, to enable peoples living under colonial rule to benefit from their natural resources, and to protect the sovereignty of newly independent states from foreign states or corporations (Schrijver 1997: 24). Reflecting this end, other documents insist that permanent sovereignty is a right that 'must be exercised in the interest of their national development and of the well-being of the people of the State concerned' (UN 1962: Art. 1). Permanent sovereignty may thus possess understandable appeal for all peoples, but perhaps especially those who have been repeatedly, and violently, excluded from enjoying the benefits of their country's resource base by colonial or authoritarian rulers. Theorist Leif Wenar appeals to such statements of international law in his own defence of resource sovereignty, going so far as to claim that 'the idea that the natural resources of a country belong to the people of that country is so intuitive that *most will need no more proof than its statement*' (2008: 10; emphasis added).

What this means is that, even if the claim that each human being has an equal right to the atmosphere may not seem to meet any obvious objections, the claim that each human being has an equal right to the *global climate sink*—regardless of whether they are the citizen of a state whose territory contains significant terrestrial sinks—is more controversial. To put it plainly, what appears to be a 'basic presupposition' of EPC—'that each human being should have an equal right to an *as yet unallocated*, scarce global common' (Grubb et al. 1992: 318; emphasis added)—cannot be assumed here without further supporting argument, because various parts of the relevant global CPR *are* considered, by some at least, to already be allocated according to their territorial location.

If resource sovereignty could be defended, two points would appear to follow. Firstly, the different countries of the world would have rights over terrestrial sinks that vary significantly in their assimilative capacity per citizen.[14] Secondly, the atmospheric commons argument would actually point towards

---

[14] It is difficult to find statistics comparing terrestrial sink capacity by country, but data from the Global Footprint Network (GFN) provides some indication of the variation that is likely to exist. GFN estimates of the 2013 forest biocapacity of approximately 190 countries (measured in global hectares per capita) range from 0 to 90.65 (GFN 2017)—where biocapacity measures 'the capacity of ecosystems to produce useful biological materials and to absorb waste materials generated by humans', including CO_2 (GFN 2012a).

a theory of climate justice that is even more atomist than EPC; one where different principles of distributive justice apply to GHGs that are assimilated by different parts of the global climate sink (with a principle of equality for GHGs such as CH_4 and N_2O that are for the most part assimilated via destruction in the atmosphere, and another principle for CO_2 since it is assimilated to a significant extent by sinks that belong—if resource sovereignty holds, that is—to different states or peoples).

Let us now return to the atmospheric commons argument, replacing references to the atmosphere with references to the global climate sink:

(1*)   distributing emission quotas equates to distributing rights to the global climate sink;
(2*)   the global climate sink is a global commons;
(3*)   rights to the global climate sink should be distributed to all human beings globally on an equal per capita basis;
(4*)   therefore, emission quotas should be distributed to all human beings globally on an equal per capita basis [from (1*) and (3*)].

Even if one accepts Grubb's 'simple' moral principle that 'every human has an equal right to use the atmospheric resource' (1990: 83), the principle he would need to support (3*)—that 'every human has an equal right to use the global climate sink'—*over*simplifies matters by neglecting the uneven territorial distribution of terrestrial climate sinks. Similarly, the claim that Agarwal now needs to make—that the *global climate sink* is a common property resource to which every human being has an equal right—requires more defence than he provides. In particular, Agarwal must show that no collectives have territorial rights to more of this sink capacity than others. And since it is not 'obvious' that all human beings will have equal claims to the global climate sink, it is unclear what Broome's 'general rule of fairness' would dictate here.

The adjusted argument also casts doubt on Athanasiou and Baer's 'foundational' ethical principle of equal per capita rights to global CPRs. This principle seems to require more defence once it is noted that amongst such CPRs is a resource system that incorporates the soils covering each separate territory's surface. The problem for all these defenders of EPC is essentially the same: they invoke principles and claims which are given *no defence* because they are assumed to be uncontroversial, but they cannot be accepted as such given that they conflict with a commitment to resource sovereignty that others likewise claim to be obviously correct.

Problems also arise for Vanderheiden, who fails in his attempt to 'set aside' territorial claims to natural resources. The restricted interpretation of the RRP that he adopts—as a principle applying only to resources that are not located within national borders—simply does not apply to the global climate sink. Even if claims to the *atmosphere* 'cannot be defended by appeal to conventional property rights [or] riparian law' (Vanderheiden 2008a: 224), claims to some parts of the *global climate sink* could be. Vanderheiden is thus incorrect to claim that 'no person or nation has any territorial ownership claims that might...justify unequal shares' (2008a: 226).

Interestingly, one place that these potential territorial claims are acknowledged is in an oft-cited paper that some have interpreted as an early, 'seminal' defence of EPC (Caney 2009: 130; Kartha 2011: 507–8. See also Athanasiou & Baer 2002: 84). Here, Anil Agarwal and Sunita Narain adopt the global commons framing for the problem of distributing emission quotas, but correctly identify the global CPR that assimilates GHGs and *do not* end up advocating EPC as an ideal solution. Instead, they claim that 'ideally', whilst shares of oceanic and atmospheric sinks should be distributed on an equal per capita basis, the sinks within a state's territory would be assumed to offset *its own* emissions. This would give an idea of 'the true emissions of each nation' (Agarwal & Narain 1991: 4). When understood accurately, then, the global commons framing does not obviously support EPC after all.[15]

2.4 Options for the Equal Per Capita View

Let us take stock of the situation faced by proponents of the commons argument for EPC. I have shown that such arguments are problematic, because the global climate sink is not in fact a territorially unbounded resource with respect to which all human beings are symmetrically situated. It is possible that some human beings and not others have territorial claims over certain parts of this sink. If these claims result in an entitlement, then the assimilative capacity of terrestrial sinks will be allocated unevenly across the global population. The inequality in emission shares resulting from territorial entitlements would only be preserved by allocating the capacity of the remaining, territorially unbounded parts of the global climate sink on an equal per capita basis.[16]

---

[15] A rare acknowledgement that Agarwal and Narain do not actually advocate EPC is given by Henry Shue, who claims to be 'dubious' of their 'nationalistic allocation of sources and sinks' (Shue 2014: 97).

[16] Some theorists may nevertheless choose to defend this position (whereby legitimate territorial claims to sinks are respected and bracketed out of the global allocation, but the remaining climate sink capacity is distributed on an equal per capita basis). As explained at the end of §2.3, Agarwal and Narain appear to adopt a view of this form: where they understand legitimate territorial claims in line with a principle of national ownership (which brackets out terrestrial sinks) and allocate only the oceanic and atmospheric sinks on an equal per capita basis (1991: 4). However, proponents of such a view must still support it with a theory of natural resource justice that explains: 1) Which territorial claims to climate sinks are legitimate and result in an entitlement; and 2) Why it is that nobody has a greater claim to any remaining, unbracketed portion of the global climate sink than anyone else.

I want to be clear that my goal here is not to undermine EPC by *defending* a conflicting principle of resource sovereignty. This is in fact a principle that I reject, but this rejection will not be outlined fully until Chapters Six and Seven. The reason I raise the principle of natural resource sovereignty here, then, is not to endorse it, but rather to show that proponents of EPC have a bigger burden of proof than they commonly recognize. The point is that since EPC conflicts with a principle of natural resource justice that some take to be obviously correct, the relatively minimal defences of EPC outlined in §2.1 cannot suffice. I thus use resource sovereignty to *unsettle* the commons argument for EPC. Ultimately, I will reject resource sovereignty but argue that EPC nevertheless fails for other reasons (to be outlined in Chapter Eight).

In the face of this critique, proponents of EPC have two pertinent options. They can either:

1. Rescue the commons argument for EPC by *rejecting* all territorial claims to climate sinks, or:

2. Accept that legitimate territorial claims to climate sinks exist but argue that they will be *trumped* by the claims of each individual to an equal share of the emissions budget.

I will argue that both options demand far deeper engagement with the question of how rights to the world's resources should be assigned.

2.4.1 Option one: rejecting territorial claims

Taking the first option, EPC theorists would attempt to save the commons argument by rejecting all territorial claims to the global climate sink, thereby removing this obstacle to the premise that rights to this resource should be equal (3*). A question then arises whether EPC theorists should reject *all* territorial claims to natural resources, or merely those to the climate sink. By limiting their original equality claim to 'global common resources' that appear to transcend territorial boundaries (such as the atmosphere), advocates of the atmospheric commons argument perhaps inadvertently offer tacit support to territorial claims over natural resources that do fall within territorial boundaries (like hydrocarbon deposits and terrestrial sinks)—and to the principle of resource sovereignty that was shown to undermine their conclusion.

If EPC theorists modify this picture by removing only the climate sink from the realm of territorial claims, then they will have to respond to charges of unfairness. Why should collectives with large hydrocarbon deposits in their territory, for example, be able to lay claim to these resources, whilst forest-rich collectives are barred from possessing territorial claims over the assimilative capacity of their climate sinks? As Brian Barry says (1989: 450):[17]

> It would hardly be surprising if, when the principle of national sovereignty over natural resources has been so recently and precariously established, Third World countries should be highly suspicious of any suggestion that natural resources should in future be treated as collective international property. They may well wonder whether this is anything more than a cover for the reintroduction of colonialism... Clearly, everything would depend on the principle's being applied across the board rather than in a one-sided way that lets the industrialized countries act on the maxim 'What's yours is mine and what's mine is my own.'

EPC theorists will therefore have to reject *all* territorial claims to natural resources, or explain how it is fair for territorial claims to extend to some terrestrial resources but not the climate sink.[18] In either case, they will need to provide a theory of natural resource justice in support of their position.

2.4.2 Option two: trumping territorial claims

Taking the second option, EPC theorists would attempt to show that any territorial claims over climate sinks should be trumped by the demand for equal shares. Here, they must do two things: first, provide an alternative, *positive* argument for distributing emission quotas on an equal per capita basis; and second, show that the pursuit of equality in this good should be given priority over respecting any territorial claims to the climate sink. I will now identify some difficulties with what might seem to be the most obvious way for the EPC theorist to adapt their natural resources approach in support of this goal.

On this defence, the EPC theorist would adopt the principle of equal division previously identified—according to which *all* natural resources should be distributed on an equal per capita basis—and argue that satisfying this principle ought to be given priority over respecting territorial claims. This would be an obvious move for Vanderheiden to make since he looks favourably on the principle of equal division, which—as explained in §2.1—he (problematically) equates with Beitz's full RRP (Vanderheiden

[17] See also Hayward 2005b: 190.
[18] Vanderheiden has adopted both strategies. In an earlier piece, he attempts to reject *all* territorial claims to natural resources, drawing on Beitz to argue 'against awarding valuable goods to parties based solely upon the morally arbitrary natural allocation of ecological wealth' (Vanderheiden 2009: 274, fn.29). For criticism, see Blomfield 2013: 293–8. See also Nine 2008 (against Beitz's moral arbitrariness claim). In a more recent piece, Vanderheiden defends a modified interpretation of the principle of permanent sovereignty that is designed to be compatible with significant restrictions on fossil fuel exploitation and 'equitable per capita emissions rights' (2017: 1286).

2008a: 224, 248). With this principle in tow, one might think that the argument for EPC can simply proceed as follows:

(1*) distributing emission quotas equates to distributing rights to the global climate sink;

(3*) rights to the global climate sink should be distributed to all human beings globally on an equal per capita basis [from the principle of equal division];

(4*) therefore, emission quotas should be distributed to all human beings globally on an equal per capita basis [from (1*) and (3*)].

To think this would be a mistake, however, because *even if* the principle of equal division is defensible, it does not straightforwardly support (3*). This is because the principle of equal division, on its most plausible reading, does not demand that each person be given an equal share of *each kind* of natural resource, but rather a *set* of resource rights deemed to be of equal value. In other words, the principle of equal division is not generally taken to demand that any *particular* resource—e.g. gold, oil, global climate sink capacity—be distributed on an equal per capita basis. Beitz himself makes this point in a later piece, explicitly mentioning 'the absorptive capacity of the atmosphere' as a resource for which one cannot assume that an 'equal-resource principle' will entail equal allocation (1999: 285).[19]

Since the principle of equal division does not obviously mandate equal per capita shares of any specific resource, it should be possible to arrive at the egalitarian distribution that it demands whilst respecting as many territorial claims to natural resources as possible. In fact, territorial claims could prove a useful means by which to determine which specific resource rights should compose each individual's equally valuable set. Thus, even if absolute priority is granted to a principle of equal division, this does not entail that rights to the global climate sink should be distributed equally. Those who are granted a smaller share of climate sink capacity due to the territorial claims of others could be compensated with rights to other resources, thereby ending up with an equally valuable bundle.

It must be conceded, however, that if given priority, a principle of equal division will trump even legitimate territorial claims to natural resources in certain situations—meaning that some of these claims will not result in actual entitlements. If, for example, a people's territory happened to contain the only source of a rare natural compound necessary for the treatment of malaria, then it seems that even a legitimate territorial claim to that resource should

---

[19] This comment appears in Beitz's discussion of Hillel Steiner's principle of equal division rather than his own RRP—both of which will be discussed in more detail in the following chapters.

not result in an all-things-considered entitlement—because many individuals worldwide could not be considered to possess an equal set of resource rights if they were not also entitled to access its benefits. Thus, if EPC theorists wish to use the principle of equal division to defend their view, they will first have to give a convincing defence of this principle, and then explain why each person's equally valuable set of natural resource rights must contain a right to an equal per capita share of climate sink capacity, specifically. Again, then, they will have to provide a theory of natural resource justice in support of this view.

2.5 Conclusion

Several theorists who suggest that EPC is a just solution to the problem of sharing the global emissions budget base their arguments on a flawed conception of climate change as a global commons problem. The *global climate sink* is the global CPR that faces overuse via anthropogenic GHG emissions—not the atmosphere alone—and it is use of *this* resource system that must be allocated fairly. I have shown that a major argument in favour of EPC fails once this fact is fully appreciated. Faced with this problem, EPC theorists have two options. Either they can argue that territorial claims to climate sinks are invalid; or, they can accept such claims, but argue that they will be trumped by the demand for an equal distribution of emission quotas.

I have argued that to see whether either of these options can succeed, the question of justice in the assignment of rights to the world's natural resources must be considered in more depth. It is this question that I will be addressing in Chapters Three to Seven. In Chapter Eight, having formulated a conception of natural resource justice, I will return to the problem of sharing the emissions budget.

Part II
Natural Resource Justice

Part II
Natural Resource Justice

3

Global Justice and Natural Resources

In Chapter Two, I showed that to address one major problem of climate change mitigation—that of sharing the emissions budget—a number of claims to natural resources must be taken into consideration. These resources include the atmosphere and the ocean, vegetation, and soils that act as a sink for anthropogenic greenhouse gases (GHGs). A theory of natural resource justice is needed for assessing and adjudicating between these claims fairly. In this middle section of the work—consisting of Chapters Three to Seven—I attempt to formulate a theory that is up to this task. In Chapter Eight, I use this theory to revisit the problem of sharing the emissions budget.

In this chapter, I engage in some necessary groundwork. I look at what natural resources are (§3.1), their place in a theory of justice (§3.2), and two forms that claims to natural resources tend to take (§3.3). I then present a simple argument for taking natural resources to be appropriate objects of egalitarian justice, because they are the subject of equal original claims (§3.4). I close by discussing how best to understand Equal Original Claims, in terms of four understandings of 'world ownership' that are common to Western political philosophy: Common Ownership, No Ownership, Joint Ownership, and Equal Division (§3.5). My own approach is in the Common Ownership camp and I defend this choice through a rejection of these prominent alternatives. No Ownership and Joint Ownership are dismissed in this chapter (§3.6), leaving Equal Division and Common Ownership as the remaining options (§3.7). In Chapter Four I reject Equal Division. With the ground cleared, Chapters Five to Seven are devoted to formulating my own, Common Ownership conception of natural resource justice.

3.1 Natural resources

Following Charles Beitz, one can identify two major elements that contribute to the advancement of human societies: the first is 'human cooperative activity', the other is what Beitz terms 'the natural component' (1979: 137). Beitz characterizes this natural component in Henry Sidgwick's words, as 'the utilities derived from any portion of the earth's surface' (Sidgwick 1908: 255). However, it is not the surface of the Earth alone from which human societies derive goods.[1] The natural things of value to humans encompass (at least): land, soils, vegetation, nonhuman biological entities, freshwater sources, the ocean and the seabed, the atmosphere, sunlight, wind, geothermal heat, extractive resources such as hydrocarbons and minerals, chemical elements, the electromagnetic spectrum, and the Earth's gravitational field.

In what follows I will be using the term 'natural resource' in a fairly loose way, to refer to anything that: a) is a part of the natural world; that b) individuals or collectives claim rights of jurisdiction or ownership over (the nature of such rights will be explicated later in this section). I follow Chris Armstrong in taking these parts of the natural world to encompass, roughly speaking, 'raw materials...comprising both matter and energy' (2017: 27, fn.3). According to clause (b), a part of the natural world *becomes* a natural resource as soon as individuals and collectives claim rights over it. These claims will not necessarily be made explicitly; I take an individual to claim a use-right over a natural object, for example, simply by using it. This definition is similar to Richard Arneson's simple characterization of natural resources as 'valued parts of the earth' (1989a: 173); or Ronald Dworkin's 'constructivist' conception, according to which people can individuate parts of the natural world in whatever way they like in order to stake claims to them (see Dworkin 1981b).[2] Whether such claims are legitimate is another question, leaving open the possibility that some things that count as natural resources according to this definition may not permissibly be owned or *used* as resources.

That natural resources are things that humans assert rights over implies that they are in some way instrumental to human well-being—as does the very terminology of 'resources'. However, I leave open the possibility that individuals or collectives may claim rights over natural resources to preserve them for non-instrumental or non-anthropocentric reasons (for example, collectives may assert the right to exclude others from certain ecosystems, or from interacting with endangered species, for such reasons). It is also important to be clear that though natural resources are valued for human ends, this does not imply that they lack any kind of intrinsic or independent value.[3] Although I will not have space to explicitly engage with concerns of environmental ethics in this work, I think various parts of the natural world have a

---

[1] As Beitz acknowledges in later work (2005: 419).

[2] The 'constructivist' terminology is from Kolers (2012: 275–6).

[3] Exactly what it would mean for a natural resource to have intrinsic value is another question. See, for example, J. O'Neill 1992.

value or status that renders certain rights that human beings might claim over them indefensible (for example, rights to destroy, or consume, or possess).[4] Where this is the case, such resources—or rather such resource rights—should be excluded from theorizing about just allocation amongst human beings.

My definition of natural resources assumes that a rough and ready distinction can be marked between natural objects and those that are human-produced (such as ideas, infrastructure, institutions, and manufactured goods), whilst recognizing the dependence of the latter upon the former. All human-produced objects will demand natural resources in their design, construction, and use (even the ideational objects of intellectual property law could not be constructed without oxygen and water). All manufactured goods will contain natural resources as essential (and sometimes recoverable) parts. Rare earths, for example, can be extracted from recycled electronic waste using 'urban mining' techniques that are likely to become an increasingly significant source of such elements in the future.[5]

The rights that are claimed to natural resources will here be understood in accordance with the canonical account of jurisdictional and property rights in Western political philosophy. The idea is not that this is the one *correct* account of rights that can be claimed to natural resources, but rather that it succeeds in identifying various important rights that human beings may claim here, which could be further supplemented or individuated as needed. On this picture, *ownership* rights comprise a number of potential incidents, including: the right to possess, the right to modify, the right to manage, the right to use, the right to consume, the right to destroy, the right to transfer or alienate, the right to security, and the right to extract income.[6] In the case of natural resources such as land and forests, important property incidents also include rights of access (the right to enter the region); withdrawal (the right to extract resources from a region); and exclusion (the right to prevent others from accessing or using a resource).[7]

Jurisdictional rights differ from ownership rights in that whilst the latter can be held by individuals, the former involve a political form of authority that I will assume can only legitimately be possessed by certain collectives. Jurisdictional rights, as Cara Nine explains, grant the 'authority to legislate,

---

[4] That *some* rights claimed over a given natural resource are indefensible does not entail that *no* rights over that object can be justified. Imagine, for example, that there exists a natural resource R (a plant or nonhuman animal, say) that humans have no right to consume or destroy. It may yet be the case that certain individuals have a right to manage or extract income from R (as might take place in a national park); or to exclude others from accessing R (in fact, it could even be the case that some individuals have not just a right but *a duty* to exclude others from R).

[5] Japan claims to possess hundreds of thousands of tons of rare earth elements in the form of used electronics (Tabuchi 2010).

[6] This list is drawn from A M Honoré's famous account of the incidents of property (1968: 112ff.), with some additions taken from Christman (1994: 29).

[7] See Armstrong 2017: 22–4; Ostrom & Schlager 1992: 250–2.

adjudicate and enforce resource rights within a geographical domain' (2013: 234). These jurisdictional rights need not be absolute and may be limited by the requirement that outsiders be considered—or included—in collective decisions. I shall use the term 'territory' to refer to a geographical domain that is bounded by some such right of jurisdiction.

There are two other kinds of territorial right besides jurisdiction over natural resources, which I will not examine in depth in the discussion that follows: firstly, the right to exercise jurisdiction over the people within a territory; and secondly, the right to determine matters of immigration including entry, residency, and citizenship status within the region.[8] I take it that each of these territorial rights is in need of separate justification; although the right of jurisdiction over resources certainly appears to entail *some* right of jurisdiction over people since, as Jeremy Waldron points out, 'property relations do not exist between persons and objects; they exist between persons and other persons' (1988: 267). I will not have time to discuss the nature and defensibility of these other territorial rights much further, but certainly do not intend to suggest, in what follows, that a collective with rights of jurisdiction or ownership over the natural resources in a given territory will necessarily possess any right to prevent outsiders from entering the region.

3.2 Natural resources in theories of justice

Natural resources are of fundamental value to human beings in the sense that humans use natural resources in everything—and everything of value—that they make and do. Natural resources comprise the ground we walk on, the air we breathe, and the water we drink. They are essential for satisfying our basic needs, exercising our autonomy, and providing us with opportunities and capabilities—including the ability to form and sustain political communities. Many contemporary political philosophers have ignored the question of how to justly distribute this 'natural component' worldwide, however, concentrating instead on how to fairly distribute products of cooperation and other goods within individual societies.[9]

Theorizing about domestic justice is an undeniably important endeavour, but if an account of global justice for natural resources is also required, then focusing on the societal case in the absence of a broader theory of natural

---

[8] This three-way distinction between jurisdiction over natural resources, jurisdiction over people, and the right to control borders appears in Miller 2012: 253–4; Moore 2015: 4; Nine 2012: 6; Simmons 2001: 300; Stilz 2011: 573; and Ypi 2013: 242.

[9] cf. Rawls 1999a. Carole Pateman points to this problem when noting that: 'discussions of the legitimacy of the modern state (always taken for granted) have said nothing about the land on which the state is created' (Pateman & Mills 2007: 36).

resource justice seems to put things backwards methodologically. Natural resources are essential inputs into all cooperative schemes, including those at the domestic level; and so, as Brian Barry says, 'Before co-operation can occur, general questions must have already been answered about rights over land, resources, and other advantages that would-be co-operators did not themselves create' (1989: 423).[10] Thus, any theory of justice concerning what co-members of a given society owe to one another must also determine which natural resources can be used in discharging those obligations.

Even statist theorists who claim that duties of justice (or at least, the most stringent of such duties) exist only at the domestic level therefore need a prior account that can identify which natural resources Canada, for example, is entitled to distribute justly amongst the Canadian people—and, furthermore, on which portion of the Earth Canadians are entitled to establish and engage in their joint endeavours. Whether one's overall theory of justice is sceptical or supportive of duties that cross state borders, then; the demands of this theory must be shown not only to be physically possible (given the state of the natural world), but also morally justifiable (given the claims or entitlements that other groups or individuals may have to the natural resources that it demands).[11]

In our world, questions of natural resource entitlement are not settled on a principled basis. The ability of current states to use or exercise jurisdiction over certain natural resources is the outcome not just of collective efforts and decision-making but also—and largely—war, conquest, colonialism, imperialism, fraud, exploitation, coercion, violent expulsion, unjustified exclusion, or just luck. But the question of how to share the world's natural resources between different individuals and societies is one that requires a normatively defensible answer. In the rest of this chapter, I continue laying some groundwork so that in Chapter Five, I can defend an account of what this normative justification should look like.

3.3 Two kinds of natural resource claim

There are two different kinds of claim that individuals and collectives tend to assert to natural resources (setting to one side, for now, the question of

[10] As Vallentyne, Steiner and Otsuka put it: 'Any *complete* theory of justice in holdings...must include an answer to the following question: What rights, if any, do individuals have to acquire property rights in previously unowned natural resources?' (2005: 214).
[11] Principles of distributive justice, as Simon Caney points out, 'standardly require, or permit, the utilization of natural resources'; and thus 'the realization of *any* proposed scheme of distributive justice is likely to have a marked effect on the natural world' (2012: 293; emphasis added).

whether the claims that get *asserted* are in fact legitimate ones). I will refer to these two kinds using the terminology of *general* claims and *particular* claims.[12] The difference between these categories can be illustrated by looking at the claims that are staked to natural resources in the context of climate change.

On the one hand, individuals and collectives make claims to *shares* of natural resources. For example, all parties to the UNFCCC claim a share of the world's climate sink capacity and it seems undeniable that all individuals have a claim to a share of the world's increasingly scarce freshwater supplies (on which climate change is expected to increase existing global stresses (IPCC 2014d: §2.3.2)). I call such claims 'general' claims because they tend to arise when the question of natural resource justice is presented as a problem of assessing fairness in the distribution of resource shares, at a level of generality abstracting from particular resource tokens.

Particular claims to natural resources, on the other hand, are supposed to link certain individuals or collectives to specific natural resource tokens. To give but a few examples: Tuvaluans claim a right to the land of the islands of Tuvalu;[13] some Canadians claim a national ownership right over the Alberta bitumen sands;[14] small-scale farmers may assert rights to their plots and crops in the face of climate change–related threats;[15] and many indigenous Amazonians claim certain rights over parts of the rainforest.[16]

Global egalitarian and statist (or nationalist) theories of justice tend to focus on either general or particular claims to natural resources, respectively.[17] Global egalitarian accounts of resource rights tend to start from an abstract perspective where the totality of the natural world is conceived as a good to be distributed fairly across all human beings. The solution to this allocation problem is often taken to be equal shares regardless of community

[12] Armstrong makes a similar distinction to this using the terminology of 'general claims' and 'special claims' (2017: 53).

[13] The island nation of Tuvalu is extremely vulnerable to climate change induced sea level rise. In 2002 Paani Laupepa—then Tuvalu's Assistant Environment Minister—was quoted as saying: 'We don't want to leave, it's our land, our God given land, it is our culture' (Price 2002).

[14] In the face of continued protests by indigenous peoples and environmental groups opposed to bitumen sands extraction, Joe Oliver—then Canada's Natural Resources Minister—wrote an open letter to *The Globe & Mail* newspaper complaining about environmental and 'other radical groups' using foreign money 'to lecture Canadians not to develop *our* natural resources' (Oliver 2012; emphasis added).

[15] A farmer evicted from his small farm in Uganda so that the land could be handed over to UK-based New Forests Company (which will use it for carbon credits and timber) is reported as stating: 'I remember my land, three acres of coffee, many trees... My land gave me everything. People used to call me "omataka"—someone who owns land. Now that is no more. I am one of the poorest now' (Vidal 2011).

[16] The Coordinating Body for the Indigenous Peoples' Organizations of the Amazon Basin has called for recognition that 'the most effective defense of the Amazonian Biosphere is the recognition of our ownership rights over our territories' (COICA 1989).

[17] For examples in the former camp, see B. Barry 1989: Chs. 16, 17, 19; and Beitz 1979: §3.2. In the latter, see Miller 2012; and Rawls 1999b.

membership. Statists or nationalists, on the other hand, reason from a world that is like our own, in the sense that it is divided into political units, each claiming jurisdiction over their respective territories. In such a world, they argue, states, nations, or peoples should be granted rights over (particular) territorial resources that are relatively unfettered (this is the principle of resource sovereignty, introduced in §2.3). This seeming conflict within the realm of natural resource rights—between particular claims (territorial claims, for example) and more abstract general claims—has been noted by a number of theorists.[18]

In what follows, I am going to look more closely at the arguments given in favour of these different positions. This examination will take place via an attempt to formulate an account of natural resource justice that is egalitarian in nature, but which pays adequate consideration to both general *and* particular claims. As will become apparent in Chapters Six and Seven, this account offers a principled defence for many of the particular natural resource rights that statists and nationalists seek to protect, thus defusing their objection to global egalitarianism for natural resources.

3.4 General claims and the argument for equality

When discussing the existence or nature of moral claims to the world's natural resources, two salient features of this good are commonly referred to. First, the world's natural resources are observed to be of fundamental value to all human beings (in the sense that they are necessary, or essential, for anything—and anything of value—that human beings make or do). Second, they are noted to exist independently of all human beings (in the sense that they do not owe their existence to human design).[19]

---

[18] See, for example, Caney 2012: 269, fn.33; Kolers 2012: 270–1; and Sidgwick 1908: 255.

[19] Brian Barry, in his critique of the current international system, objects that it 'makes the economic prospects of a country *depend*, to a significant degree, on something [natural resources] for which its inhabitants (present or past) can take *absolutely no credit* and to whose benefits they can lay no just claim' (1989: 451; emphases added). Beitz claims that 'adequate access to resources is a *prerequisite* for successful operation of (domestic) cooperative schemes', but that 'no one has a natural prima facie claim to the resources that *happen to be* under one's feet' (1979: 141; emphases added). Michael Blake and Mathias Risse consider study of the moral status of the world's original resources pertinent 'for two reasons: such resources, first, are *necessary* for any human activities to unfold; second, they have come into existence *without human interference*' (2007: 159; emphasis added). Paula Casal identifies several features of natural resources 'which make them a fit subject for distributive principles', including that they are '*non-produced* and so invulnerable to the claim that producers are morally entitled to their products' and 'uniquely *essential* for human survival' (2011: 313). Peter Vallentyne, in his introduction to left-libertarianism, defines natural resources as 'resources which are *not* the results of anyone's choices and which are *necessary* for any form of activity' (2000: 1; second emphasis added). See also Reitberger 2017: 1.

If the totality of the world's natural resources (or, more accurately, the totality of *rights to natural resources that human beings can legitimately claim*) is viewed as a good to be allocated fairly across all individuals, then these two features can be used to formulate a simple argument for a view that I will refer to as 'Equal Original Claims'. Firstly, given their central value to human beings, each individual must have *some* claim to the world's natural resources. Secondly, since natural resources exist independently of human beings (thus ruling out any particular claims that human beings may have as designers or creators of natural resources), no individual originally has a better claim to natural resources than any other.[20] Thus, each individual originally has a claim to the world's natural resources that is equal to that of everyone else (Equal Original Claims).

It is important to be clear about the sense in which such claims are *original*. Following Mathias Risse, I will take such claims to be original in the sense that: (1) they are possessed by individuals regardless of their time and place of birth; (2) they exist prior to the moral claims that individuals or groups can acquire by forming certain relations to resources; and, (3) they take as their object resources that exist independently of human beings (2012: 108). This state of original claims is theoretical rather than historical—defined by the claims of individuals with no specific characteristics, and no relations to resources that could give rise to any particular claims.

This *original* symmetry of claims to natural resources, though itself immutable, will be built upon as soon as individual human beings enter existence and come to acquire additional, particular claims to specific natural resources. Even though—from an atemporal standpoint, abstracting from the contingencies of individual circumstance—each human being originally has an equal claim to natural resources; somebody born in a place where potable water is limited to a single spring will presumably have a better claim to *that* water than a person born on the other side of the planet where drinking water is abundant. One might also think that individuals who are biologically disposed to need more of a certain resource or those who come to value particular instances of natural resources, develop attachments to them, incorporate them into their way of life, become dependent upon them, or improve them in some way, may acquire claims to them that others do not— at least when certain conditions are satisfied.

'Equal Original Claims' thus only characterizes the *original* situation with respect to the world's resources. This landscape of moral claims to natural resources, though simple to begin with, will soon become modified by human

---

[20] Brian Barry also characterizes the argument for 'an equal claim on natural resources' negatively (1989: 515). Casal terms this view—affirming 'the equal claim of all humanity to land and other planetary resources'—*geoism* (2011: 308–9).

existence and activity. A number of accounts can be given regarding how these equal original claims might restrict the morally permissible ways that individuals can use or interact with natural resources, and the particular rights that they can gain to them. The challenge here, as theorists have long recognized, is that of explaining how it is justifiable for certain individuals or groups to acquire rights to natural resources at the exclusion of others, given that this places those others under a duty of forbearance with respect to resources to which nobody originally had any better claim. In what remains of this chapter, I begin my defence of a particular way to understand Equal Original Claims and its implications for natural resource justice.

3.5 Original ownership and Equal Original Claims

In the Western political philosophy tradition, many discussions of rights to use and appropriate natural resources start by attempting to establish what *original ownership status* the Earth should be thought to possess. Those who do not think the Earth is something that can be owned may well find the terminology of 'ownership' troubling. I share this worry but think that if one interprets these discussions charitably, what original ownership debates really concern (what they could only concern) is the question of *what human beings originally owe to one another with respect to the natural world*. As stated in §3.1, I am following Waldron in taking property relations to exist between persons, rather than between persons and objects (1988: 267). This means that discussions of original world ownership, if they succeed in saying anything, say something about what property relations originally exist *between persons* with respect to natural objects. The ownership worry can hopefully also be further defused by recognizing that various property relations—those of full private ownership, for example (where all incidents fall to one agent)—cannot simply be assumed, but rather must be *proven* legitimate with respect to natural resources.[21]

A residual concern is that discussing original ownership *of the Earth* seem to assume that the whole world of natural objects is up for grabs in this debate. This is not an assumption that I intend to make here since, as stated in §3.1, I am presupposing that resource rights that cannot be legitimately possessed have already been excluded from our theorizing about just allocation amongst human beings. The project of identifying such illegitimate claims is an important task of environmental ethics that will have significant implications

---

[21] It may turn out, for example, that the only justifiable resource rights are collectively rather than privately held.

for the substance of the conclusions that I draw here, but which deserves extensive treatment of its own.[22]

The subject of original world ownership has recently been given an instructive treatment by Risse (2012: Ch. 6). I follow Risse in terming the four commonly identified options Joint Ownership, Equal Division, Common Ownership, and No Ownership; and in using capitalization to distinguish *original* ownership conceptions from general principles of ownership (2005: 361, fn.19). Effectively, each of these alternatives offers a different way to map the original moral terrain between human beings with respect to natural resources. All or some of these four conceptions—sometimes given slightly varying interpretations and referred to using different terminology—are discussed by Michael Blake and Mathias Risse (2007: 159ff), Gerald Cohen (1995: Ch. 4), John Cunliffe (2000: 5), Attracta Ingram (1994: 46), Darrel Moellendorf (2009: 475ff), A. John Simmons (1992: 238), and Peter Vallentyne, Hillel Steiner and Michael Otsuka (2005: 202–3). My discussion here is most notably informed by Risse's, but also departs from it in significant ways; one major difference being that although we both attempt to defend Common Ownership through a rejection of three prominent alternatives, we understand Common Ownership very differently.[23]

Joint Ownership and Equal Division construe the original relationship between humans with respect to natural resources in terms of a scheme of moral *rights* that individuals possess in this initial situation, where these rights are assigned in accordance with principles of joint ownership and equal division, respectively. According to the first principle, each human being has a right to the *whole* of the Earth's resources; a right that is as extensive as full private ownership. Because this right is shared by all, however, each intended use of the world's resources can be vetoed (and thereby made morally impermissible) by another individual.[24] According to the principle of equal division, on the other hand, each person has a right to *an equal portion of* the Earth's

---

[22] Risse excludes wildlife from the set of resources that are originally collectively owned for perhaps this reason (2012: 109). As explained in fn.4, I think it is more likely that concerns of environmental ethics will mean that certain *rights* with respect to wildlife must be excluded (e.g. rights to possess), but others may be included (e.g. rights to manage).

[23] Common Ownership, as Risse understands it, encapsulates the 'core idea ... that all co-owners ought to have an equal opportunity to satisfy basic needs to the extent that this turns on collectively owned resources' (2012: 111). I instead understand Common Ownership to be the view that the world's natural resources originally belong to everyone in the weak sense that each individual has a moral claim to *use* the natural world, and where exclusive rights to natural resources can only be gained by groups or individuals if such appropriation can be justified, somehow, to all other human beings. Risse construes this view (that 'we must justify the acquisition of resources to each other') as a form of Joint Ownership, which he rejects (2012: 121). A fuller defence of my own view (against Risse's) will take place in Chapter Five, where I will argue that Risse's conception of Common Ownership is too minimal, given a commitment to Equal Original Claims.

[24] See Cohen 1995: 14; Blake & Risse 2007: 160–1; Risse 2012: 110.

resources 'or, perhaps, its value equivalent' (Blake & Risse 2007: 160). If appropriation takes place beyond these limits, this is a moral transgression for which redistribution or compensation is in order.[25]

Common Ownership and No Ownership, on the other hand, are not characterized by principles of justice that assign *rights* over natural resources. Rather, these views specify the original relationship between humans with respect to natural resources in terms of the moral *claims* that individuals possess in this initial situation. On the Common Ownership view, the world's natural resources originally *belong to everyone* in the very weak sense that each individual has a moral claim to *use* the natural world, but lacks any rights of exclusion.[26] According to No Ownership, the Earth originally *belongs to no one* in the very strong sense that we begin with a vacuum of moral claims. Despite the belonging to everyone/belonging to no one distinction, Common Ownership and No Ownership are quite similar conceptions. Both deny that individuals have any original rights of *exclusion* over natural resources, so both are committed to the idea that the original relationship between human beings with respect to natural resources is one of no *private* ownership. The difference is that Common Ownership affirms, whilst No Ownership denies, that individuals still have *some* moral claims with respect to resources in this original situation.

These four options are not jointly exhaustive. Waldron, for example, suggests another possibility: an 'extreme version of original communism', from which no exclusive rights can arise (1988: 149). I will not be discussing alternatives to the four major approaches in what follows, however; in part because most other views can be construed as variations of the Common Ownership conception. Waldron's extreme original communism, for example, can be understood as a conception of original ownership according to which: (a) everybody originally has a claim to use natural resources, but lacks any rights of exclusion (Common Ownership); and (b) nobody can gain exclusive rights to natural resources. The second part of this schema (part (b)), concerning how original claims may be modified, can be filled out in a variety of ways, to create different forms of the Common Ownership view (Lockean interpretations, where exclusive rights can be gained provided 'enough and as good' is left for others, being one option).

As conceptions of the *original* ownership status of the Earth these four options are, however, mutually exclusive: the world's natural resources are *originally* either subject to a principle of joint ownership, *or* subject to a principle of equal division, *or* commonly owned, *or* unowned (or something else). It should be noted, though, that the *principle* of joint ownership and the

---

[25] See Steiner 1994: 268.
[26] See Blake & Risse 2007: 160; Cohen 1995: 79; and Ingram 1994: 46.

principle of equal division can be defended not only as original principles, but also as derivative principles; and that as derivative principles, they could be compatible with a No Ownership or Common Ownership conception of original ownership. For example, one could formulate a view according to which the world is *originally* owned in common and attempt to derive a principle of equal division as a proviso on appropriation from this state (in §3.7, I discuss Tim Hayward's view as an instance of this approach).

Daniel Butt claims that 'An interesting facet of the disagreement over ownership of the earth's resources is that it might be thought that there is no immediate way in which it can be resolved, short of recourse to some intuitive belief' (2009a: 150). Furthermore, he objects, 'It is not even clear to me that people do have intuitive beliefs on this issue, given the complexity of ideas relating to joint ownership. What is more common is to find writers simply asserting one position or the other to be the correct one' (2009a: 169, fn.31).[27] The argument of the previous section, however, has handed us one tool with which to approach this problem. Any conception of original ownership must at least be *compatible with* Equal Original Claims. Better still, a conception of original ownership might be shown to be *derivable from* Equal Original Claims. Perhaps, that is, one could argue that it is *implied by* Equal Original Claims, or else that it can be understood as an *interpretation of* Equal Original Claims. In §§3.6–3.7, I will use this approach to assess each of the four conceptions of original ownership. I will argue that the principle of joint ownership and the No Ownership conception are incompatible with Equal Original Claims. Equal Division, on the other hand, might be implied by Equal Original Claims; and Common Ownership could be an interpretation of Equal Original Claims.

3.6 Rejecting Joint Ownership and No Ownership

I first reject the principle of joint ownership. According to this principle, each human being has a right to the Earth's resources that is as extensive as full private ownership, although shared with every other human being. This means that any individual's intended use of the Earth could be vetoed by another owner. As many have pointed out, Joint Ownership is thus not only impracticable, but implausibly restrictive.[28] Whilst the universal consent required for any use of resources appears impossible to attain, vetoes from one's immediate neighbours are all too easy. But 'people can do (virtually) nothing without using parts of the external world' (Cohen 1995: 93). If every

---

[27] Similar comments are made by Leif Wenar (2016: 344).

[28] See, for example, Blake & Risse 2007: 160–1; Vallentyne 2012: 161–2.

use of natural resources (every breath of air, movement from one bit of land to another, or gathering of wild food) could be vetoed by another person, individuals would have no 'substantial control over their own lives' (Cohen 1995: 14); or, at least, no *morally permissible* control (the constraints supposedly placed by Joint Ownership are *moral* rather than physical, so it would remain possible for individuals to exert control over their lives by ignoring the vetoes of others, but in doing so they would violate the rights of joint owners).[29]

These considerations imply that the principle of joint ownership cannot do justice to Equal Original Claims. These claims, recall, were based on the value of natural resources to human beings, and so are not respected by a principle according to which individuals cannot *realize* any of this value without violating the rights of others. This principle, and the corresponding conception of original ownership, should therefore be rejected; given a commitment to Equal Original Claims.

Similar reasoning can be used to reject the No Ownership conception of original ownership. No Ownership is adopted by Michael Otsuka, Robert Nozick, and (perhaps) Jean-Jacques Rousseau, amongst others.[30] As Otsuka points out, it might appear a reasonable assumption regarding the original moral status of the Earth's resources if one does not share Locke's theological view that the Earth was given to humankind by a supernatural being (Otsuka 2003: 22, fn.28). However, it appears that if No Ownership is correct, then Equal Original Claims cannot be. No Ownership is the view, recall, that there is originally a vacuum of moral claims and rights with respect to natural resources. But if there are no claims at all originally, then there cannot be equal claims originally. For this reason, No Ownership tends to be the conception of original ownership advocated by theorists who wish to deny Equal Original Claims.[31] Those with a commitment to Equal Original Claims should reject No Ownership.

This rejection of No Ownership may concern those who hold that natural resources should not be subject to private property relations, who might view

[29] Locke thus speaks somewhat hyperbolically when objecting of Joint Ownership that 'If such a consent as that was necessary, Man had starved, notwithstanding the Plenty God had given him' (1690: V.28). The point is not that humans would starve if Joint Ownership is correct, but rather that it may well be impossible to eat without violating the rights of others.

[30] See Nozick 1974: 174ff. Rousseau may be thought an advocate of No Ownership due to an oft-cited passage deploring acts of enclosure, in which he states that 'the fruits are everyone's and the Earth no one's' (1775: 161). Wenar takes the first clause of this sentence to imply that Rousseau's view is in fact a hybrid of Common Ownership and No Ownership (Wenar 1998: 803–4). If Rousseau intends the second clause of the sentence to relay the idea that nobody has *private* ownership of the Earth, then he could instead be read as advocating a purely Common Ownership conception (since Common Ownership is also a no private ownership view).

[31] Otsuka combines No Ownership with a rejection of Equal Original Claims (2003: 27ff.); and right-libertarians commonly do likewise (for discussion, see Vallentyne 2012: 162; Risse 2012: 115–16).

No Ownership as the best representation of this commitment. Scepticism about private ownership of natural resources does not, however, tell in favour of No Ownership over Common Ownership. As explained in §3.5, both these conceptions are committed to the claim that individuals originally lack any rights of exclusion, and thus lack any rights of private property, over natural resources. Neither is it clear that rights of private property could more easily emerge from a starting point of Common Ownership. In fact, many who defend a No Ownership conception (right-libertarians, in particular) appear to do so because they hope that private property—and the accumulation of private property—can be more easily justified if we start from a vacuum of moral claims over natural resources. From this starting point, there are fewer claims that need to be taken into account in justifying private property rights.[32] Those concerned about private property over natural resources, or inequalities resulting from it, would thus do better to support a Common Ownership conception; where original rights of exclusive property are still denied, but original claims to use the world's resources are acknowledged and understood to place restrictions on appropriation.

3.7 Equal Division and Common Ownership

Since the principle of joint ownership and the No Ownership conception have been rejected, the choice remaining is between the Equal Division and Common Ownership conceptions of original ownership. Only one of these conceptions can be correct concerning the *original* ownership status of the Earth. In this work, I seek to formulate a Common Ownership account and must therefore reject Equal Division.

One initial worry about Equal Division is that the view, in itself, says nothing about particular claims to natural resources. The principle of equal division endows every individual with a right to an equal portion of the Earth's resources (or its value equivalent), but not 'possession of or a claim on any particular share' (Simmons 1992: 238).[33] This makes the principle of equal division a means of 'undifferentiated redistribution' and leaves it ill-

---

[32] Nozick, for example, hopes to defend a very liberal picture of private ownership over natural resources from an assumption of No Ownership. According to his worsening proviso on appropriation, 'A process normally giving rise to a permanent bequeathable property right in a previously unowned thing will not do so if the position of others no longer at liberty to use the thing is thereby worsened'—where such worsening is assessed relative to a very permissive baseline (Nozick 1974: 178ff.).

[33] As Steiner puts it, under Equal Division raw resources are 'owned in the weak sense that a specified *proportion* of them belongs to each person. But they're unowned in the strong sense that none of them is specifically ascribed to any particular person as an item in a property title' (1994: 235, fn.11).

equipped to deal with particular claims (Armstrong 2013a: 57). In other words, whilst the principle of equal division purports to tell us what *distribution* of natural resources is just (one of equal per capita shares), it says nothing about which natural resources should be assigned to each person. This is a problem, because many of the claims to natural resources that people press with urgency in real-world conflicts are particular (see the list of climate change–related particular claims detailed in §3.3). If Equal Division cannot tell us anything about the legitimacy of such claims—beyond saying whether the claimants have more or less than their fair share of natural resources—then it is at best an incomplete account of natural resource rights for our purposes.

The principle of equal division does, however, succeed in the important task of setting egalitarian limits on appropriation, and could be supplemented with a method by which to identify and assess claims to particular natural resources. And most importantly, the principle of equal division is prima facie compatible with Equal Original Claims. In fact, one could attempt to defend Equal Division by arguing that the equal original claims of all constrain every individual's entitlement to no more than an equal share, so co-owners can have the same.[34] Equal Division thus appears to be a serious contender, given acceptance of Equal Original Claims. The entirety of Chapter Four will be devoted to rejecting it.

What about Common Ownership? This, recall, is the view that each individual originally has a moral claim to use the world's resources, but lacks any right of exclusion. As it stands, Common Ownership does not appear to be incompatible with Equal Original Claims, but neither does it appear to be a straightforward implication of the view. However, Common Ownership could perhaps be taken as an *interpretation* of what Equal Original Claims amounts to. To be a plausible interpretation, a Common Ownership approach must be able to explain when appropriation is permitted—i.e. how certain jurisdiction or ownership rights can be acquired by some to the exclusion of others—by showing how principles of appropriation can be justified in some sense to all human beings. Some appropriation *must* be justified, because otherwise the original claims possessed by human beings will be empty. Such appropriation must be *justified*, however, in line with principles that respect the equal original claims of all.

I argued in §3.6 that the principle of joint ownership is incompatible with Equal Original Claims. Any principle of appropriation justified from the perspective of Common Ownership will therefore, if successful, demand less than unanimous consent. This makes justification a thorny issue, given that one must explain how it is legitimate for individuals to appropriate natural

---

[34] This appears to be Steiner's approach to defending Equal Division (1994: 235–6). It will be discussed further in Chapter Four.

resources, and thereby impose duties of forbearance on others, in a unilateral manner.[35] There are many candidate principles of appropriation that one might attempt to justify from the perspective of Common Ownership, both substantive (e.g. appropriation is permitted provided everybody else is left with enough for subsistence) and procedural (e.g. appropriation is permitted provided it is justified via some kind of democratic or hypothetical agreement). To succeed in justifying any particular principle of appropriation, one must explain how it can be upheld in accordance with Equal Original Claims. The illustration just given of a substantive principle of appropriation, for example, arguably is not justified in this sense, because its minimal focus on subsistence cannot do justice to the equal original claims of each individual.[36]

When understood this way—as an approach by which one seeks to justify principles of appropriation in accordance with Equal Original Claims—it is possible to argue that Common Ownership will in fact entail a principle of equal division. A theory of this form is suggested in the work of Hayward. Though Hayward does not explicitly discuss the original ownership status of the Earth, he appears to adopt a Common Ownership conception, stating that (2006: 352):

> Prior to engaging in the requisite labour no-one can have any special claim to anything, perhaps, as Beitz says, but in those circumstances, if ethical considerations can apply at all, then a reasonable one is that everyone is entitled to try to make the most of what they find round about them without interference from others.

Hayward then offers a Lockean justification of 'individuated property rights' (to what is originally held in common), claiming that appropriation must take place in accordance with a proviso leaving enough and as good for everyone else. Acknowledging that the focus on 'enough' appears to make this a sufficientarian rather than egalitarian principle of appropriation, Hayward nevertheless argues that in a world of scarcity, enough and as good can only be an *equal* share (2006: 360–1). Thus, although apparently adopting Common Ownership as the original ownership status of the Earth, Hayward ends up using this conception in an attempted justification of the principle of equal division.[37]

---

[35] Worries about such unilaterality are expressed by Kant, who concludes that due to its unilateral nature, original acquisition 'can be only *provisional*' (1797: 415ff.).

[36] As Vallentyne puts it, this subsistence-based principle 'fails...to recognize the extent to which natural resources belong to all of us in some egalitarian manner' (2012: 163–4).

[37] See also Hayward 2005a: 326. Hayward's argument is somewhat more complicated than this and invokes his distinctive conceptualization of natural resources, but this sketch will suffice for my purposes here.

In order to avoid confusion in what follows, it is important to be clear about the structure of any given form of global egalitarianism for natural resources. As just explained, one might claim that the principle of equal division is directly entailed by Equal Original Claims (thus ending up with an Equal Division conception of original ownership). On the other hand, one might attempt to justify the principle of equal division more circuitously—as a principle that is claimed to derive from the Common Ownership conception of original ownership. Thus, to reject the principle of equal division—which I aim to do—it is not sufficient to show that it cannot be defended directly from Equal Original Claims (my project in Chapter Four). One must also show that a principle of equal division cannot be justified from the perspective of Common Ownership (which I will do in Chapter Five).

3.8 Conclusion

In this chapter I defended the view that each human being has an equal original claim to the world's natural resources. I then used this view to assess four conceptions of the original ownership status of the Earth: Joint Ownership, No Ownership, Equal Division, and Common Ownership. I showed that a commitment to Equal Original Claims should lead us to reject the principle of joint ownership and the No Ownership conception. The choice one is left with is that between Equal Division and Common Ownership. It is the latter that I defend in this work.

In Chapter Four I reject Equal Division, in order to clear the ground for an alternative, Common Ownership conception of original ownership. Then, in Chapter Five, I formulate a particular interpretation of the Common Owner-ship approach. This interpretation, which I term 'Contractualist Common Ownership', will be defended on the basis that it invokes an appropriate understanding of the way in which human beings can be said to have original claims to natural resources that are equal. In addition, I show that the principle of equal division cannot be justified from the perspective of Contractu-alist Common Ownership, thereby concluding that the principle of equal division should be rejected as an interpretation of natural resource egalitarianism.

4

Against Equal Division of Natural Resources

In Chapter Three, I used a commitment to Equal Original Claims to reject the Joint Ownership and No Ownership conceptions of original world ownership. In this chapter I take on the more challenging task of rejecting Equal Division, to clear the way for my alternative, Common Ownership, account.

Equal Division is a very prominent interpretation of natural resource egalitarianism. It is held by left-libertarian Hillel Steiner, who defends a right to equal 'bundles' or portions of natural resources (Steiner 1994: 235–6, 270); and liberal egalitarian Brian Barry, who states a commitment to 'equal shares' (Barry 1989: 515–16).[1] The principle of equal division is also relevant to discussions of climate justice since, as discussed in §2.1, Steve Vanderheiden invokes a restricted version of this principle when attempting to justify the equal per capita emissions view. And when David Miller attempts to refute global egalitarianism concerning natural resources, he takes Equal Division to define this position (2007: Ch. 3).

This chapter seeks to undermine Equal Division, primarily through a critique of Steiner's view, along with potential extensions to it. I focus on Steiner's work because I believe he provides one of the strongest and most carefully formulated defences of Equal Division. Steiner's development of the theory also provides a trajectory by which to understand Equal Division and the challenges that it faces. My aim, however, is to reject Equal Division itself, and not just Steiner's formulation of it, and I will critique several other proponents of the principle of equal division along the way.

---

[1] At this point, Barry is discussing justice between generations and takes equal shares to require that each generation have an equal range of opportunities with respect to natural resources (1989: 515). Elsewhere, Barry suggests that 'countries, as collectivities, should have their fair share of the world's resources' (1989: 492), where this fair share seems to be understood in terms of 'equal access' (1989: 489). For individuals, he talks of 'an equal right to enjoy their benefits' (B. Barry 1989: 448).

I start by providing some further explanation of why one might take Equal Division to follow from Equal Original Claims (§4.1). I then seek to reject Equal Division by drawing on Miller's objection that there is no defensible metric by which resource shares can be made commensurate (see Miller 2007: Ch. 3). What the metric problem shows, I argue, is that Equal Division is insufficiently impartial to satisfy the equal original claims that motivate the view in the first place. I make this case by critiquing each of three principal metrics proposed to amalgamate individual valuations of natural resources and thereby render Equal Division both coherent and defensible; namely, economic value, opportunity cost, and ecological space (§4.2). I conclude that to respect Equal Original Claims, the best approach will be to formulate a Common Ownership conception of justice for natural resources (§4.3).

4.1 The argument for Equal Division

A commitment to Equal Original Claims is likely to be the major motivation for adopting Equal Division. Steiner takes the right to an equal share of natural resources to be *'near-foundational'*, directly implied by (or perhaps, one might say, forming a part of) each individual's foundational right to equal negative freedom (2011a: 111, fn.5). In more detail, Steiner holds that our foundational right to equal freedom entails the possession of 'equal original property rights' and that it is just 'evident' that these equal original property rights entitle us to *equal shares* of 'initially unowned things' (1994: 235–6).[2]

---

[2] Though he generally talks in terms of equal original *rights*, I take Steiner to be committing himself to roughly the same view that I have termed Equal Original Claims—and he does elsewhere talk of 'an equal claim to natural resources' (Steiner 1994: 248, fn.25). The brief sketch given here is an oversimplification and does not do justice to the intricacies of Steiner's complete theory. A full explanation of Steiner's commitment to Equal Division requires a detour through his views regarding the necessity of rights compossibility; that is, his claim that any set of rights must be mutually consistent (what he describes as the 'linch-pin' of his argument in *An Essay on Rights* (1994: 2–3)). Rights compossibility requires the set of rights possessed by each individual—their 'domain' of negative freedom—to be compossible also; and Steiner argues that this will only be the case when these domains are title-based (title-based domains are constituted by property rights, where 'no two persons simultaneously have rights to one and the same physical thing') (Steiner 1994: 90–2). Any *current* set of such domains, Steiner claims, must—if it is valid—ultimately be derived from a compossible set of original property rights that include legitimate rights to initially unowned things (1994: 105–7; 235). The (prescriptive) question of how these original rights should be allocated thus arises, with Steiner holding that 'Persons are assigned equal freedom when they are assigned *equal* original rights' (1994: 228; emphasis added). Equal original rights, Steiner argues, must include a right of self-ownership (1994: 231–2) and (here is the 'evident' step in Steiner's argument) a right to an equal bundle of initially unowned things (1994: 235). These two kinds of original right, when combined, are supposed to continuously generate the mutually consistent rights domains that Steiner's historical entitlement theory of justice requires (1994: 236).

Another simple-looking argument for Equal Division justifies the move from Equal Original Claims to equal shares by invoking a principle that may seem plausible to many: that when people have an equal claim to a good, that good should be divided between them equally (or, perhaps, that each should have *the opportunity to acquire* an equal share). This principle follows from John Broome's 'general rule of fairness' (introduced in §2.1), according to which 'when some good is to be divided among people who need or want it, each person should receive a share that is proportional to the claim she has to the good' (2012: 69). Therefore (the argument might go), if original claims to natural resources are equal, then natural resources should originally be divided between all human beings on an equal per capita basis (see Miller 1999: 191).

This argument for Equal Division appears somewhat deceptive in its simplicity, because it does not explicitly acknowledge the different incidents of resource rights (identified in §3.1). Equal Division, as Mathias Risse suggests, seems to gain plausibility 'from the idea that there is a (figurative) *heap* of resources to which each person has an equal claim' (2012: 122; emphasis added). This idea is, however, misleading. The world's natural resources are not a good that can be divided up and distributed like a heap of sand, a cake, or a pot of money. What we are discussing when we talk about the fair distribution of natural resources is not actually how to parcel up the resources themselves (so as to hand them over to individuals who will then be full owners). What we are really discussing is how to allocate jurisdiction and ownership *rights*: rights which place individuals under a system of rules concerning what they can *do* with natural resources.[3] Because resource rights consist of many incidents, it is not necessarily the case—as Equal Division might appear to imply—that each individual should be given full ownership rights over a distinct bundle, portion, or share of natural resources.[4] This is a problem that Steiner avoids to some extent, since he does acknowledge the presence of different property incidents on various occasions. But even Steiner tends, for simplicity's sake, to talk in terms of rights that individuals have

---

[3] As Jeremy Waldron points out, the concept of property just *is* 'the concept of a system of rules governing access to and control of material resources' (1988: 31).

[4] This appears to be an instance of what Gerald Gaus identifies as a problematic tendency for philosophical debates about property to recognize the fragmented nature of this concept, but continue to draw on the ideal of full ownership in discussion of substantive issues (2012: 94–5). This would worryingly appear to privilege—without defence—a full ownership private property system; that is, one where 'the rules governing access to and control of material resources are organized around the idea that resources are on the whole separate objects each assigned and therefore belonging to some particular individual' (Waldron 1988: 38). Fabian Schuppert raises a related problem with the conceptualization of natural resources as 'some stack of stuff to be divided' (2012: 218): that this neglects 'the fragile and mutable nature of many natural resources and their complex interconnectedness'; a nature that (he suggests) makes many of them inappropriate objects of full private ownership (2012: 220ff.).

over individual physical *objects*, rather than their possession of individual property *incidents* (1994: 98–100, 102, fn.60).

It is also important to bear in mind that the step from Equal Original Claims to Equal Division is not as obvious as some might think. Anybody wishing to defend this move owes an explanation of why an equal claim to a good (in this case, the world's resources) is best satisfied by an individuated equal share of that good. One might instead think that equal claims would be better respected by a system that gives an individual equal standing with respect to that good: perhaps via an equal say in how it is used, or an equal right to use it in certain ways. I will ultimately defend a theory of natural resource justice along these lines. However, first I will argue not merely that Equal Division fails to possess clear support from Equal Original Claims but, more problematically, that the two are inconsistent.

4.2 The Metric Problem for Equal Division

Having clarified the nature of the allocation problem that Equal Division theorists purport to solve, we can now consider the main problem with the way that they attempt to do so. This problem arises because natural resources are an extremely heterogeneous good and thus there is significant difficulty in specifying what an equal per capita distribution would look like. This is where Miller's metric problem surfaces to suggest that Equal Division cannot even be rendered coherent, since there is no defensible common measure by which to compare shares of resources and determine whether they are equal (1999: 191ff.; 2007: Ch. 3). It is important to note the 'defensible' caveat in this statement. Clearly it is possible to come up with various metrics by which to compare resource shares—two examples would be weight and volume. The problem, as I will explain, is that such metrics fail to make shares equal in a way consistent with Equal Original Claims.

Let us look at this objection in more detail. The claim that two shares of natural resources are equal could be understood in the following ways:

1. The shares of natural resources are identical (containing the same physical quantity of each resource: the same amount of gold, oil, water etc.).
2. The shares of natural resources have the same value (where that value might be measured in terms of opportunity, access, benefit,[5] welfare,

---

[5] As explained in fn.1, Brian Barry suggests each of these first three metrics.

opportunity for welfare,[6] market value,[7] ecological space,[8] weight, volume, or something else).

No defender of equal shares, to my knowledge, adopts (A). Steiner rejects this option because 'it is unreasonable to assume that each quantity of each kind of resource is physically divisible into the requisite equal portions' (Steiner 1987: 65; see also Dworkin 1981b: 285). Aside from the issue of physical impossibility, (A) appears absurd,[9] impractical and difficult to formulate (Miller 2011: 99, fn.30), and looks to be guilty of fetishizing particular resources, 'which matter not in themselves but for what they enable people to do' (Miller 2008: 142).

Defenders of Equal Division therefore appeal to (B) instead, interpreting equal shares of natural resources as those with the same value.[10] (B), however, must be cashed out in terms of a particular metric, and this poses serious difficulty. As Miller points out, the value of a natural resource seems relative to individual and societal wants, abilities (technological and knowledge-based), and beliefs about appropriate use (1999: 191ff.).[11] Essentially, there will be significant global variation in many factors relevant to determining the value of natural resources, including: personal and societal conceptions of the good; ideas about how human beings should relate to the natural world;[12] views about what natural resources are and how they are individuated; understandings of resource rights (e.g. which incidents the concept of property should fragment into for natural resources, how these incidents should be bundled together, and which should be given priority in cases of conflict); beliefs about whether natural resources are fungible; assessments of the relative value of different natural resources (for example, extractive resources

---

[6] One might think that Michael Otsuka's view falls into this category (see Otsuka 2003). I will not, however, be discussing Otsuka in what follows because he is not a proponent of Equal Division. Otsuka defends global equality of opportunity for welfare *overall*—with natural resources in particular to be distributed to this end—rather than equal division of natural resources on an opportunity for welfare metric (2003: 27ff.). Peter Vallentyne's view—according to which 'justice requires that the value of natural resources be used to promote effectively equality of opportunity for a good life'—is likewise a form of global welfarism rather than Equal Division; as Vallentyne notes (Tideman & Vallentyne 2001: 452). A welfarist version of egalitarianism concerning natural resources is also defended by Chris Armstrong (2017: 3).

[7] See Dworkin 1981b; Steiner 1994. In §4.2.2, I explain that Ronald Dworkin has a somewhat idiosyncratic understanding of market value. It would be more accurate to say he has a metric of *opportunity cost to others* (see Dworkin 1981b: 338; 2000: 149).

[8] As I discuss in §4.2.3, this metric is suggested in the work of Tim Hayward and Steve Vanderheiden.

[9] Risse thinks the idea that 'every nugget of gold found on the ocean floor [must] be divided among all humans' is typically raised in an attempted *reductio* of the claim that humanity has some form of collective ownership of the Earth; an unsuccessful one given that there are other—more plausible—ways of conceptualizing such collective ownership (2012: 109).

[10] See Steiner 1987: 65ff.   [11] See also Risse 2012: Ch.6, §7; Ypi 2008: 449ff.

[12] As Krushil Watene points out, 'There are deep differences in how different cultures value, and think about their obligations to, the natural world' (2016: 204).

compared to land); views about the appropriate and permissible use of resources (whether they should be used at all, or for certain purposes); and available technology and knowledge.

I will refer to this as the fact of reasonable value pluralism concerning natural resources; which, following Joshua Cohen, can be understood roughly speaking as the idea that there are distinct understandings of the value of natural resources, 'each of which is fully reasonable' (Cohen 1993: 281–2; see also Rawls 1993b: 36–7). This means that different people and different collectives may reasonably disagree about the value of any given set of natural resources (or resource rights). But in the face of such disagreement, it is very hard to see how two natural resource bundles could be judged to have *equal* value. Note the claim is not that *any* value disagreements will undermine Equal Division. It would not be reasonable, for example, for an individual to object that from his personal perspective, any arrangement where he did not have rights to nearly all the world's resources would be 'unequal'. But a significant amount of this disagreement will be reasonable—and some of it unavoidable—and such *reasonable* value pluralism must be respected by any theory of natural resource justice.

One could mistakenly assume that Equal Division deals successfully with such reasonable disagreement. If an individual is given an equal share of natural resources, they are left free to use those resources in a way that reflects their own particular understanding of value (conservationists can preserve their resources, whilst developers can convert theirs, and so on). However, the problem of reasonable value pluralism is deeper than this assumption recognizes, undermining the very idea that we could identify such 'equal' shares in the first place. The problem is that the metric used to individuate resource shares must be sufficiently impartial if Equal Division is to be consistent with Equal Original Claims. The idea behind this defence of Equal Division, recall, was that each individual's equal original claim to the world's resources can be satisfied by giving them an equal share of this good. But if Equal Division individuates these shares using a metric of valuation that favours some individuals over others, those who are disadvantaged by this metric can legitimately object that their equal original claims have not been respected after all.

A metric will favour some individuals over others if it fits with the former's, but not the latter's, understanding of what makes natural resources valuable; thereby guaranteeing the former, but not the latter, an equal share of what they value. To illustrate this using a toy example: if what W values most about natural resources is their weight, whilst V most values their volume; then equal distribution with a weight metric will prioritize the claims of W over V; because W is guaranteed an equal share of what they value, whilst V has no such assurance. A weight metric thus fails to be impartial and there is no clear sense in which a division by this measure respects the equal original claims of *V*. More realistically (and reasonably), some people will consider natural resources valuable due to the opportunities that they provide, whilst others will believe that their fundamental value should be assessed in terms of their contribution to welfare. Distributing on a welfare metric will treat the former unjustly, whilst an opportunity metric will be unfair to the latter.

One could, of course, argue that all but one of these understandings of natural resource value are simply wrong. Somebody advocating equality of natural resources with a welfare metric might, for example, claim that it is mistaken to value natural resources for the broader opportunities they provide. However, given the apparent intractability of the long-running 'equality of what' debate,[13] it seems difficult for any theorist to claim that their favoured valuation of resources is the globally correct one. For Equal Division to be rendered consistent with Equal Original Claims, proponents must therefore find a way to formulate a metric that passes the *impartiality test*: i.e. a metric that is neutral between different reasonable understandings of the value of natural resources (and resource rights).

The essential task then, as Steiner himself concedes, is to find a metric that does not 'better serve some persons' interests than others' (1987: 67).[14] Proponents of Equal Division have attempted to accomplish this by formulating metrics that *amalgamate* the varying valuations of different individuals. In what follows, I argue that each of the three principal metrics proposed to amalgamate individual valuations of natural resources and thereby render Equal Division both coherent and defensible—namely, economic value, opportunity cost, and ecological space—fail the impartiality test.

Before proceeding, it is important to explain a distinction between substantive and procedural conceptions of natural resource justice. Equal Division is what I will term a substantive conception of justice, but defenders of the view sometimes attempt to solve the metric problem by formulating a *procedure* for making resource shares commensurate. In an earlier paper, for example, Steiner contemplates a procedure of *universal agreement*, stating: 'It may well be that the only commensuration standard that is properly construable as an amalgam of all rightholders' own commensurations is one directly agreed to by all of them' (1987: 68).[15] Another procedure that is appealed to—and

---

[13] See, for example, Dworkin 1981a, 1981b; Arneson 1989b; Cohen 1989; Roemer 2003; Page 2007.

[14] Steiner also acknowledges the importance of impartiality in Steiner 2011a: 121.

[15] Steiner does not pursue this approach, instead retaining hope that the 'pure rent' (or unimproved value) of resources can be calculated and used as a metric (1987: 68). This is an understandable hope since, as Miller points out, making universal agreement necessary to the choice of metric would effectively turn Steiner's Equal Division conception into something resembling Joint Ownership. If appropriation is not permitted until a metric has been universally agreed, each person essentially 'has a veto right against anyone else's appropriating resources from the common' (Miller 2011: 100).

which will be discussed in §4.2.2—is a *hypothetical auction* (Dworkin 1981b; Steiner 2011b: 332, fn. 12). The essential role played by these procedures may create confusion regarding whether Equal Division is appropriately understood as a substantive or a procedural conception of justice.

The way I shall use the term, however, a conception of justice is only procedural when *its very principles* are identified using a (potentially hypothetical) fair procedure (a procedure that will in turn be constructed on the basis of one's substantive normative commitments). Beitz's conception of natural resource justice is thus procedural because—as explained in §1.2.1—his RRP is defended as the *outcome* of a hypothetical contract. My own conception of natural resource justice will also count as procedural, for similar reasons. Steiner's Equal Division conception, on the other hand, is given the substantive defence explained at the start of §4.1. For Steiner, the defining principle of Equal Division—that each individual is entitled to an equally valuable share of natural resources—is non-negotiable and does not require a procedural defence. The role of any procedure is limited to determining how the (substantively) equal shares mandated by the principle can be individuated, which is not sufficient to render Equal Division a procedural conception of justice.[16]

4.2.1 *Economic value*

Steiner's appeal to economic value emerges directly out of further concerns about the inadequacy of solution (A), according to which equal shares would be identical shares. Even if natural resources *could be* divided equally between all currently existing people on this basis (say because they were homogenous), a problem arises when new people—with their own rights to an equal share—are born. At first, each of the original generation might be able to redistribute sufficient natural resources to maintain an equal distribution, but Steiner worries that this solution will soon be unavailable as natural resources are laboured upon by their owners. Once individuals have

---

[16] As Steiner puts it: 'Vesting a collectivity with the authority to decide the values of natural resources—coupled with the *requirement* that each receive an equal part of that value—is very different from vesting a collectivity with the authority to decide which resources should compose each share, who should get it, and what may or may not be done with it' (1987: 68; emphasis added). Dworkin too is clear that his arguments 'are constructed against the background of assumptions about *what equality requires in principle*'—i.e. equality of resources (1981b: 345; emphasis added). In the auction thought experiment through which Dworkin attempts to render Equal Division coherent, the bidders are committed from the start to a substantive principle of justice according to which the available resources shall be 'divided equally among them'. The auction procedure is only needed to individuate those shares, given that the resources cannot be separated into the right number of 'identical bundles' (Dworkin 1981b: 285). Dworkin contrasts this approach to that of Rawls in which, he says, a procedure is used to 'establish that background' of what equality requires. Unlike Rawls, Dworkin intends his procedure merely to 'enforce rather than construct a basic design of justice' (Dworkin 1981b: 345).

transformed their shares through use, their duties to newcomers can no longer be discharged by the transfer of raw resources (Steiner 1994: 270–1).

What the original appropriators must owe instead, Steiner concludes, is something *equivalent* to the natural resources they would have had to transfer. Steiner claims one can then generalize that 'in a fully appropriated world, each person's original right to an equal portion of initially unowned things amounts to a right to an equal share of their total *value*', by which he means '*economic value*, i.e. price' (1994: 271). In other words, to implement Equal Division in a world of 'countless persons who are generationally differentiated', each person's entitlement cannot be 'one in kind' (i.e. to what is literally an equal portion of natural resources), but must instead be 'one to cash' (i.e. to an equal share of the *economic value* of natural resources) (Steiner 1998: 67). Equal Division is thus satisfied either when each of n (existing) individuals can appropriate natural resources of $1/n$ economic value (where 1 represents the total value of the natural resources to be distributed), or when those who appropriate natural resources of economic value greater than $1/n$ give sufficient cash compensation to those with less.

It appears that Equal Division can be satisfied on this metric even in cases where some individuals have no rights over *any natural resources at all*. Imagine that you live a world composed of ten people and natural resources of economic value 90, where the nine others possess all the natural resources—of value 10 each—and you possess none. Equal Division appears to be satisfied provided each transfers cash of value 1 to you when you arrive on the scene. However, if *what you want* is natural resources—not money—this hardly seems fair, especially if the others will not sell any of their natural resources to you.[17] This solution thus does not appear duly sensitive to the equal original claims of those who view natural resources as *non-fungible* sources of value, for whom cash compensation 'does not provide them with as good as that from which they are excluded' (Moellendorf 2009: 479).[18]

Other initial worries about the economic value metric are raised by Steiner himself. Firstly, the market value of a good depends both on the existing

---

[17] And Steiner suggests that nobody has a duty 'to offer for sale what is rightfully [theirs]' (1977: 46).

[18] It is also unclear how Steiner then escapes the incoherence with which he charges right-libertarianism, that: 'permitting a subset of self-owning persons unilaterally to acquire unencumbered ownership of *all* natural resources...implies that, in the absence of those owners' waivers, later arrivals are encumbered with *unperformable duties of non-trespass*'; which, if enforced, would violate the self-ownership that Steiner also takes to be a near-foundational right of each human being (Steiner 2011a: 111, fn.3). As Henry George puts it: 'Place one hundred men on an island from which there is no escape, and whether you make one of these men the absolute owner of the other ninety-nine, or the absolute owner of the soil of the island will make no difference to him or to them. In the one case, as the other, the one will be the absolute master of the ninety-nine—his power extending even to life and death, for simply to refuse them permission to live upon the island would be to force them into the sea' (2009: Book VII, Ch. II).

distribution of holdings and the personal valuations of those who possess them (Steiner 1977: 46; 1981: 563). Change the distribution or the preferences and the market value of the goods will usually change as well—so which set of prices do you use? It is hard to see how prices *can even be determined* for natural resources that are yet to be distributed. Furthermore, economic value differs from personal value, and so 'My loss, due to someone else's appropriation, may be greater than the economic value I might have received in the market for the object in question had I been its appropriator' (Steiner 1977: 46). If natural resources are distributed equally on an economic value basis, an individual might reasonably be able to complain that everybody else possesses bundles that she, personally, values more highly than the one she was given.

Steiner later rejects these worries as 'groundless' (1994: 271–2, fn.11). I am not convinced they are so easily allayed.[19] Either way, there are other reasons for rejecting Steiner's economic value solution to the metric problem. Steiner ultimately proposes to implement Equal Division on this metric by means of a financial mechanism termed the '*Global Fund*'. Natural resources are now conceptualized as 'geographical sites' (Steiner 2011b: 28), understood more precisely as 'portions of physical space' including 'all global surface areas and the supra- and sub-terranean spaces contiguous to them, as well as the natural objects they contain' (Steiner 2011b: 330).[20] The owners of these sites (effectively, states) are required to pay tax into the fund at a rate of 100 per cent of their *unimproved value*: 'their gross market value *minus* the value of the improvements added to them by human effort' (Steiner 2011b: 328).[21] The total fund—intended to be equivalent to 100 per cent of the unimproved value of the geographical sites owned globally—is then disbursed worldwide on an equal per capita basis. States in possession of territory that grants them lower than average unimproved value per capita will be net beneficiaries, whilst states whose territory embodies higher than average unimproved value per capita will pay more into the fund than they receive back.[22]

There are normative and epistemic difficulties with determining the 'unimproved value' of geographical sites. We are supposed to calculate this metric by: (1) establishing the gross market value of a site and then; (2) subtracting

---

[19] Steiner claims to have been concerned that the distribution-relative character of prices would make this metric biased against 'later arrivals' (1994: 271, fn. 11; 2011a: 121). Whether or not this is the case, the worry remains that market price 'cannot consistently be treated as a parameter for determining the very distributive entitlements of which it is necessarily a function' (Steiner 1980: 252). At this earlier juncture, Steiner believes the same problem to apply to the Georgist solution he later adopts; that of attempting to calculate the unimproved value of the land by subtracting the value of improvements from the market value (Steiner 1980: 264, fn.30).

[20] Elsewhere Steiner simply talks in terms of 'land' (see Steiner 1998).

[21] Subtracting the value of improvements is intended to protect the entitlement of self-owned individuals to the products of their labour (Steiner 1998: 70, fn.13), reflecting Steiner's desire to construct a theory of justice that is responsibility sensitive (1997; 2011a).

[22] This approach is also defended by Nicolaus Tideman (Tideman & Vallentyne 2001).

the value of human improvements. Step (2) mainly poses problems of an epistemic nature (namely, how to disentangle these values).[23] The problems posed by step (1) go deeper, however, because they show that whether or not step (2) is epistemically feasible, unimproved value is not a suitably impartial metric.

Steiner characterizes the gross market value of a site in terms of its 'full competitive value'—that is, 'the maximum amount that would be paid by bidders in a *global* auction' (2011b: 332, fn.12). Other things (i.e. the value of human improvements to that site) being equal, the *unimproved* value of a site is thus entirely a function of its full competitive value. This, however, depends on what bidders are willing and able to pay for it. As Steiner points out, this will largely be determined by the most economically valuable use that site can be put to, which will vary with changes in technology, individual preference functions, global consumption patterns, the depletion or discovery of natural resources and—presumably—changes to other geographical sites (Steiner 1994: 272; 1998: 68). Imagine, for example, that we use our land as an allotment and that one day, our neighbours build a supermarket on their adjacent site. Because our land could now be used as a supermarket car park, the maximum bid for it is likely to increase (and our tax liabilities with it).[24]

The question therefore arises whether this metric is sufficiently impartial between individuals and collectives with differential access to technology, knowledge, and finance; and reasonable variation in their preferences and beliefs regarding natural resource use (see Miller 2007: 58ff.). By allowing the unimproved value of natural resources to be dictated by global high-bidders, Steiner's proposal does not appear to do justice to significant diversity in worldviews and capacities concerning natural resources. Take the example of oil: this resource is prized highly by lots of individuals and groups, many of whom are very wealthy, so geographical sites containing oil are going to have relatively high unimproved value, and relatively high Global Fund liabilities. This holds regardless of whether the people inhabiting a geographical site containing oil wish to exploit it, are able to exploit it, or even think that it is permissible to exploit it. Thus, many are going to find they are credited with—and consequently liable for taxation on—resources that only have a high 'unimproved value' given uses that they themselves are unable, or unwilling, to make.

When Steiner responds to Miller's concerns about the cultural relativity of natural resource values, I think he reveals that the fundamental disagreement

---

[23] For discussion, see Miller 2007: 57ff. As Lisa Herzog puts it, Miller's essential point here appears to be that this epistemic problem is intractable: Steiner's view invokes 'a conceptual distinction that cannot be cashed out in concrete terms at the non-ideal level' (Herzog 2012: 279).

[24] This alone may create worries about the unimproved value metric. See Miller 2007: 60–1.

here concerns whether—or perhaps rather which—individuals and societies should be held responsible for their different outlooks and abilities regarding resource use. Steiner denies that the value of resources should be allowed to vary on this basis. The correct value of a production good like a natural resource, he insists, is given by 'standard economic theory', according to which it is 'entirely a function of the *most valuable* use to which it could be put' (Steiner 1997: 299, fn.10; emphasis added). The value of a natural resource is thus totally independent of any less economically valuable uses to which states or individuals are desiring, willing, or able to put it. Steiner assumes *no* limits on the use of natural resources, so that states 'must bid successfully for the ownership of sites *before* they can acquire owners' powers and liberties to impose restrictions on their use' (2011b: 332, fn.12). The financial cost of any restrictions put in place is thus supposed to be borne by the owner alone.

At first glance this might seem reasonable. Is it not important to prevent collectives appropriating the most valuable geographical sites and then sitting on those resources, restricting the ability of others to access their benefits?[25] Equal Division theorists might attempt to motivate this idea with an example. Imagine a world composed of three apparently identical geographical sites: A, B, and O. Three groups of equal population size—a, b, and o—appropriate one site each.[26] It is later discovered that O contains the only accessible oil in the world; a resource highly valued by individuals in groups a and b, but which can only be extracted via a process that destroys the land above the reserves. In a global auction, this site would now receive a maximum bid of x whilst sites A and B would only get maximum bids of y, where $x \gg y$. Imagine, however, that group o refuses to extract due to its own beliefs (or abilities) regarding resource use. Furthermore, o insists, on this basis, that the natural resources of each site have equal value from its perspective. If o is thereby excused from any

---

[25] One reason for extreme caution here is that concerns along these lines were invoked in some perverse attempts to justify colonialism. Aimé Césaire (2000: 38–9) outlines some of these arguments as follows:

M. Albert Sarraut, the former governor-general of Indochina, holding forth to the students at the Ecole Coloniale, teaches them that it would be puerile to object to the European colonial enterprises in the name of 'an alleged right to possess the land one occupies, and some sort of right to remain in fierce isolation, which would leave unutilized resources to lie forever idle in the hands of incompetents.' ... Rev. Barde assures us that if the goods of this world 'remained divided up indefinitely, as they would be without colonization, they would answer neither the purposes of God nor the just demands of the human collectivity' ... as his fellow Christian, Rev. Muller, declares: 'Humanity must not, cannot allow the incompetence, negligence, and laziness of the uncivilized peoples to leave idle indefinitely the wealth which God has confided to them, charging them to make it serve the good of all.'

[26] In this example and the next I assume the groups in question are of constant equal size and that the values of human improvements to each territory are equal unless otherwise stated.

redistributive duties, it looks rather like a and b are unfairly having to bear the costs of o's value-set.[27]

Unfortunately for Equal Division theorists, one can imagine similar cases that may elicit opposing intuitions. Let us return to the example but make two alterations: firstly, instead of oil, O turns out to contain the only major reserve of opal; secondly, A and B also contain a small amount of opal. a, b, and o again take one site each and at first all are happy with their lots: opal is yet to be discovered, so the sites are seemingly identical and would receive equal maximum bids in a global auction. Sometime later, due to technological advancements made by groups a and b, opal is first discovered and extracted in their territories—again via a process that destroys the land. This resource has no known practical use, but individuals of a and b develop a taste for opal jewellery. After their limited supplies are quickly exhausted, they somehow discover that much larger amounts are available in O.

We can assume now that as before, at a global auction, site O would receive a maximum bid of x whilst the others only receive maximum bids of y, where $x \gg y$. Group o may again insist, however, that their natural resources are no more valuable than those composing A or B: imagine that they do not share a desire for opal jewellery, see no value in the extraction or use of this resource, and have no interest in selling it. For group o, their reserves of opal are no more valuable than the rocks that lie beneath the corresponding areas of A and B. What do we say in *this* situation?

On Steiner's view, it appears that group o is going to have to start paying a much greater amount into the Global Fund than groups a or b in order to retain possession of its territory. Effectively, the Fund is going to set up ongoing transfers from o to a and b, just so long as bidders in a global auction would pay more for the former's territorial site—which could continue indefinitely (so long as groups a and b retain their desire for opal). Group o could have significant difficulty financing these Global Fund contributions. They cannot borrow the money,[28] because a and b are the only available creditors. Maybe they could labour harder on the natural resources they *are* willing to use so as to become an exporter to A and B. If this does not generate enough revenue, perhaps o will have to permit companies from A or B to come and extract some of the opal, despite their desire to avoid the destruction this will wreak on their land. They may even be forced to give up the territory (or at least a part of it) because they cannot keep up with the payments. Whichever

---

[27] For worries about nations having to subsidize others' value-sets, see Steiner 1999: 184ff.

[28] This 'simple answer' for states that appear to be disadvantaged in global auctions by their relative poverty is borrowed from Steiner & Wolff 2006: 250.

option they take, however, I think it now looks more like o is unfairly bearing the burdens of the value-set of the global majority.[29]

If I am right about this example, this suggests that unimproved value is simply not an impartial metric.[30] Steiner's Global Fund appears biased in favour of the value-sets of those willing—or able—to bid more for geographical sites in a global auction. Those who bid the most for a site thereby increase its unimproved value, thus exerting influence over the distribution of Global Fund contributions. In most cases, the highest bidders will be the rich or the global majority, leaving poor minority groups vulnerable to being priced out of the geographical sites that they value. And furthermore, this pattern is likely to recur with pernicious results. Groups that fully exploit their own natural resources and become economically powerful do not only thereby gain a privileged ability to determine the pattern of Global Fund contributions; they also drive up the unimproved value of the geographical sites of those who conserve by making those natural resources increasingly scarce, and thus of greater market value. Steiner thereby unfairly favours those who value wealth creation and unrestricted resource use over those who value conservation.

Thus, Steiner's economic value metric—assuming it could even be operationalized—fails the impartiality test. This metric threatens to neglect the equal original claims of those who view natural resources as non-fungible sources of value and those whose personal valuations differ significantly from economic valuations of resource bundles. The Global Fund threatens to be unfair to those unwilling or unable to use natural resources in the most economically valuable way, who may be priced out of the natural resources that they most value. Finally—and particularly worrying in a time of environmental crisis—this account is biased against those who value resource conservation.

---

[29] Avery Kolers uses a similar example to argue that a Dworkinian conception of Equal Division will leave 'ontological minorities' (those who have a different understanding of the material world; for example, by valuing the site of an oil field as a place to live rather than a commodity to be sold) 'vulnerable to outside efforts to commodify their land' (2012: 276). An example along these lines is also discussed by Cécile Fabre (2005: 154ff.). I think Steiner's opposition to a procedural conception of justice for natural resources arises—in part—because he perceives a threat to freedom if collectives are able to dictate how individuals can use their natural resource shares (1987: 68). It appears in this example, however, precisely that a global collective *is* getting to determine what can be done with natural resource shares, but through market forces rather than a fairly designed procedure.

[30] One thought that may be operative in eliciting different responses to these examples is that to adjudicate between conflicting claims over natural resources, we need to think about which solution will best support claimants in the exercise of certain valuable activities. Steiner does not allow any such considerations to play a role in his theory. What determines the unimproved value of a site is the maximum that would be paid for it by global bidders, but it does not matter whether those bidders want the site in order to produce luxury disposable goods or medical equipment.

4.2.2 *Opportunity cost*

Equal Division theorists might instead attempt to make natural resource shares commensurate by appealing to a Dworkinian auction—an approach that Steiner appears to approve of (Steiner 2011a: 122). Ronald Dworkin attempts to render equality of resources coherent using two contrivances: first, the notion that a distribution of resources can be deemed equal if it is 'envy-free', in that nobody prefers anybody else's bundle to their own; and second, a device for generating such a distribution. This device is the hypothetical auction (Dworkin 1981b).

We are to imagine shipwreck survivors washed up on an as yet unclaimed island. These new arrivals decide that the island's natural resources should be divided between them equally, in the envy-free sense. To implement this distribution, they hold an auction. The island's resources are separated into lots by allowing the bidders to individuate them as finely as they wish: if you want to bid on one item, but somebody else wants only a part of it, then that part becomes its own lot. Each survivor is given an equal number of (otherwise worthless) clamshells with which to bid. A set of prices must then be found such that: each survivor bids all their shells; the market is cleared (each lot is sold to a unique high-bidder); and every individual is happy with what they have won, thus satisfying the envy-test (the process is to be run repeatedly until this happens).

At the end of this hypothetical process, Dworkin claims, each individual's bundle of resources can be understood as equal according to the metric of 'opportunity costs', understood as the value others must forgo by that individual having that bundle (2000: 149–51). Dworkin believes he has thereby rendered Equal Division coherent (this is the full extent of the support he gives to the view: Dworkin is clear that his aim is not to provide a defence of Equal Division, except insofar as providing a coherent interpretation of the view serves as some defence (1981b: 283)). Taking the survivors and the island as a model for human beings and the world's resources, the question we must now consider is whether the opportunity cost metric can succeed in rendering Equal Division not only coherent, but also suitably impartial.

One respect in which Dworkin's account *is* more impartial than Steiner's is that the survivors enter his hypothetical auction 'on equal terms' (Dworkin 1981b: 289). Each possesses the same economic power (in the form of an equal number of clamshells), so nobody is unjustly disadvantaged by relative poverty. There are, however, other ways in which individuals could claim to be treated unfairly here. Firstly, Dworkin assumes (for this exercise, at least) that equality of resources 'is a matter of equality in whatever resources are owned *privately* by individuals' (1981b: 283; emphasis added). The auction will therefore determine a scheme of full private ownership, where all the property incidents of each object are possessed by a single individual.[31] Those who believe we should allow property incidents to be fragmented and possessed by different people thus seem able to object that their claims have not been given fair consideration.[32]

Steiner has an easy solution to this problem, however, because he believes equal freedom to dictate that each property incident should constitute a *separate* lot in the hypothetical auction (2011a: 122–3).[33] Steiner characterizes these incidents in accordance with A M Honoré's canonical list and they thus will include: 'the right to possess, the right to use, the right to manage, the right to the income of the thing, the right to the capital, the right to security, the rights or incidents of transmissibility and absence of term ... and the incident of residuarity' (Honoré 1968: 113).[34] With each incident up for grabs separately, the action will not necessarily give rise to a system of full private ownership, thus assuaging the initial accusation of bias. However, this is achieved at the cost of complicating matters significantly.

Each lot must be clearly specified before the auction can begin, and this is now going to be somewhat more difficult. Dworkin, as explained, allows the bidders to individuate natural objects into lots as finely as they please. But this time each natural object identified as worth bidding on must also have each of its incidents separated into lots, creating potential for conflict.[35] Imagine that one of the items confronting bidders is a geographical site encompassing woodland and, beneath it, a reserve of oil. A bidder who only values the woodland (or the oil) requests that the oil and the woodland be divided into separate lots. These resources are not individuated any further by the bidders, except insofar as their incidents are made separately purchasable.

Consider the choice faced by those considering whether they wish to bid on the following three incidents: 1. the right to manage the woodland; 2. the right to use the woodland; and 3. the right to extract income from the oil.

---

[31] For a definition and detailed discussion of full ownership, see Gaus 2012.

[32] This objection might be raised by everyone apart from a few libertarian philosophers since, as Gaus points out, 'the very idea of unified ownership' is now 'passé', both in philosophy and in contemporary property systems (2012: 94–5).

[33] The idea is that anyone allowed to parcel incidents together in their preferred manner thereby enjoys greater than equal freedom compared to others. In a similar vein, Gaus argues that 'liberty upsets full ownership', because individuals acting freely will inevitably choose to 'fragment' their property rights (2012: 100).

[34] Honoré actually includes two more incidents—'the prohibition of harmful use [and] liability to execution'—but I assume Steiner would exclude these from the auction because he holds that they 'are respects in which an owner may *not* enjoy his property' (Steiner 1994: 98, fn.53).

[35] This separation must be done on a case-by-case basis because not every object will be subject to each of the nine incidents of property (Steiner 1994: 99). Gaus similarly warns that we should not think of property being straightforwardly fragmented into Honorian incidents: each of these incidents 'itself fragments into a variety of rights, liberties, and powers in particular contexts' (2012: 102). If Steiner is correct that these incidents can be 'temporally differentiated' (1994: 99), then they appear to multiply to infinity.

The bidders will have a very hard time determining what value these lots hold for them unless they know more about what each incident would enable them to *do* with the resource in question. A right to manage the woodland could be extremely valuable if it enabled the possessor to prevent oil extraction from proceeding except on their terms, but much less valuable without the ability to resist extraction by those with rights to the oil. The value of a right to *use* the woodland—for recreation or foraging, say—will also vary depending on what the possessor of the management right is permitted to do with it (e.g. if the manager is able to build an oil extraction facility there). The right to the income from the oil will also vary on these bases—and furthermore will depend on whether sufficient knowledge and technology is available to make extraction and sale possible.

These indeterminacies must be resolved before bidding begins because, as Dworkin points out, 'no one can intelligently, or even intelligibly, decide what to bid for in an auction, or what price to bid for it, unless he makes assumptions about how he will be able to use what he acquires' (2000: 143). The auctioneer must therefore specify what technology will be available and what each property incident will enable bidders to do with a resource, along with a set of what Gerald Gaus terms 'priority rules' (2012: 105): rules that determine which rights should give way in cases of conflict. Dworkin, who acknowledges from the start that property is 'an open-textured relationship many aspects of which must be fixed politically', gets around this problem by assuming it out of his thought experiment. Only being interested in defining equal division *within* a society, Dworkin stipulates that the society in question has determined the 'general dimensions of ownership' such that citizens possess sufficient understanding of 'what powers someone who is assigned a resource thereby gains' (1981b: 283–4). He presumably also takes the available knowledge and technical ability to be fixed by the characteristics of that society.

Whether or not it is defensible to assume that the society in Dworkin's thought experiment has determined the dimensions of ownership in a justified manner (given that reasonable value pluralism concerning natural resources may well hold locally as well as globally); at the global level, there certainly is not any such shared system—or understanding—of property rights and no common level of technological ability. These parameters will have to be specified as necessary background features of the auction, but this stipulation must be a justified one. Different background assumptions can change the values that lots hold for individuals and thus 'reverberate' through the auction to produce different results (Dworkin 2000: 143–5). When the envy test is satisfied given one set of background assumptions, individuals can argue that they would have preferred an envy-free distribution resulting from an alternative stipulation. The auctioneer thus needs to be able to defend a unique choice. Otherwise equality of resources risks becoming a 'hopelessly indeterminate'—and thus empty—conception of equality (Dworkin 2000: 150).

The problem with making stipulations about available knowledge and technology, however, is that this makes the island thought experiment a poor model for our real-world distribution problem. Globally, individuals and collectives differ significantly in such capacities; but the value of management, income, and use rights—to extractive resources, for example—will vary greatly depending on whether you possess the requisite expertise to take advantage of them in certain ways (Miller 1999: 192–3). If we assume that everyone has access to the most advanced technology currently available, those who lack this technology will complain that the hypothetical auction credits many of the resources in their possession with too high a value. If we instead assume the lowest common denominator of technological capacity, then some individuals will complain that the opportunity cost *to them* of allowing others to 'sit on' extractive resources that they cannot exploit is being greatly underestimated (because these resources would have received a much higher bid in a hypothetical auction where greater technological capacity was assumed). And stipulating that things simply are as they are would build existing inequalities into the thought experiment in a way that seems to assume their defensibility.

Similar problems arise in any attempt to specify how the different property incidents should play off against one another. Stipulating, for example, that management rights should trump income rights will lead to cries of injustice from those who view natural resources primarily as supports for wealth creation. The contrary would lead to claims of unfair treatment from those who believe that human beings should relate to the world as stewards rather than extractors of economic value. *Any* particular stipulation of priority rules for property incidents is bound to conflict with the worldview of certain individuals and collectives. Even the choice of incidents itself may be open to criticism.

To conclude this section: a Dworkinian auction can only succeed in rendering Equal Division coherent given various background assumptions about how natural resources can be used. When called on to determine global equality of natural resources no choice of background assumptions can be defended as sufficiently impartial, due to variation in technology, knowledge, and reasonable views about how the dimensions of resource ownership should be arranged and balanced against one another. To put it in Dworkin's terms, at the global level his auction cannot treat each individual 'as an equal in the division of resources' (1981b: 285). Without defensible background features the outcome of this hypothetical procedure is indeterminate and thus it cannot solve the metric problem for Equal Division.

4.2.3 *Ecological space*

Another potential solution to the metric problem can be extracted from the works of Tim Hayward and Steve Vanderheiden (see Hayward 2005a; 2006; 2007; Vanderheiden 2008b). As explained in §3.7, Hayward actually appears to be an advocate of Common Ownership rather than Equal Division, but he has argued that the principle of equal division applies in situations of natural resource scarcity. When applying this principle to assess the global distribution of natural resources, Hayward argues that we should compare shares by conceptualizing them in terms of *ecological space*.[36] According to the resulting view, *'in present circumstances'*—at least—'justice requires entitlements to equal shares of ecological space' (Hayward 2006: 360).

Hayward has distanced himself from the principle of equal division in more recent work.[37] However, one might suppose that proponents of Equal Division could nevertheless borrow the notion of ecological space from Hayward's earlier view and deploy it to solve their metric problem. Ecological space looks, on the face of it, like a physical metric able to endow judgements of natural resource equality with the impartiality that they require. This all turns, however, on how 'ecological space' is defined. In what follows, I identify problems with the most obvious way to understand the ecological space metric.

The challenge of operationalizing this concept has been taken up by ecological economists, who have attempted to find ways of quantifying and comparing the amount of ecological space represented by various uses of different natural goods. The method that appears most established at present is Ecological Footprint accounting.[38] This approach was pioneered by William Rees and Mathis Wackernagel (see Wackernagel & Rees 1996), the latter of whom set up the Global Footprint Network (GFN) to promote use of the Footprint concept internationally. The GFN's work encouraging sustainable resource use worldwide is commendable and I do not wish to deny that Ecological Footprint accounting may play an important role in the practical pursuit of environmental goals. I argue, however, that this concept is unable to provide the requisite metric for Equal Division at the level of principle. In other words, whilst I agree with Steve Vanderheiden that Ecological Footprints are a useful 'empirical tool for assessing efforts to improve environmental performance', I reject his attempt to portray this concept as 'a

---

[36] The equality of ecological space view is also discussed by Edward Page (2007: 459ff.).

[37] Here, Hayward insists that the equality he has in mind is 'not conceptualised on the model of slicing a cake into equal shares', but is more akin to a notion of equal respect (2014: 1).

[38] Hayward appeals to this understanding of ecological space on a number of occasions (2005a: 324, fn.20; 2005b: 195; 2006: 359), but has formulated an alternative interpretation in more recent work (2013; 2014). He is clear that this more recent interpretation is ill-suited to support Equal Division (Hayward 2014: 9).

normative ideal of global resource egalitarianism' (Vanderheiden 2008b: 435; emphasis added).

It is important, first, to distinguish between the Ecological Footprint of a given population and the biocapacity available to it in virtue of its natural resource rights. Biocapacity, measured in units of global hectares (gha), refers to 'the capacity of ecosystems to produce useful biological materials and to absorb waste materials generated by humans, using current management schemes and extraction technologies' (GFN 2012a). Despite being a spatial term, a global hectare is not equivalent to a physical area. The five different kinds of land that are included in the accounts—built-up land, cropland, grazing land, forest land, and fishing ground—are deemed to have different capacities to produce useful materials. Grazing lands, for example, are judged to have lower productivity than cropland, so a physical hectare of the former will translate into fewer gha than a physical hectare of the latter. Converting physical hectares of each land type into gha (multiplying by an equivalence factor supposed to reflect their differing productivities) makes comparison across these different land types possible—thus enabling the GFN to estimate the biocapacity of the territories of 150 different countries. They also estimate total global biocapacity in each year and, divided by world population, the per capita biocapacity available (GFN 2017).

The ecological space *used* by a population, on the other hand, is called its *Ecological Footprint*. Likewise measured in terms of biocapacity, in a given year this Footprint can be understood as the aggregate area of land (across the five categories) that is required in order to produce the biophysical products that a population consumes—adjusted for imports and exports of biophysical materials (GFN 2012a). Thus, whilst the Ecological Footprint is a measure of human demand, biocapacity is a measure of natural supply. To put it in Elinor Ostrom's terminology (introduced in §2.2), the Ecological Footprint accounts are concerned with investigating a somewhat peculiar type of resource system: the resource system that is an entire country, or even the whole world. Biocapacity is a measure of the flow of resource units—units of useful biological materials and assimilative capacity—that these resource systems can produce each year, given in generic units of gha. The Ecological Footprint, on the other hand, is a measure of a population's appropriation of those resource units, again in gha.

Clearly, a population can *possess* natural resources with more biocapacity than it *demands*—either because it does not fully exploit the biospherical resources in its territory, or because it is a net exporter of those resources. Such countries are termed 'ecological creditors'. Equally, a country can be a net importer of biocapacity, or overuse its own biospherical resources, making its Ecological Footprint of consumption *greater* than the biocapacity supplied by its territory. This turns it into an 'ecological debtor'. The question therefore arises whether Equal Division on an ecological space metric should compare countries on the basis of the resources that they *consume* (i.e. their Ecological Footprint of consumption), or the resources that they *possess* (i.e. the capacity of their territorial resources to produce useful biological materials). The values of these two measures will rarely be the same for any one country—most countries are either ecological creditors or (more often) ecological debtors. We must consider, then, which value the Equal Division theorist should use for their metric.

Due to environmental concerns, the measure that is usually focused on in discussions of ecological space use is the *Ecological Footprint*—the major question being whether a given population, or the world as a whole, is placing excessive demands on biocapacity and thus depleting the planet's resources. When talking of fair resource distribution, however, attention needs to be paid to the biocapacity of the natural resources in a population's *possession*. Assuming for now that ecological space should be equal per capita in some sense, one can envisage cases where Equal Division theorists should have no objection to *unequal* per capita Ecological Footprints; and cases where Equal Division theorists should take *equal* per capita Ecological Footprints to be masking an unfair distribution of ecological space. Let me illustrate this with two examples.

First, imagine two populations of equal size—*X* and *M*—each in possession of equal territorial biocapacity, where such possession is respected internationally (i.e. other countries do not use any of *X* or *M*'s natural resources without their consent, say by consuming their forest biocapacity through excess carbon emissions). *X* and *M* engage in fair and mutually advantageous trade with the result that *X* becomes a net exporter of biocapacity and *M* a net importer (perhaps they both fully exploit their biospherical resources, but due to reasonable variation in consumption preferences *X* exports many of its high-Footprint products to *M* in exchange for low-Footprint services). In this case, *M* will have a greater per capita Ecological Footprint of consumption than *X*, but it does not appear that an Equal Division theorist should view this as unfair.

Now instead imagine a world with total biocapacity of 2gha per capita and two equally sized populations, one of which (*B*) possesses territorial resources of 3gha per capita, whilst the other (*b*) possesses resources of only 1gha per capita. By working very hard, members of *b* may be able to afford imports from *B* that will increase *b*'s Ecological Footprint of consumption to 2gha per capita. Both countries may now have equal Ecological Footprints per capita, but this does not seem fair. By virtue of its greater possession, *B* is able to consume 2gha per capita *and* have biocapacity leftover for export. *b*, on the other hand, can only consume this amount by purchasing biocapacity from elsewhere.

If we should be aiming to equalize shares of ecological space for reasons of justice, it therefore appears that we should primarily be doing so in terms of per capita *possession* of biocapacity rather than per capita *consumption* of biocapacity. Territories of equal biocapacity per capita should *in theory* provide each population with an equal opportunity for consumption.[39] Each country *could* fully exploit its biospherical resources and end up with an equal per capita Ecological Footprint. Alternatively, countries could choose to leave some of their resources unexploited and end up with a smaller Footprint, or engage in fair trade of biocapacity with others, thus resulting in unproblematic inequalities of consumption.

But now, familiar problems are going to arise. First, we encounter a difficulty that afflicted the economic value approach: even if natural resources could be distributed so that each person possessed a bundle deemed to be of equal biocapacity, an individual could legitimately complain if everybody else possessed a bundle that she, personally, reasonably endows with more value. If you have a way of life centred on fishing, but your bundle contains no fishing ground, for example, then being told that you have been treated equally in terms of biocapacity will be little consolation. Second, the global variation in technological capacity that undermined the Dworkinian approach is also going to cause problems here. Collectives without access to the 'current' technology assumed in the GFN's biocapacity estimations will be unable to draw the same quantity of biospherical materials from territory that is deemed to be of equal biocapacity. They thus do not appear to be treated fairly by this metric.[40]

Another problem derives from what Hayward perceives to be a benefit of the ecological space approach; namely, that this concept 'is specified by reference to its usefulness to human ends' (2007: 446). This appeal to 'human ends' and 'usefulness' may instead prove problematic since it means, as before, that variation in individual and societal values and understandings will render the ecological space metric insufficiently impartial. The GFN does seem to attempt a neutral understanding of 'useful materials'. They define them as those *actually demanded* by the 'human economy', which may appear to offer an impartial amalgamation of the varying valuations of different individuals. As the GFN acknowledges, however, this means that 'what is considered "useful" can change from year to year' in accordance with global consumption patterns. For example, if corn stover (the leaves and stalks left over when corn grain has been harvested) begins to be used in the production of ethanol, this

---

[39] This is very much in ideal theory, understood as full compliance theory. In our nonideal world, many countries consume the biocapacity of others without their free, prior, and informed consent.

[40] For similar worries, see Kolers 2012: 275.

will serve to 'increase the biocapacity of maize cropland' (GFN 2012a). Countries with a large proportion of cropland in their territory will find that they are now credited with a greater share of global biocapacity, whether or not they wish to use corn stover for this purpose.[41]

Thus, just as we found with Steiner's economic value approach, global market forces can drive up the value of a collective's territory and make that collective liable for redistributive duties, whether or not *they* take the value of their resources to have changed. This suggests that ecological space does not offer a defensible means of valuation after all, because reasonable global variation in technology use, personal valuations, and resource use once again undermine the impartiality of this metric.

Another major problem with the ecological space concept is that it simply cannot be used to quantify the value of all natural resources. Ecological space only provides estimates of the planet's biospherical productive capacity, excluding water, 'materials that are extracted from outside the biosphere' (such as minerals and extractive resources), and 'deserts, glaciers and the open ocean' (GFN n.d.). But all these resources can be of value to human beings, as can particular portions of geographical space, the electromagnetic spectrum, the Earth's gravitational field—and many other aspects of the natural world.[42] The seeming inability of the ecological space metric to value such resources is a problem, because Equal Division is the view that the *totality* of the world's natural resources are originally subject to a principle of equal division. There is no straightforward route from here to the conclusion that the biosphere alone—or any other part of the natural world—should be distributed equally. Once we bring other natural resources such as water into the picture, the question arises of how they are to be incorporated into our judgements of equality. Could an individual or collective possessing a less than equal share of biocapacity nevertheless be considered to have an equally valuable set of *natural resources* if they were compensated with extra rights over certain rare earths? What quantity of rare earths would it take?

The Ecological Footprint accounts, as they stand, provide no answer to these questions; and it is very difficult to see how an answer could be provided without running up against the familiar problem of reasonable value pluralism (this time, involving reasonable disagreement about the relative values of

---

[41] Corn stover plays an important role replenishing field nutrients after the harvest. When it is instead removed for ethanol production, farmers must increase their use of fertilizers (Marshall & Sugg 2009). It is likely, then, that a group which valued stover as a fertilizer rather than a fuel would choose not to adopt this new practice.

[42] To conceptualize natural resources in terms of ecological space is thus, as Steiner puts it, to take an 'unduly "geological-cum-biological" view' of such goods, one that 'fail[s] to appreciate—as persons in real estate markets do not—that portions of sheer (surface and aboveground) space also possess value' (1999: 190, fn.15).

biospherical and other natural resources). Thus, *even if* the ecological space metric could be defended against my objection that it cannot justly render shares of *biospherical* resources commensurate, it does not provide a way to compare shares of natural resources in general. Therefore, ecological space fails to offer a solution to Equal Division's commensuration problem.

4.3 Conclusion

I have given various reasons to think that proponents of Equal Division will not be able to identify the defensible common metric required to render claims of resource equality coherent. It is not that metrics are hard to come by. Rather, no metric is sufficiently impartial to be consistent with the equal original claims of all human beings to natural resources (the claims that plausibly motivate Equal Division in the first place)—even when those metrics are designed to amalgamate the varying valuations of different individuals.

Underlying this failure is the fact of reasonable value pluralism concerning natural resources. If all human beings originally have an equal claim to the world's resources, then at the very least the principles assigning rights to such goods should be impartial among these claimants. A principle of Equal Division *may look* impartial. However, it promises to treat individuals equally *only in the sense* that they will be given a right to an equal share of natural resources. If individuals are then given shares that are only perceived to be equal by some, whilst others can reasonably object that they *do not* believe their share to be of equal value, it appears that not everybody is being treated equally—or impartially—after all.

This should not, however, cause us to abandon any attempt to formulate impartial principles for the assignment of natural resource rights. An obvious alternative is available, in the form of a theory more closely aligned with Charles Beitz's approach to this topic. When Miller posed the metric problem he intended it to undermine both Steiner *and* Beitz's accounts of natural resource justice (Miller 1999: 319, fn.5). However, in classing these theorists together Miller overlooks an important difference between their views. The metric problem is essentially an objection to a *substantive* principle of equality for natural resources, but what Beitz is fundamentally committed to is a *procedural* conception of justice for this good—where principles of natural resource justice are derived from a global Rawlsian original position. Equal Division can be jettisoned without necessitating any rejection of the contractualist framework from which Beitz seeks to justify a principle of resource redistribution. Thus, though the metric objection is decisive against Steiner, it does not require us to abandon Beitz's approach to natural resource justice.

In defending his RRP, Beitz uses a method of justification designed to identify principles that are impartial between all those represented in a hypothetical contract; such impartiality being ensured by having the parties assess principles from 'an initial situation of equality' (Rawls 1999a: 19; see also 165–6). I will explore and defend this approach in Chapter Five, where I argue that to identify truly impartial egalitarian principles for the assignment of natural resource rights, we should return to—and improve—Beitz's global original position.

5

Contractualist Common Ownership and the Basic Needs Principle

In Chapter Four I concluded that due to the metric problem, Equal Division can only be rendered coherent at the price of becoming incompatible with Equal Original Claims. If every human being has an equal original claim to the world's natural resources—as I have argued and as proponents of Equal Division ought to accept—then we must formulate impartial principles of justice for the assignment of natural resource rights; but Equal Division cannot instantiate such impartiality in a world characterized by reasonable value pluralism concerning natural resources. Proponents of natural resource egalitarianism should therefore abandon Equal Division and explore the more promising alternative of a Common Ownership conception of justice: one that allows exclusive rights over natural resources to be gained by groups and individuals by showing how such appropriation can be justified, in some sense, to all other human beings.

In this chapter I draw on Charles Beitz's account of natural resource justice to defend a method of justification that can be used to elaborate on the Common Ownership view (§5.1). This method employs an original position device, familiar from contemporary social contract theory, and I therefore term the resulting view 'Contractualist Common Ownership'. I motivate this particular version of Common Ownership by arguing that it is an apt interpretation of Equal Original Claims (§5.2). I also anticipate and reject two objections to this approach (§5.3).

With Contractualist Common Ownership thus defended, I then use it to reconsider, and again reject, the principle of equal division—since this principle now appears to be a potential object of agreement from the perspective of Contractualist Common Ownership's cosmopolitan original position (§5.4). I claim that the parties would instead first secure agreement on a principle of basic needs, and I discuss what form this principle could take and what some of its implications will be (§5.5). I also argue, however, that this sufficientarian principle would not be accepted in isolation; parties would seek agreement on further principles of justice for the assignment of rights to natural resources, beyond what is necessary for the satisfaction of basic needs (§5.6). In Chapter Six, I will argue that a principle of collective self-determination would also be agreed to, resulting in a conception of natural resource justice composed of two principles.

5.1 Rehabilitating Beitz's resource rights contract

Many theorists have employed Rawls-inspired original positions in defence of principles of global justice.[1] My account differs from almost all of these in an important respect. Those proposing the use of a global original position in theorizing about justice generally hold that it should be used to determine the global distribution of a range of rights and resources—social, political, and economic. In my thought experiment, on the other hand, the parties will only debate principles for the assignment of rights to one particular kind of good: natural resources. In this respect, at least, the original position I am suggesting is most similar to the international original position once put forward by Beitz.[2]

Beitz also appears to accept Equal Original Claims, holding that 'each person has an equal prima facie claim to a share of the total available resources'. He seems to understand Equal Original Claims as a form of Common Ownership, believing it requires the appropriation of resources to be given 'a justification against the competing claims of others and the needs of future generations', and he proposes to model this justification by means of a global original position (Beitz 1979: 141). The resource redistribution principle (RRP) that Beitz defends as an outcome of his hypothetical procedure has often been interpreted as a principle of equal division. In §2.1 we saw that Steve Vanderheiden accepts it as such, and in §4.3 I explained that David Miller attempts to reject it given the same reading.

However, it is not actually clear what Beitz's RRP amounts to. Beitz implies several interpretations of the principle and is ultimately ambiguous between distributing natural resources on an equal per capita, more loosely egalitarian, or even sufficientarian basis. The principle of equal division is suggested by Beitz's talk of 'equitable shares' and distribution on the basis of 'population size'. However, he then wonders whether departures from equality should be permitted 'if the resulting inequalities were to the greatest benefit of those least advantaged by the inequality'—a version of Rawls's difference principle (Beitz 1979: 139–41). Beitz also suggests that the RRP 'provides assurance to persons in resource-poor countries that their adverse fate will not prevent them from realizing economic conditions *sufficient* to support just social

---

[1] See, for example, Beitz 1979: §3.2–3; Brock 2009: §3.1.2; Carens 1987: 255ff.; Moellendorf 2002; and Pogge 1989: §22.

[2] Waldron uses a similarly restricted original position when discussing whether a Lockean principle of justice in acquisition can be defended (1988: Ch.7, §5).

institutions and to protect human rights', implying a sufficientarian principle of distribution (1979: 142; emphases added). In later work, Beitz claims that under the RRP, 'each person is equally entitled to benefit from the earth's resources' (2005: 420). Again, it is unclear what this means. Saying that each person is *equally entitled to benefit* is not equivalent to saying that they are entitled to *equal benefits*, or *entitled to benefit equally*.

Furthermore, as Simon Caney has pointed out, Beitz's argument cannot be accepted in its existing form (Caney 2012: 267, fn.29). Beitz formulated his RRP with the express aim of undermining Rawls's scepticism about global principles of distributive justice, attempting to show that this scepticism is mistaken *even if* one is generous enough to accept certain of Rawls's more controversial idealizing assumptions. To serve this goal, Beitz adopts the international original position briefly specified by Rawls in *A Theory of Justice* (see Rawls 1999a: 331–2); one where the parties are *representatives of states*, and where Beitz takes Rawls to be conceiving these states as self-sufficient (Beitz 1979: 136). But both the assumption of self-sufficiency and this characterization of the parties are problematic (as Beitz himself recognizes).[3]

Firstly, the assumption of self-sufficiency prevents us from concluding that the principles agreed to in Beitz's original position would apply in various situations where principles of justice are required (for example, the situation in which we actually find ourselves). Even if parties selecting principles for a world without international interdependence would agree to Beitz's RRP, this does not show that parties selecting principles for an interdependent world like our own would do likewise.[4] In addition, by adopting Rawls's formulation

---

[3] Beitz is clear that he explores the international original position formulated by Rawls for the sake of argument, and later gives reasons to reject certain of the assumptions that he takes it to embody. In a correctly formulated global original position, Beitz argues, nations will not be characterized as self-sufficient, but rather interdependent; and the parties will be representatives of 'persons' rather than states (1979: 151–3, fn.58).

[4] Caney suggests that Beitz only ever intended the RRP to apply in 'a world without extensive interdependence', and that in a world like our own it would be replaced with a global difference principle for socio-economic goods more generally. In order to show that the RRP is applicable, Caney claims, one would have to show 'that we do *not* live in a highly globalized world' (2012: 267, fn.29). However, it is not actually clear that Beitz intends to abandon the RRP in a world of interdependence. Beitz continues to appeal to the RRP after the assumption of self-sufficiency is dropped, as a principle that would still be in play even if arguments could be given to undermine or restrict the operation of a global difference principle (1979: 162, 169). Even in later work reflecting on Caney's criticism, Beitz states that he does not consider his reasoning about natural resources to be 'wrongheaded' and suggests that it could prove relevant to the problem of climate change in our world of interdependence (Beitz 2005: 419–20). It would thus seem that Beitz intends to defend the RRP as a principle that would apply even if (rather than only if) there was no global interdependence; the idea being that interaction between states gives rise to additional principles of justice, rather than alternative principles. Caney is correct that this reasoning is flawed (Beitz fails to show that we do not end up with a disjoint set of principles in a situation of global interdependence), but incorrect that the only way to save the RRP would be to contest global interdependence. Rather, in order to determine whether the RRP also applies in our world, one would have to reconsider the arguments in its favour in light of a suitably adjusted original position.

of a global original position, Beitz appears to commit himself to a controversial form of global contractualism.[5] On this approach, which might be termed *international* contractualism, the parties to a global contract are representatives of *states or societies*. Such international contractualism will be rejected by those who believe that a global original position should rather incorporate representatives of *persons*—a view that I term *cosmopolitan* contractualism.

If seeking principles to assign rights to the world's natural resources, it is cosmopolitan contractualism that one should adopt. This is because it is individuals that possess equal original claims to the Earth's resources—not societies—and therefore individuals that must be given equal representation in any hypothetical contract. In fact, if we are seeking principles of justice for natural resources that will be valid for *all* individuals, then we must not assume a world consisting of separate states at all. Many individuals throughout time have not, and perhaps will not, inhabit such a world. Furthermore, the equal original claims that human beings possess may well place limits on the kind of political associations that can be justly formed. We should not assume that the territorial states Beitz appears to take for granted will turn out to be justified once equal original claims to natural resources are taken seriously.[6]

Correcting for these problems, we end up with a global, cosmopolitan original position where representatives of *all* individual human beings debate the just assignment of natural resource rights in a world that, like our own, has varying levels of interdependence. This is the approach that I term 'Contractualist Common Ownership'. I explain why it is an appropriate interpretation of Equal Original Claims in §5.2.

5.2 Contractualist Common Ownership

The Earth itself can be conceptualized as a common-pool resource (CPR): a resource system prone to overuse and from which it is impossible to exclude potential appropriators. And as Elinor Ostrom points out, when appropriators are dependent on the same CPR, many of their activities will affect one another. Coappropriators of a single CPR are 'tied together in a lattice of interdependence' and each individual must take the choices of others into account when assessing their own choices (Ostrom 1990: 38). If I appropriate a

---

[5] I say 'appears', because Beitz is not entirely clear on this point. Later in his book, he suggests that it may in fact be 'incoherent' to construe the parties to an international original position as representing sovereign states (Beitz 1979: 152–3; fn.58). But Rawls certainly appears to be construing them this way, and Beitz claims to be following Rawls's design at this point.

[6] In other words, we *should* attempt to determine, from the perspective of justice, whether—or at least in what form—'there should be states . . . at all' (Rawls 1993a: 42).

natural resource for my exclusive use, then you are no longer at liberty to use it. Each appropriation modifies the moral landscape and thus requires justification regardless of whether it appears to have any immediately troubling effects. My act of appropriation may not appear to affect anybody at the time, but it could yet have an impact on later arrivals, or be combined with other acts of appropriation in a process of accumulation that turns out to be morally problematic.

Those who wish to acquire exclusive rights over natural resources must therefore be able to justify their appropriative acts to others who are no longer at liberty to use those resources in certain ways (or at all), and this justification must treat those others as persons with an equal original claim to natural resources. In some cases, such justification will be easily offered. If the stream that we share produces enough water for us to all drink our fill without subjecting it to overuse, then I can easily justify my appropriation of sufficient water to stay well hydrated (this act can be offered two justifications: first, that it is reasonable for me to take what I need to survive, provided this does not jeopardize anybody else's ability to do likewise; and second, that my appropriation does not modify anybody else's ability to use this resource in a morally significant way). But what about more difficult cases: cases where acts of appropriation are not necessary for survival, or where resources are not sufficiently abundant to avoid conflicts of interest? How can we justify the acquisition of exclusive rights then?

What we need to do is identify specific principles of justice that assign natural resource rights in a way that is fair to all individuals. Use of an original position is one method by which to justify such principles; a particularly appropriate method since, as I will explain, it is a form of justification that represents each individual as a person of equal standing. An original position is a hypothetical choice situation that can guide us in identifying a conception of justice: an expository device designed to 'make vivid to ourselves the restrictions that it seems reasonable to impose on arguments for principles of justice, and therefore on these principles themselves' (Rawls 1999a: 16). To ensure that the principles emerging from this choice procedure might correctly be understood as principles of justice, the restrictions that we impose on our arguments must reflect the substantive moral commitments with which those principles should conform. Individuals acting in accordance with principles that are justified from the perspective of a suitable original position can then be viewed as taking others into account in an *ethical* sense, insofar as they are acting in a way that is intended to pay adequate consideration to the interests of all.

This understanding of the justificatory purpose of an original position accords with Aaron James's interpretation of Rawlsian political constructivism. Political constructivism, James claims, is a method of justification that draws on an original position—or some other device—'to represent all morally relevant criteria in the form of a procedure of judgment which clearly leads to particular principles'. Which criteria are morally relevant will vary depending on the social practice for which governing principles are sought. That certain principles are selected by reasoning in accordance with a suitable original position gives us sufficient reason to accept them as principles of justice for the social practice in question. This method of justification can make the reasonableness of those principles 'manifest to all involved' and thus renders the principles themselves potential objects of public agreement (James 2014: 252).[7]

In reasoning from an original position, we find 'a way of moving from a conception of agents and their moral relations to definite principles' (Wenar 2001: 91). When seeking principles of justice to govern the assignment of natural resource rights, the appropriate conception of agents and their moral relations to begin with is that of the Common Ownership interpretation of Equal Original Claims. This conception defines a moral predicament in which all human beings, abstracted from their individual characteristics and circumstances of birth, are related to one another in virtue of their symmetrical claims to the natural resources that they must share. Originally (in what we might consider the 'state of nature' situation), each individual has a moral claim to *use* the natural world, but lacks any rights of exclusion. It appears that everyone could gain by establishing principles according to which exclusive rights to resources can be justly acquired by individuals and groups. Conflicts of interest arise, however, because the preferred principles for each individual might well ensure that whilst they can appropriate whichever resources they want, others cannot do likewise.

To resolve this conflict in a way that respects the original symmetry of natural resource claims, parties to the original position must be representatives of individuals who seek agreement from 'an initial situation of equality' (Rawls 1999a: 19). This initial situation of equality is ensured by stipulating that no party to the hypothetical contract is in a superior bargaining position, a result achieved in part by use of a Rawlsian veil of ignorance.[8] The veil of ignorance denies parties any access to information that they can use to unjustly favour themselves, which in this case includes facts such as: their time of birth (and thus the potential use that certain natural resources can be

---

[7] As James makes clear, it is left an open question whether the correctness of these principles consists in their being so chosen, or whether they could have been justified in other ways. The resulting principles can be taken as requirements of justice 'simply because there is a good argument for regarding them as such' (James 2014: 261).

[8] This equality is also secured by the condition that parties 'all have the same rights in the procedure for choosing principles; each can make proposals, submit reasons for their acceptance, and so on' (Rawls 1999a: 17).

put to, since this depends on the existing state of technology, knowledge, and discovery); their place of birth (and thus the social, cultural, and political situation into which they are born—both at the local and global level); and their individual characteristics (beyond their common interest in securing a beneficial assignment of rights to the Earth's resources). Parties should not know their preferences and beliefs regarding the value of resources and their appropriate use, or their abilities to convert resources into well-being or wealth. This information is restricted because it is irrelevant to the original claims that human beings possess to natural resources and because defending principles on the basis of such features—for example, by reasoning that 'I will defend principle P because it promotes what I value', or 'I will defend principle P because it will benefit those (like me) who possess characteristic c'—is unacceptably biased.

Parties are, however, granted as much general information as is available. They are permitted to know, for example, the kinds of natural resources that exist in the world and the various different uses they might be put to; that most of these uses require coordinated group activity; that natural resources are distributed unevenly across the Earth's surface and that many of them need to be discovered before they can be used; that knowledge and technology are required for many uses of natural resources and that these too may be unevenly distributed (both temporally and geographically); that resources are limited and can become scarce relative to the demands humanity places on them; that global limits may only become known once a certain level of scientific understanding is reached; that natural resources serve various fundamental interests of both individuals and groups; but also that there will be various other important goods that can promote these interests—including manufactured, social, and political goods.

Parties to this original position must attempt to select principles of justice for the assignment of natural resource rights that will best promote the interests of the individuals that they represent, despite the restrictions on their knowledge. The veil of ignorance is supposed to ensure that in seeking to promote their own interests, equal consideration is given to the interests of all (since the parties must consider the possibility of being revealed as any one of these individuals, once the veil is lifted). The principles selected are supposed to be justified because they are ones that all human beings—in their status as equal original claimants of natural resources—would agree to if they thought about things in an impartial way. To restrict one's appropriation in accordance with principles chosen from the original position then offers a form of justification to others: justification designed to respect their equal moral standing as claimants of the Earth's resources.

In what follows, then, I will use the idea of a hypothetical contract to defend principles for the assignment of natural resource rights. I will again be following Rawls in that I will not take the choice of principles to be open-ended (Rawls 1999a: 105–9). A short list of familiar principles will be considered, chosen due to their prominence in debates about global justice: a principle of equal division, a basic needs principle, and a principle of resource sovereignty. For any of these principles to be accepted from within the original position framework, it must hold appeal for the parties despite the epistemic restrictions of the veil of ignorance. In this chapter, I argue that equal division fails this test but the basic needs principle passes it. In Chapters Six and Seven, I show that although a principle often appealed to in support of resource sovereignty would be accepted—namely, a principle of collective self-determination—resource sovereignty does not follow.

Before I proceed, however, it is important to deal with two potential objections.

5.3 Objections to Contractualist Common Ownership

Cosmopolitan contractualist theories of global justice have been extensively criticized. Such criticism comes largely, and understandably, from statists—but this approach to global justice has also been rejected by some global egalitarians. One major objection, which threatens to undermine my own approach, is that an original position is only appropriately used at the domestic level, because the domestic and global realms are disanalogous in some important respect. These disanalogy objections aim to show that at the global level, individual human beings do not stand in the right relations—or cannot be said to possess the right features—for cosmopolitan contractualism to be appropriate. In this section, I start by addressing this critique, and then consider a further objection to Contractualist Common Ownership as a *particular breed* of cosmopolitan contractualism.

One important worry that I will not confront in depth concerns whether contract theory is essentially—and unavoidably—a tool for justifying and perpetuating oppressive power structures; sexual, racial, and colonial power structures being central examples. Carole Pateman and Charles W Mills—key figures in this critique of contract theory—disagree on this point, with Pateman arguing that contract theory should be abandoned, but Mills insisting that it can still be of use to progressives (see Pateman & Mills 2007: 4–7). I here follow Mills in holding that although contract theorizing has often been used to justify oppression in the past, it remains a device that egalitarians can deploy for emancipatory, and potentially even radical, ends (Pateman & Mills 2007: 104ff.). I hope that this work serves as some validation for this conviction.

5.3.1 *The disanalogy objection*

Objections in the first category can take various forms. Some critics start by pointing out that Rawls primarily designed the original position to formulate principles of justice for the institutions constituting the *basic structure* of a society (see Rawls 1999a: 6ff.). They then argue that there is no basic structure—or at least no basic structure of the right sort—at the global level, and thus no need for a cosmopolitan original position.[9] Others reject the use of a cosmopolitan original position by claiming that individuals do not stand in the right relations to one another globally,[10] or that individuals at the global level cannot be assumed to possess certain essential features that would make their equal representation in a global original position appropriate.[11]

Proponents of cosmopolitan contractualism have two ways of addressing this kind of objection: one relationist and the other nonrelationist. A first option is to accept that original position reasoning is only appropriate when selecting principles of justice for individuals that stand in certain practice-mediated relations, but to argue that all human beings *are* related to one another in this way at the global level. Those pursuing this relationist defence might argue that there is indeed a global basic structure, or that individuals at the global level are related to one another analogously to those who are subject to the same domestic basic structure.[12] Alternatively, one might offer

---

[9] Michael Blake, for example, understands the basic structure to equate to a state's coercive legal system and argues that cosmopolitan contractualism is inappropriate given the absence of such a coercive system at the global level (2001: 279–80, 283–4). An original position, he argues, 'is not a device to be used every time there is a division of a good' (Blake 2001: 292). Though I agree with the latter claim—as will become apparent in §5.3.2—I believe that Blake is mistaken to claim that an original position should only be used in the context of a coercive legal system.

[10] Andrea Sangiovanni, though he accepts cosmopolitanism (2007: 3), suggests that one can appeal to the notion that only co-nationals stand in a particular kind of reciprocal relationship to argue that the parties behind a veil of ignorance should be citizens and residents of the same state, 'rather than individuals *qua* human beings' (2007: 27)—at least, that is, in the absence of a world state (2007: 38).

[11] Rawls does accept that there is a global basic structure—which he terms the *'Basic Structure of the Society of Peoples'*—but he believes that it is essential for this structure to maintain mutual respect between peoples, where this includes 'decent nonliberal peoples' (1999b: 61–2). He argues on this basis that it is peoples, rather than individuals, that should be represented as equals in a global original position; because to use a cosmopolitan original position would be tantamount to assuming 'that only a liberal democratic society can be acceptable' (Rawls 1999b: 82–3). Rawls appears to be worried that a cosmopolitan original position encapsulates the idea that we should treat 'all persons, regardless of their society and culture, as individuals who are free and equal'; and that taking all human beings to be free and equal in this way only makes sense from a liberal perspective that is not accepted globally (1993a: 55).

[12] Pogge accepts that if societies were self-contained, there would be no global basic structure and it would remain to be shown 'that the construct of the original position is relevant'. He takes Rawls's contractualist device to be applicable at the global level 'only if there is significant global interdependence' (Pogge 1989: 241). Pogge argues, however, that there is indeed a global basic structure—understood as a global institutional scheme (1989: §22). Beitz argues that Rawls's contractualist approach is appropriate for identifying principles to justly govern those who stand in cooperative relations, and argues that 'global economic and political interdependence shows the existence of a global scheme of social cooperation' (Beitz 1979: 151).

a *nonrelationist* defence of cosmopolitan contractualism. Here, one would argue that even if principles of domestic justice—given that they apply—apply to the basic structure, it is not the existence of the basic structure (or any other practice-mediated relations) that makes the use of an original position appropriate. It is something else that justifies the contractualist approach—some property that individuals also instantiate at the global level.[13]

Both responses can be used in defence of Contractualist Common Ownership. Firstly, one could follow Thomas Pogge in claiming that any global regime of natural resource rights *is* an institutional scheme that forms part of an existing global basic structure; one that should be governed by principles identified from a cosmopolitan original position (1989: 252).[14] This argument, however, is open to a further objection that territorial rights or norms are not the right kind of thing to prove the existence of a global basic structure (see Meckled-Garcia 2008: 261; Freeman 2007: 307–8).

Although I am not convinced by this further objection, I think that the alternative, nonrelationist justification of original position reasoning provides a better defence of Contractualist Common Ownership. Regardless of what institutions or practices *actually* relate individuals at the global level, all human beings should be represented in an original position to determine the assignment of rights to natural resources purely in virtue of their equal original claims to this good. The essential point here is that if we accept this original symmetry of moral claims to natural resources, then we should accept that principles of justice are required to ensure that these claims are respected. Regardless of whether the regime of natural resource rights is a global institution, the appropriation of resources from the commons should be assessed from the standpoint of justice. The reasons for using an original position in this assessment were given in the previous section. The lack of a global basic structure—or other practice-mediated global relations—does not, therefore, make the use of a contractualist device inappropriate when formulating principles for the just assignment of natural resource rights.[15]

Before moving on, however, it is important to consider a further objection that can be made to Contractualist Common Ownership as a *particular breed* of cosmopolitan contractualism.

---

[13] Beitz later rejects his earlier, cooperation-based argument for a cosmopolitan original position, instead stating that the original position should include all human beings in virtue of their possession of Rawls's two moral powers (Beitz 1983: 595). This change of view is partly a result of Brian Barry's objection that the global system of trade originally appealed to by Beitz 'does not constitute a co-operative scheme of the relevant kind' (Barry 1989: 446).

[14] In Pogge's words: 'the institutional distribution of natural assets is included in the master pattern in terms of which a Rawlsian criterion of global justice would assess any particular global basic structure' (1989: 252).

[15] Although it may, of course, affect the implementation of such principles.

5.3.2 The unjustified restriction objection

In a discussion of Beitz's international original position, Caney argues that Beitz fails to defend his restricted focus on principles for the distribution of natural resources. This restriction, Caney argues, is in fact one that Beitz has reason to reject given the Rawlsian framework that he adopts, where all individuals are assumed to be seeking to maximize their shares of certain *primary goods* (that is, goods that every rational individual can be presumed to want—including income and wealth). Such parties to the original position would not distinguish between natural and economic goods ('the goods and capital that result from human creation') at all, but would seek to distribute both in a way that serves to advance their primary goods (Caney 2005b: 391). By restricting the use of my own original position to justifying principles of natural resource rights, I may thus be making the same mistake as Beitz, thereby formulating a theory of justice that is problematically isolationist (the error that I accused the equal per capita emissions view of in §2.1).

However, it is not actually clear that a cosmopolitan original position is an appropriate tool with which to justify principles for the distribution of all economic and natural resources *in combination*. For such principles to be on the table in the first place, we need a reason to be considering the distribution of these particular goods as a whole, in abstraction from any practices and relations that currently produce them. We also need a reason to think that the principles for distributing these goods should be justified using the egalitarian reasoning of the original position. It is particularly important to provide such reasons given the possibility—receiving increasing attention in theoretical debates about global justice—that a more complex and discriminating approach is appropriate at the global level: one where principles of justice could pertain for different reasons, take different forms, apply to different sets of people, and relate to different goods, institutions, and practices.[16]

Defending the use of a single cosmopolitan original position to formulate one's theory of global justice could prove difficult. For a start, a set of global primary goods—goods that every rational person can be 'presumed to want'

---

[16] That justice should be pluralist in this way is suggested by Cohen and Sabel (2006). De Bres (2012) attempts to motivate a highly pluralist approach to global distributive justice. Armstrong suggests that egalitarian principles of justice may apply to different goods at the domestic and global levels (2009: 313)—citing, as an example, Moellendorf (2006). A pluralist approach also seems to follow from James's suggestion that 'original position reasoning' should only be used to identify principles of justice for existing social practices and the goods that they are meant to realize (2005: 282). Whether or not this restriction to existing practices is justified, it could well be that different forms of reasoning are appropriate for justifying principles to apply to different practices and goods. Risse provides an account of global justice in a pluralist vein, taking 'common ownership of the earth' to provide a distinct ground for global justice; one that generates its own specific principles (2012: ix). A pluralist approach is also endorsed elsewhere by Caney (2006b: 753–5).

(Rawls 1999a: 54)—might not be that easy to define.[17] Natural resource rights are one of the least controversial candidates here given that they are essential for all human beings at all times and places. The value of income, on the other hand, will vary depending on one's access to and reliance upon contingently existing market systems.

Furthermore, though it seems clear that the global distribution of human-produced goods should be assessed from the standpoint of justice, some might question whether an original position is the correct means by which to do so. An original position is a device designed to give the interests of each represented individual equal consideration when selecting principles for the allocation of rights to certain goods. This is appropriate in the case of natural resources, with respect to which individuals are originally symmetrically situated. But individuals are not symmetrically situated with respect to all human-produced goods. Manufactured and social goods have been contributed to by some people and not others; and the institutions that create and distribute them involve, and impact on, some more than others. It is thus quite possible that individuals *will not* have equal claims to these goods, even originally.

In saying this, I do not intend to draw on a 'dubious' or 'empirically implausible...Group Desert Argument' (Caney 2005b: 393). The claim is not that those who contribute to human-produced goods are *entitled* to them (and thus that those who have not contributed to them have no claims, or that any claims they have are trumped by those of contributors). The idea is rather that plausibly, those who contribute to human-produced goods (or are related to their creation in other morally significant ways) thereby acquire *particular* claims to them; claims that others do not possess. This does not mean that other individuals have *no* claims—far from it. Non-contributors will frequently have claims—on the basis of need, for example—and such claims may well trump those of producers. The problem is rather that it is harder to argue that all individuals globally are symmetrically situated with respect to human-produced goods—and thus harder to defend the idea that all individuals should be given equal representation in an original position justifying principles for their distribution.

It is therefore far from obvious that we should adopt a single cosmopolitan original position to justify principles for the distribution of a set of global primary goods, allocating both natural and human-produced resources. Beitz might not have shown that there is anything *wrong* 'in distributing the products of a system of social cooperation amongst absolutely everyone in the world whether or not they had taken part in the productive process' (Caney 2005b: 392). But it is a somewhat different—and more difficult—task to show that *we*

---

[17] See Heath 2005: 218; Ypi 2008: 460.

are required to distribute the products of a system of social cooperation amongst absolutely everyone in the world *considered as having equal claims*, regardless of each individual's relationship to the production of those goods.

Perhaps to identify a full set of principles of global justice one would employ several different original position-style justifications, along with arguments of other forms. I think, for example, that my approach could be fruitfully paired with that of Joseph Carens, who uses original position reasoning to defend principles of justice in migration (1987: 255ff.; see also Bertram 2018: Ch. 2). Then, as James points out, where original position reasoning is not appropriate—for example, because not everybody can be taken to have equal claims to the goods in question—this does not mean that principles of justice do not apply (2005: 309–10). Those who do not have equal claims may yet have claims of justice that are justified in some other way (and perhaps using a different contractualist method). It is possible, that is, to take 'original position reasoning to be only one *part* of reasoning about what justice requires' (James 2005: 311).

There is, finally, something to the left-libertarian idea that 'the question of the fair division of the fruits of social cooperation' must be posterior to, or at least informed by, the question of how natural resources can be legitimately claimed or acquired (Vallentyne, Steiner & Otsuka 2005: 213–14). Natural resources are essential inputs into the design, construction, and use of all human-produced goods. Any restrictions that justice places on rights to natural resources thus have the potential to influence what social and economic products can justifiably be made and how they can legitimately be used. Considering natural resources first therefore appears to be an acceptable move. By taking this approach we also retain more prospect of identifying principles of global justice that should gain broad agreement given that—as noted by Elizabeth Cripps (2011a: 126)—even those with otherwise libertarian commitments can accept that natural resources are appropriate objects of egalitarian distribution (as demonstrated by theories of left-libertarianism).[18]

Having thus defended Contractualist Common Ownership as an appropriate understanding of Equal Original Claims, I will now proceed to discuss which principles for the assignment of natural resource rights will be chosen in this hypothetical contract.

5.4 Reconsidering the principle of equal division

The Equal Division conception of original ownership was rejected in Chapter Four, for lacking sufficient impartiality to be consistent with Equal

---

[18] In Risse's words, taking individuals to have equal claims to natural resources is 'Maximally uncontroversial', whilst including human-produced goods is not (2012: 114).

Original Claims. Having defended Contractualist Common Ownership as an alternative, however, I appear to have opened up a new—impartial—way of justifying a principle of equal division; because it is now possible to argue that this principle would be agreed to by parties to my cosmopolitan contract.[19] Given that the parties are symmetrically situated, is the obvious choice not a principle assigning natural resource rights on an equal per capita basis? Rawls reasons along such lines in his use of a domestic original position. Symmetrically situated parties, he suggests, will take 'equal division of income and wealth...as the starting point' and then ask whether there are good reasons for departing from this baseline (Rawls 2001: 123).

However, the argument of Chapter Four suggests that the principle of equal division will not gain traction even as a starting point in this cosmopolitan contract. This is because parties to the original position *will know* that the persons they represent may differ significantly in many factors relevant to determining the value of natural resources. Parties do not know the technology and knowledge they will have available, or the values they—and those in their society—hold. Given this lack of information, agreement on any particular metric will be very hard to come by; particularly in the case of the opportunity cost metric, which can only be rendered determinate if parties also agree to a shared conception of property (including how its incidents are to be understood and which will take priority in situations of conflict).

Agreement on a single metric does not just pose practical difficulties, however. It also poses risks to those behind the veil of ignorance. What if you agree to equal shares on an economic value metric and then find, once the veil is lifted, that your valuations of natural resources differ significantly from economic valuations—or that you are part of a collective that values conservation over wealth creation? What if you agree to an ecological space metric and then discover that you lack the technology to realize the value of your resources? The market value and ecological space metrics also make the value of the natural resources possessed by political communities very sensitive to the valuations of others (as determined by, say, the maximum bid those resources would receive at a global auction, or the demand placed on those resources by the global economy). This means that the value of a collective's territorial resources can be driven up by factors beyond their control, thus making that collective liable for redistributive or compensatory duties—whether or

---

[19] Steven Luper-Foy gives an argument along these lines, claiming that representatives in a cosmopolitan original position would opt for a 'resource equity principle', which (roughly speaking) would permit 'everyone to divide resources equally among themselves' (1992: 49–51). And although he rejects contractualism, Steiner too explores such an argument in defending his Equal Division–based Global Fund over Pogge's Global Resources Dividend; his aim being to show that the Global Fund is superior even allowing Pogge's use of a global original position occupied by individuals (Steiner 1999: 191, fn.32, 184–8).

not *they* take the value of their resources to have changed. Prudent parties will prefer principles of justice that grant resource rights more stability than this.

The principle of equal division thus threatens to undermine important interests of those represented in a hypothetical contract in two ways: firstly, because they could turn out to represent individuals, or members of societies, whose valuations of natural resources significantly differ from the chosen metric; and secondly, because with a principle of equal division in play, resource rights lack stability. Parties in the original position will therefore reject this principle.

5.5 The basic needs principle

A more promising object of agreement from this cosmopolitan original position is a basic needs principle. As Gillian Brock suggests, anybody party to such a hypothetical contract would most likely think first about 'the *minimum* set of protections and entitlements [they] could reasonably be prepared to tolerate'. It would be a grave mistake to agree to anything one might find unbearable once the veil is lifted. Thus, whatever else is chosen from the original position, parties seeking to promote the fundamental interests of those they represent 'would find it prudent and reasonable for each person to be able to enjoy the prospects for a decent life, and much discussion would be about the (minimum) content of such a life' (Brock 2009: 50). Brock suggests that this minimum will secure for individuals the ability to meet their basic needs, understood as those needs that are 'essential to our ability to function as human agents' (2009: 65).

Reasoning along these lines, Contractualist Common Ownership would appear to justify the following principle, as an object of agreement from the original position:[20]

> The Basic Needs Principle (BN): The system of natural resource rights must grant every human being the entitlements over natural resources that are necessary for satisfying their basic needs.

[20] In keeping with the understanding of original position reasoning outlined in §5.2, the claim is that Contractualist Common Ownership provides sufficient (but not necessary) justification for this basic needs principle. There are other ways that one might attempt to justify a principle of this form. For example, one could argue that basic needs are fundamental interests that rights—by their nature—must protect. Caney gives such an argument in favour of the right to subsistence (2005a: 120). One could also offer an alternative contractualist defence of such rights, claiming that a basic needs principle is reasonable to propose, and unreasonably rejected. This argument is suggested in Scanlon's brief example of a debate over water rights (1998: 192). Moore states simply that it is a 'very plausible insight...that resources are important to subsistence, and subsistence is a basic right of everyone' (2015: 181). Armstrong similarly suggests that 'humans are entitled to sufficient shares of those natural resources necessary for them to meet their basic human rights' (2017: 74).

According to this principle, individuals can acquire exclusive rights over natural resources whenever this is necessary for their basic needs satisfaction. Those who appropriate natural resources for the satisfaction of their basic needs do no wrong to co-claimants. And all have a duty to ensure that their use of natural resources does not prevent others from satisfying their basic needs.

A conception of natural resource justice containing a basic needs principle can already be seen to have an advantage over Hillel Steiner's view in that—as we saw in §4.2.1—it appears possible on Steiner's account for an individual not to have any rights to natural resources at all, including those necessary to meeting her basic needs. As Beitz similarly notes, for Steiner 'there is no human right to subsistence or to any particular minimum level of welfare' (Beitz 1999: 283; see also Fabre 2002: 256).

One might worry, however, that the metric problem will re-emerge as soon as we try to specify what these basic needs encompass. Is the concept of a basic need not also hopelessly indeterminate, in that it is relative to societal and individual values? It is important to remember, however, what the metric problem for Equal Division really shows. The fundamental problem for Equal Division is not the *practical* one that metrics are difficult to suggest or to implement, but rather a problem of *principle*—that no given metric can be shown to be sufficiently impartial due to reasonable global variation in various factors relevant to determining the value of natural resources. That some form of metric is required to assess whether the system of natural resource rights satisfies BN would thus only pose an equivalent problem if no impartial metric can be offered. The necessary metric will presumably be a multifaceted one—identifying a number of basic needs that resource rights must be designed to protect—and I concede that the specification and implementation of this metric will not be easy. However, the requisite *impartiality* of the basic needs metric would be secured by the agreement of parties to the hypothetical resource rights contract. Thus, a metric problem only arises at the level of *principle* if one can show that the parties would not, in fact, agree to any principle of basic needs.

Not knowing the values of the individuals they represent, the parties to the original position may well find it difficult to specify a list of basic needs, and may well worry about whether they will be content with any given list once the veil is lifted. The alternative, however—of agreeing to no such list—will be unacceptable to the parties, because it leaves open the possibility that the most fundamental needs of those that they represent will be unprotected. Discussion in the original position will therefore continue until agreement is reached on a set of basic needs—thereby providing an impartial defence of this list and solving the metric problem at the level of principle.[21] Furthermore,

---

[21] See also Moore, who argues that the metric problem 'is not a source of concern if we can agree on a crosscultural or intercultural list of an appropriate minimum' (2006: 658).

the challenge of reaching such agreement may turn out to be overstated.[22] The notion of basic needs may not be so difficult to render coherent across different worldviews, being a concept with boundaries that, as Brock suggests, 'can be drawn in principled ways'. In particular, if we understand basic needs as necessary conditions for human agency, this concept will be constrained by the nature of such agency. To draw up a list, we can therefore start by examining 'what it is to function as a human agent'. Though the goods that *satisfy* our basic needs may well be culturally variable, the needs themselves will not (Brock 1998: 17).

I therefore assume that the parties to the original position will agree on a list of basic needs to be protected by the first principle of natural resource justice. Several candidates illustrate what form this list might take: for example, one could appeal to Martha Nussbaum's set of 'Basic Human Functional Capabilities' (1992: 222), or a set of commonly accepted human rights. I do not intend to take a position on which account of basic needs is the most defensible, but use the conception formulated by Len Doyal and Ian Gough as an example because it is accepted by both Brock (2009: 64) and Mathias Risse (2012: 114).

According to Doyal and Gough, basic needs are universal preconditions that enable individuals to participate in a social form of life. Most fundamentally, these basic needs are taken to encompass physical health and autonomy (understood, roughly speaking, as the ability to make informed choices about what to do and how) (Doyal & Gough 1991: 50–4). To satisfy these basic needs, all individuals will require intermediate goods including: adequate food and water, shelter, a safe environment, security, 'significant primary relationships', and appropriate healthcare and education (Doyal & Gough 1991: 157–8). Reflection on these intermediate goods immediately suggests that certain rights to natural resources would be established by BN if basic needs are understood in line with Doyal and Gough's conception. Individuals will, for example, have rights of secure access to non-hazardous environments and potable water, and various rights over the natural resources on which they depend for food.

At this point, someone might object that many basic needs require, for their satisfaction, not only natural resources but also (and often primarily) human goods such as technology, social systems and care. This is particularly apparent in the case of the intermediate goods of primary relationships, healthcare, and education. However, BN does not rely on the implausible idea that it will always be possible to satisfy basic needs using natural resources alone. It merely invokes the idea that all individuals will require *some* access to natural

---

[22] As Christian Barry and Laura Valentini suggest in their own discussion of the metric problem, the importance of certain basic goods is 'hard to deny ... and thus may be acceptable to a relatively broad range of cultural groups' (Barry & Valentini 2009: 505).

resources if their basic needs are to be satisfied. The requisite natural resource entitlements will vary depending on what non-natural goods an individual has access to. For example, those with fewer human goods at their disposal may require more extensive rights to natural resources to satisfy their basic needs, and vice versa. BN simply states that nobody can be denied whichever natural resource entitlements they require to satisfy their basic needs. This is compatible with accepting that the entitlements of different individuals will differ along various dimensions, including: their personal characteristics, their situation, and their access to human-produced goods and relationships.

5.6 Beyond basic needs

It is important to note that there is likely to be a surplus of natural resources left over after entitlements for basic needs have been allocated. We must therefore consider whether parties to the original position will agree on further principles for the assignment of rights to these remaining natural resources.

Risse—who also holds a view according to which each co-owner of the Earth has 'equality of status' but not necessarily any claim to an *equal share* of natural resources (2012: 111)—argues that the principles of natural resource distribution chosen from an original position like the one that I propose would be minimal (2012: 121–2). He claims these principles would embody nothing beyond the 'core idea...that all co-owners ought to have an equal opportunity to satisfy basic needs to the extent that this turns on collectively owned resources' (Risse 2012: 111);[23] this restriction to basic needs satisfaction being necessary in order to limit the content of natural resource rights 'to what would be acceptable to every reasonable person' (2012: 112). Reasonable people, Risse claims, can reject stronger conceptions of justice for natural resources (2012: 122).

In rejecting conceptions of justice stronger than that constituted by a basic needs principle alone, Risse claims to be motivated by concerns of cultural diversity. Principles identifying rights to use resources for purposes other than

[23] Risse actually defines Common Ownership in terms of this core idea. Our use of terminology is therefore rather different. Furthermore, although the original position that Risse discusses appears to be the same as my own, he claims that it is a means of interpreting the *Joint Ownership* conception of original ownership (2012: 121). As an interpretation of Joint Ownership, however, this contractualist approach is open to Ronald Dworkin's objection that a hypothetical contract 'is no contract at all' (1973: 501). If one accepts Joint Ownership—according to which each individual has a full private property right to all of the world's resources—then co-owners could only be bound by principles or contracts that they have *actually* agreed to. This hypothetical contract conception of original ownership is therefore more accurately understood as a form of Common Ownership, on the more expansive interpretation of Common Ownership that I advocate.

basic needs satisfaction, he believes, can only be agreed to when they reflect shared understandings of how natural resources should be used (Risse 2012: 112, 118). Clearly, I agree with Risse that such diversity is relevant to the justification of principles of natural resource justice (as seen in Chapter Four). However, I think he is mistaken in claiming that there is such significant absence of shared understandings at the global level that no further principles would be agreed to in the original position.

In fact, it seems that parties to the original position would be cautious of endorsing BN in isolation, despite knowing that those they represent have divergent understandings of natural resources. A conception of natural resource justice incorporating nothing but a concern for basic needs looks far too weak. Parties to the hypothetical contract would recognize that distribution on the basis of this single principle might condemn those they represent to a minimally acceptable existence: an existence where they have no rights to natural resources beyond those necessary to satisfy their basic needs (and no sphere of control within which shared and cultural understandings of natural resources can be given expression). Risse is thus incorrect. Discussion will continue after the selection of BN, to ascertain whether there are other principles that can gain the requisite broad agreement by offering to improve the prospects of all.

5.7 Conclusion

In this chapter I motivated the Contractualist Common Ownership method by which to justify principles of natural resource justice, defending it from two key objections. I then used this approach to identify a primary principle of justice for the assignment of natural resource rights. This is the basic needs principle, according to which:

> BN: The system of natural resource rights must grant every human being the entitlements over natural resources that are necessary for satisfying their basic needs.

Unlike Risse, however, I deny that parties to a hypothetical contract would agree to a conception of justice consisting of this principle alone. In Chapter Six I will argue—through examination and rejection of the principle of natural resource sovereignty—that another principle of justice would also be selected; namely, a principle of collective self-determination.

6

Collective Self-Determination without Resource Sovereignty

In Chapter Five I defended the Contractualist Common Ownership method, by which principles of natural resource right can be justified. I used this approach to reject a principle of equal division and defend a principle of basic needs. I also argued, however, that parties to a hypothetical resource rights contract would not accept a principle of basic needs in isolation. In this chapter, I defend another principle that I claim would be chosen, together with the principle of basic needs, to constitute a conception of global justice for natural resources: the principle of collective self-determination.

My defence of a principle of collective self-determination will emerge from my critique of a principle of natural resource justice with which collective self-determination is often assumed to be closely linked, both in political theory and in international law; namely, the principle of natural resource sovereignty. I first explain why the principle of resource sovereignty is a candidate that should be considered from the perspective of Contractualist Common Ownership's cosmopolitan original position (§6.1.1). I then identify what I take to be the two most promising reasons why resource sovereignty might be accepted from this perspective. First, it may be thought that resource sovereignty encourages responsible stewardship of resources (§6.1.2); second, it may be thought that resource sovereignty is necessary for collective self-determination (§6.1.3). I reject the stewardship defence but suggest that the argument from collective self-determination is worthy of further consideration.

There are two steps to this argument: first, that collective self-determination is an important value that must be supported by resource rights; and second, that a system of resource sovereignty best supports collective self-determination. I argue that parties to the original position would accept a principle according to which natural resource rights should support collective self-determination (properly understood), thus supporting the first step of this argument (§6.2). However, the claim that collective self-determination demands resource sovereignty is questionable. The exercise of self-determination certainly appears to require some right of exclusive territorial jurisdiction over natural resources (§6.3.1). However, this right will only be a presumptive one, which must be abnegated or moderated if it conflicts with basic needs satisfaction or the self-determination of other collectives (§6.3.2). In Chapter Seven, I examine such restrictions at more length to demonstrate that the conception of justice here defended does not demand resource sovereignty, but rather a system of *limited territorial jurisdiction* over natural resources.

6.1 The principle of natural resource sovereignty

The principle of natural resource sovereignty was introduced in Chapter Two. Roughly speaking, this principle states that the natural resources of a country belong to its people. More precisely, this means that states, nations, or peoples possess a full right of jurisdiction over the natural resources within their territory, where this includes the exclusive authority to determine patterns of ownership. This fits with a common understanding of sovereignty *simpliciter* as 'supreme authority within a territory' (Philpott 2011). As explained in §2.3, resource sovereignty receives support not only from political theorists but also in international declarations, where one finds numerous commitments to the principle of permanent sovereignty over natural resources.

In what follows I will be examining the defensibility of the principle of justice that I have termed *natural resource* sovereignty, rather than the principle of international law known as *permanent* sovereignty. This is both because the legal principle is somewhat open to interpretation (for in-depth discussion, see Schrijver 1997), and because it is the potential normative grounding for such a legal principle that is really of interest. The two principles are closely related in that their vision of a just world is one separated into distinct and clearly bounded political units, each with strong, exclusive, and relatively unimpeded rights over its territorial resources. In both political theory and international declarations, it is generally held that a right of resource sovereignty must be exercised for the good of the people that possesses it, is limited by a prohibition on harmful use, and may be further circumscribed by other important considerations.[1] However, full and

---

[1] See, for example, the Stockholm Declaration: 'States have, in accordance with the Charter of the United Nations and the principles of international law, the sovereign right to exploit their own resources pursuant to their own environmental policies, and the responsibility to ensure that activities within their jurisdiction or control do not cause damage to the environment of other States or of areas beyond the limits of national jurisdiction' (UN 1972: Art. 21). See also UN 1962: Art 1.1 (quoted in fn.2).

exclusive resource rights are the starting point and good reasons must be given for departing from this. Some political theorists instead refer to a principle of *national ownership*, but I opt for the terminology of natural resource sovereignty because it helps me to remain neutral on the question of whether it is states, nations, peoples, or other collectives that should be granted full rights over 'their' territorial resources (if, indeed, any should).[2]

Some might presume that a commitment to Equal Original Claims entails outright rejection of resource sovereignty. Such sovereignty may appear to be in opposition to any egalitarian assignment of natural resource rights, because it grants collectives full rights over territories that seem very unequal in natural wealth. I do not think that resource sovereignty is so easily rejected, however. In this section, I explain why it should be considered as a *candidate* for agreement from the perspective of Contractualist Common Ownership's egalitarian original position. Having provided reason to pay this principle serious consideration, I then argue that parties to the original position would, nevertheless, not accept it.

6.1.1 *The appeal of natural resource sovereignty*

Resource sovereignty possesses broad and understandable appeal. As Leif Wenar notes, 'The principle that the resources of a country belong to the people of that country is widely accepted and embedded deep within international law' (2008: 9). Permanent sovereignty was cemented in international relations during a period of decolonization, with many viewing the establishment of such sovereignty as a key component of that process.

Frantz Fanon suggests that 'For a colonized people, the most essential value, because it is the most meaningful, is first and foremost the land: the land, which must provide bread and, naturally, dignity' (2004: 9). There are obvious reasons why peoples seeking independence, after having long been excluded from their country's resource base by colonial oppressors, might embrace a principle affirming a 'right of peoples and nations to permanent sovereignty over their natural wealth and resources', to be 'exercised in the interest of their national development and of the well-being of the people of the State

---

[2] Leif Wenar defends a principle of national ownership in earlier work (2008), but more recently has opted for the terminology of 'popular resource sovereignty' (2016: Ch. 11). The question of the relevant rights-bearer does not have a clear answer in international declarations, where statements of permanent sovereignty have referred variously to peoples, states, and nations—sometimes in the very same sentence. UN General Assembly resolution 1803 ('Permanent Sovereignty Over Natural Resources'), for example, states that: 'The right of *peoples* and *nations* to permanent sovereignty over their natural wealth and resources must be exercised in the interest of their national development and of the well-being of the people of the *State* concerned' (UN 1962: Art. 1.1; emphases added). For more on this inconsistency, see Daes 2004: 21, n.4; Schrijver 1997: 369–70. For further discussion (and critique) of permanent sovereignty, see Armstrong 2015; Schuppert 2014.

concerned' (UN 1962: Art. 1). This is the wording give to the 1962 UN General Assembly resolution 1803 ('Permanent Sovereignty Over Natural Resources'), the adoption of which was 'virtually unanimous' (Schrijver 1997: 372). Permanent sovereignty has been affirmed in numerous UN resolutions and decisions since (Schrijver 1997: Appendix I. See also Daes 2004: §I).

Even Brian Barry, who is highly critical of resource sovereignty,[3] is forced to admit that 'no substantial body of opinion in either the North or the South (or, perhaps more remarkably, in the East or the West) is adverse to the principle that each country is entitled to benefit exclusively from its own natural resources and to take decisions about their exploitation'. Furthermore, Barry concedes, this support is understandable in several respects. Resource sovereignty has a 'simplicity and definiteness' suitable for international relations;[4] and, in the absence of a world state, it will be 'relatively easy to enforce' (given that, *ceteris paribus*, a people may be presumed best placed to control the natural resources within its own territory) (Barry 1989: 449–50).

International support for the legal principle of permanent sovereignty suggests that the principle of natural resource sovereignty is thus, at least, a *candidate* for agreement from the standpoint of a cosmopolitan original position. One can, in addition, assume that any principle of resource sovereignty agreed to from this perspective would apply equally to all relevant political communities. Some might argue that this alone constitutes a kind of egalitarian justification of the principle. Daniel Butt, for example, points out that if one shares Rawls's view that 'inegalitarian holdings of natural resources does not affect a given people's ability to develop',[5] then it may well seem that 'by dividing the world up into sovereign, self-governing communities, each with control over a given territory, we have afforded each community "enough and as good" as one another' (Butt 2009a: 156).

If the principle of natural resource sovereignty *could* be justified using the Contractualist Common Ownership approach defended in this work, it would be paired with a lexically prior basic needs principle. This should mitigate some concerns about the potentially problematic consequences of granting collectives near *absolute* control over the natural resources within their territory.[6] Furthermore, a commitment to resource sovereignty does not entail

---

[3] Elsewhere, Barry deems it a principle 'without any rational foundation' (1980: 36).

[4] Given the metric problem for Equal Division (discussed in Chapter Four) one might note, in particular, that resource sovereignty does not require us to compare shares of natural resources using a common measure, but only to identify which natural resources belong to each sovereign community—on a conventional or pragmatic basis if necessary.

[5] See Rawls 1999b: 108, 117. See also Heath 2005: 215.

[6] Even without a lexically prior basic needs principle, the principle of resource sovereignty will never grant collectives *absolute* control over the resources within their borders due to the prohibition on harmful use. One can imagine that our world would look very different were this prohibition observed.

acceptance of current state borders, so the principle could be defended in a form according to which the area over which political communities can exercise this right is much diminished.[7] Significant resources could then remain under common ownership, outside of state jurisdiction.

Resource sovereignty thus cannot be rejected by claiming that it is plainly incompatible with Equal Original Claims. In the present context, one might further note that this principle validates some of the particular claims to land and other natural resources that those vulnerable to climate change press with the most urgency—the claim of Tuvaluans to the islands of Tuvalu, for example. But still, the principle of resource sovereignty looks a questionable choice for parties to the original position given that, for all they know, they might represent members of collectives with scant territorial resources. To defend resource sovereignty from the perspective of a cosmopolitan original position, one must identify supporting considerations that can reasonably be assumed to hold generally. I will consider two main ways that theorists might attempt such a defence. One is to claim that resource sovereignty encourages responsible stewardship of resources. The other is to argue that resource sovereignty is necessary for collective self-determination.[8]

6.1.2 The stewardship argument

The stewardship argument essentially claims that resource sovereignty should be instituted because it encourages responsible resource management. The basic idea here is that 'unless a definite agent is given responsibility for maintaining an asset and bears the loss for not doing so, that asset tends to deteriorate'; the asset in this case being 'the people's territory and its capacity to support them *in perpetuity*...their land and its natural resources' (Rawls 1999b: 39). Granting a people full control over the natural resources within its territory is claimed to encourage sustainable long-term use, whereas global redistribution would remove the incentive for conservation by undermining national responsibility (Miller 2012: 264; 2007: 70–1). Why, David Miller asks, would any collective conserve its own resources only to see them redistributed to those that have ended up with less due to profligacy? He suggests that such redistribution would result in a tragedy of the commons type scenario: 'any one state that tried to conserve per capita resources, either through environmental or through population policy, would find that it lost almost everything that it had saved—so no state would make the attempt' (Miller 1999: 194).

---

[7] Wenar claims that an oil field one hundred miles off the coast of New Orleans 'of course' belongs to the US (2016: 203). However, this view clearly stands in need of justification.

[8] See, for example, Miller 2012: 264. Margaret Moore (2012: 86–9) and Chris Armstrong (2017: 133) also identify these two arguments for state sovereignty over natural resources.

It should be noted that the stewardship argument at least appeals to an end that parties behind the veil of ignorance can be presumed to support—namely, a global drive towards responsible resource management (though such appeal is somewhat undermined by the fact that most of the benefits of natural resource conservation will accrue to the people of the territory within which those resources are located, rather than being globally dispersed). The argument fails, however, because resource sovereignty does not actually appear to be necessary or sufficient for good stewardship of natural resources.

Even if natural resources will deteriorate unless a definite agent takes responsibility for them, there is no need to think that the agent in question must be a territorial state or similar such entity. Elinor Ostrom provides many empirical examples in which smaller communities of individual appropriators have succeeded in implementing robust and lasting institutions of sustainable resource management without—or perhaps in spite of—the state (see Ostrom 1990: Ch. 3). In fact, Ostrom concludes that one element appearing to account for successful community resource management is that 'The rights of appropriators to devise their own institutions are not challenged by external governmental authorities' (1990: 101). The requisite agents could alternatively be identified above state level, or created as a body representing local, national, and global interests. There will be ways to hold such agents responsible for negligent resource management. In the case of resources that sub-state or supra-state collectives depend upon (e.g. local water sources or the ozone layer) losses will often be felt directly. In other cases, suitable monitoring and sanctioning institutions can be established.

In some cases, assigning a people the sole responsibility for preserving their territorial resources will *undermine* incentives toward good stewardship. In the case of what Michael Glennon terms 'global environmental resources' (GERs)—that is, natural resources 'located within the territory of one country but broadly enjoyed, and arguably needed, by the world community as a whole' (1990: 34)—resource sovereignty is likely to incentivize exploitation, because any benefits will accrue almost entirely to the country in question whilst the costs are often dispersed more widely. Fossil fuels are a good case in point. Currently, any state with large hydrocarbon reserves faces a significant incentive to extract this extremely valuable resource in order reap the profits, regardless of whether exploitation benefits those beyond (or, indeed, many of those within) its borders. This is a significant problem in the current context, where some researchers are warning that as little as 20 per cent of the world's fossil fuel reserves can be burned between now and 2050, to have a reasonable chance of preventing global average temperature from rising more than 2°C above pre-industrial levels (Carbon Tracker 2013: 4). If collectives with significant reserves have full rights over such resources and can manage and exploit them as they please, this creates a serious obstacle to climate mitigation.

Claims of resource sovereignty have indeed been used to oppose action on climate change. When the US Environmental Protection Agency suggested that the US and Canada should cooperate in efforts to reduce greenhouse gas emissions from the Alberta bitumen sands, for example, the TransCanada Corporation accused them of ignoring 'the fundamental sovereignty of the Canadian government' (quoted in McCarthy 2013). The Organization of the Petroleum Exporting Countries (OPEC) countries, on the other hand, have demanded compensation if mitigation measures prevent them from selling the fossil fuels beneath their territory—a claim which is presumably based on the assumption that permanent sovereignty grants them an exclusive right to exploit, alienate, and extract income from these resources (OPEC 1998).

Defenders of resource sovereignty might hope they can avert these concerns by reminding us that this resource right is commonly understood to be limited by a prohibition on harmful use. However, this prohibition does not remove the obstacle that resource sovereignty presents for climate action. The suggested 20 per cent restriction on fossil fuel exploitation is designed to prevent harm. But countries with territory containing fossil fuel reserves will nevertheless struggle to come to an agreement on which should forgo extraction, because their assumed right of resource sovereignty creates a strong incentive for each state to claim the greatest possible share of any restricted global budget, giving rise to a significant problem of divergent interests. As Canadian Prime Minister Justin Trudeau is reported to have said, 'No country would find 173bn barrels of oil in the ground and just leave them there' (quoted in McKibben 2017); at least, not under the present system of resource sovereignty, where that country is assumed to have a primary claim to the benefits of exploitation.

In a world with local and global environmental collective action problems, resource sovereignty will often thus be a hindrance—rather than an aid—to the responsible management of natural resources. Concerns of stewardship can only be used to support resource rights on a case-by-case basis, and thus cannot be used to mount a general defence of resource sovereignty.[9]

6.1.3 The self-determination argument

The self-determination argument for resource sovereignty makes two claims. First, that collective self-determination for certain political communities below the global level is an important capacity that any theory of justice must support.[10] Second, that such self-determination can only be secured if these collectives are accorded full and exclusive rights over their territorial

---

[9] Similar conclusions are drawn by Armstrong (2017: 140–2); and Fabian Schuppert (2014: 82).
[10] Armstrong identifies several ways in which this claim might be defended (2010: 317–18).

resources, where the assumption appears to be that this right extends to both supra- and subterranean resources. Miller, for example, defends resource sovereignty by stating quite simply that: 'because of the way that the availability of natural resources influences the general course of the society's development, for reasons of self-determination it will normally be desirable that the resources should remain under the collective control of the society's members' (2012: 264).

Self-determination and resource sovereignty are also linked in international law, where both constitute central organizing principles. UN resolution 1803 notes that the Commission on Permanent Sovereignty over Natural Resources was originally set up on the basis of resolution 1314—titled 'Recommendations concerning international respect for the right of peoples and nations to self-determination' (UN 1958)—in order to conduct 'a full survey of the status of permanent sovereignty over natural wealth and resources as a *basic constituent* of the right to self-determination' (UN 1962; emphasis added).[11] This link, and the centrality of these principles, is demonstrated in the International Covenant on Civil and Political Rights and the International Covenant on Economic, Social and Cultural Rights. The first article of both covenants is identical in stating that (UN 1966a, 1966b):

(1.1)   All peoples have the right of self-determination. By virtue of that right they freely determine their political status and freely pursue their economic, social and cultural development.[12]

(1.2)   All peoples may, for their own ends, freely dispose of their natural wealth and resources without prejudice to any obligations arising out of international economic co-operation, based upon the principle of mutual benefit, and international law. In no case may a people be deprived of its own means of subsistence.

However, though collective self-determination and resource sovereignty are often assumed to be linked, the precise nature of the relationship between collective self-determination and resource rights requires further examination. Here, it is vital to note that the self-determination defence of resource sovereignty proceeds in two stages, such that one might accept the first step of this argument but reject the second. That is, one could agree that

---

[11] Antonio Cassese dates this linking of self-determination and resource rights back to 1952, when 'Chile, in the Commission on Human Rights, proposed an important addition to the draft article on self-determination' (Cassese 1995: 49). The proposed addition included the claim that 'The right of the peoples to self-determination shall also include permanent sovereignty over their natural wealth and resources' (Chile 1952).

[12] A right to self-determination is also enshrined, with almost the exact same wording, in the UN Declaration on the Granting of Independence to Colonial Countries and Peoples (UN 1960: Art. 2); and the UN Declaration on the Rights of Indigenous Peoples (UN 2007: Art. 3). The right of indigenous peoples to self-determination is also maintained in the Kari-Oca Declarations (1992; 2012).

self-determination for certain political communities is an important value that should be supported by natural resource rights, but hold that this value will be best served by a system of rights different from that of resource sovereignty.[13]

To keep open this possibility, the parties to Contractualist Common Ownership's original position should not be asked about the principle of natural resource sovereignty directly, but should instead be asked to consider a principle like the following:

> The Principle of Collective Self-Determination: The system of natural resource rights must grant every political community the entitlements over natural resources that are necessary for engaging in the legitimate exercise of collective self-determination.

In §6.2, I argue that this principle would be agreed upon. However, it remains to be seen what system of natural resource rights is demanded by the principle of collective self-determination; and, in particular, whether resource sovereignty follows.

6.2 Reformulating the argument from self-determination

I have argued that parties to the cosmopolitan original position should consider what I have referred to as *the principle of collective self-determination* (SD). To determine whether the parties would accept this principle, more needs to be said about which political communities SD refers to; what self-determination, and its legitimate exercise, consists in; and why the system of resource rights mandated by SD would promise to serve the interests of those the parties represent. In this section, I address each of these issues to make the case that the parties would indeed accept this principle.

6.2.1 Collective self-determination

Collective self-determination is 'by definition, about the people ruling themselves' (Nine 2012: 16). Put simply, it is the capacity of a group to govern its

---

[13] Schuppert (2014), for example, argues that whilst some control over natural resources is necessary for self-determination, resource rights are divisible and their importance for self-determination must be assessed on a case-by-case basis. Oliviero Angeli argues that 'the value of collective self-determination justifies a claim to *some* rights over natural resources, but not to the entire set of rights' (2015: 124). In particular, whilst it succeeds in justifying a claim to control rights (including 'rights to use, manage and exclude others from accessing a natural resource'), it is less successful in justifying 'rights to gain income or benefits from the use or transfer of natural resources' (Angeli 2015: 131–2). And Moore similarly argues that 'At best, the idea of collective self-determination offers a limited and defeasible right to *control* the rules governing the acquisition, transfer and use of natural resources but does not justify a right to the full stream of benefit from the resource' (Moore 2015: 174). The view that I will ultimately defend is similar to Angeli and Moore's, but is more stipulative about the limits of this presumptive right of control.

collective way of life by exercising control over certain aspects of its physical, political, social, and economic environment.[14] This capacity of self-rule is widely recognized to have both an internal and an external aspect.

Internally, a collective can only be deemed *self*-determining if the group's decision-making is exercised by the corporate body of members. This would most plausibly be achieved through some form of democratic governance.[15] At least, it is hard to see how a political community can be deemed self-determining without processes in place to ensure that collective decision-making is determined, in some sense, by the community as a whole; where this will involve, at a minimum, that members have freedom of thought, expression, association, assembly, and avenues for political participation.

Externally, there is a presumption against outside interference in a self-determining collective's decision-making. This is sometimes taken to entail that the collective be granted an absolute right of non-interference, or full sovereignty, within a given domain.[16] However, as Iris Marion Young notes, 'A theory of self-determination for peoples should recognize that peoples are interdependent and, for this reason, that non-interference is inadequate as an interpretation of self-determination' (2002: 258). In an interdependent world, where it is impossible to insulate any given collective from the actions of outside agents, external self-determination will realistically involve a more tempered form of self-government; one where external interference is presumed against and international relationships are subjected to certain protective restraints. In short, then, a self-determining collective is one that can govern itself, within a certain sphere, based on the interests of its members, and free from undue external interference.

Principles of global justice are sometimes claimed to be *incompatible* with meaningful collective self-determination below the global level—self-determination, that is, which genuinely enables political communities to choose between different ways of life.[17] The self-determination objection to global redistribution works both synchronically and diachronically (see Tan 2004: 100). At any *given* time, self-determination may be claimed to imply—by its very nature—that a collective has a right over its own resources, and thus that those resources can only be reallocated if it so chooses. *Over* time, collective self-determination is claimed to undermine principles of global justice through its connection to collective responsibility. The idea here is that,

---

[14] See Buchanan 2004: 206; Margalit & Raz 1990: 440.
[15] See Philpott 1995.   [16] See Altman & Wellman 2009.
[17] See the discussion in Armstrong 2010. As Armstrong points out, one of the main proponents of this incompatibility claim is Miller, who holds that there is 'a *fundamental* conflict between national self-determination and global justice' (Miller 2000: 162; emphasis added). This incompatibility claim is also made by Andrew Altman and Christopher Wellman (2009: 123–4); and Jon Mandle (2006: 621–2).

even if it were possible to instigate a globally fair distribution of resources at a certain moment, the different choices that each collective makes about what to do with those resources—choices that they are both permitted to make and responsible for as a self-determining group—will soon result in justifiable departures from that initial pattern. Redistributing later in pursuit of greater equality, Miller argues, would then undermine collective responsibility and collective self-determination with it (Miller 1999: 193–7).[18]

This purported incompatibility between collective self-determination and principles 'that seek to treat people equally regardless of which community they belong to' (Miller 2005: 388) might appear to suggest that, if one accepts the importance of collective self-determination, then one must reject global egalitarianism for natural resources. This, at least, is Miller's conclusion (1999: 195):

> global equality of resources, even if it can be coherently defined in the abstract, must be defeated over time by the different policies followed by autonomous political communities, which give rise to fair inequalities in per capita shares of natural resources.

However, Miller's argument gains much of its plausibility from the fact that he again assumes that natural resource egalitarianism must embody a commitment to a *substantive* 'principle [of] per capita equality of natural resources' (Miller 1999: 194).[19] I have argued that natural resource egalitarianism should instead be understood in terms of Contractualist Common Ownership. If SD would be agreed to by the parties in Contractualist Common Ownership's cosmopolitan original position, we can conclude that this principle is after all compatible with Equal Original Claims; because it can be defended from a perspective that respects those claims.

The question, then, is whether SD would be accepted by the parties. In what remains of this section I argue that it plausibly would be—*if* we understand the value of collective self-determination and the political communities with a claim to this capacity appropriately.

6.2.2 Which political communities

In considering which political communities have a claim to self-determination, one first thing to note is that many theorists construe it as a

---

[18] Elsewhere, Miller terms this the 'dynamic objection' to global equality (Miller 2007: 74). As some might recognize, this is effectively a version of Robert Nozick's Wilt Chamberlain argument against within-state redistribution, replayed at the global level (see Nozick 1974: 160ff.). Avery Kolers, who designs his own global analogue of this problem, terms it: 'How state autonomy upsets global patterns' (2002: 41, fn.26). A version is also presented by Rawls (1999b: 117–18).

[19] Which is not to say that Miller succeeds in showing that collective autonomy and substantive equality of natural resources are incompatible either. For an argument that he does not, see Hayward 2006: 355–6.

capacity of *nations* in particular, where nations are often understood as 'encompassing cultural groups that associate themselves with a homeland and in which there is substantial (though not necessarily unanimous) aspiration for self-government of some kind (though not necessarily full independence) in that homeland' (Buchanan 2004: 235, fn.32).[20]

The aspiration for self-government condition makes the matter of a right to self-determination pertinent for such collectives. However, if one construes the collectives with a claim to self-determination as nations, this problematically appears to suggest that shared culture is a pre-requisite for the possession of this right; and that one of the primary purposes of self-determination is protection of the national culture. This would rightly concern parties in the original position, who do not know whether they represent members of cultural minorities within a larger national group, or members of groups that construe their collective identity on other—perhaps merely political— grounds (and who may therefore find themselves at a distinct disadvantage in a world where only cultural nations have resource rights in support of their self-determination).[21]

If collective self-determination is to be acceptable from the perspective of Contractualist Common Ownership it must therefore be *uncoupled* from nationality and defended on political, rather than cultural, grounds; as a capacity of value to political, rather than necessarily cultural, communities.[22] With this aim in mind, I here draw on Margaret Moore's non-statist, *political* conception of a people to define the political communities with a claim to collective self-determination.

Moore defines a people in terms of its satisfaction of three key conditions: political identity, political capacity, and political history. Political identity

---

[20] Buchanan here borrows terminology from Avishai Margalit and Joseph Raz, who argue that 'the right to self-determination derives from the value of membership in encompassing groups' (understood, roughly speaking, as 'groups with pervasive cultures...membership of which is important to one's self-identity') (Margalit & Raz 1990: 456, 448). I take the sharing of a common culture to be a necessary condition for a group to count as a nation, but it should be noted that others reject this condition (in fact, though Buchanan takes this as a working definition, he disputes the idea that nations are necessarily cultural groups (2004: 235–6)). The national culture defence of self-determination is exemplified by Yael Tamir's claim that 'the right to national self-determination...stakes a cultural rather than a political claim, namely, it is the right to preserve the existence of a nation as a distinct cultural entity' (1995: 57). Miller also defends national self-determination (and, ideally, statehood) by claiming that it is necessary for protection of the national culture (1997: 87–8).

[21] Concerns about the nationalist defence of self-determination—in particular, its implications for members of minority or other cultural groups—are also expressed by Cara Nine (2012: 64–5) and Anna Stilz (2015: 3).

[22] The 'uncoupling' terminology is used by Buchanan (2004: 244). Avner de Shalit (1996) also argues that self-determination should be understood in political rather than cultural terms. To avoid the assumption that self-determination is necessarily a right of nations, one might instead refer to the collectives with a claim to this capacity as 'peoples' (Moore 2015: Ch. 3; Nine 2012: §3.8; Rawls 1999b; Young 2002: Ch. 7) or 'political communities' (Moore 2006).

exists when individuals 'share a conception of themselves as a group', in a relationship 'marked by a shared aspiration to exercise collective self-government'. This means that they 'subjectively identify with co-members, in terms of either being engaged, or desiring to be engaged, *in a common political project* and they are mobilized in actions oriented towards that goal'. Political capacity requires that the group also possesses the ability to create and maintain political institutions through which self-determination can be exercised. Finally, to count as a people, a group must have a history of political cooperation with one another, with 'bonds of solidarity, forged by their relationships directed at political goals or within political practices' (Moore 2015: 50). This history could involve organization under a state or state-like structure, but could also be 'a history of sharing a substate unit or a history of political mobilization against an oppressive colonial state' (Moore 2015: 52).

I intend to read all three of Moore's conditions loosely. I take it that a group could meet the political identity condition by sharing an understanding of themselves as, for example, 'the people of this land'; desiring to engage in the common project of coordinating their lives alongside one another within a region, shielded from external interference. The political institutions referred to in the capacity condition could be relatively simple collective decision-making processes, resource-sharing schemes, and conflict resolution mechanisms. And a history of political cooperation could similarly consist in such basic practices of social coordination. On this loose reading, political identity, capacity, and history are not straightforward to identify, so it may not always be obvious to external observers that a group constitutes a people. In some cases, for example, it may only become clear to observers that a group constitutes a people once that group is threatened with outside interference. A group identity that has previously been somewhat tacit may at this point be brought to the fore, along with the aspiration to exercise collective self-government (through resisting such outside interference).

The peoples picked out by Moore's definition are relevant to the question of self-determination because they have the desire and the wherewithal to exercise this right. Political identity not only marks out a group with an aspiration for self-government, but also a collective agent that can be the bearer of rights and duties, with the ability to decide and act as a group. Political capacity requires that the ability to exercise self-determination has been demonstrated or else can be predicted. Capacity is here understood generously: if burdensome circumstances are preventing a group from being able to exercise effective governance, that group will still count as having political capacity if those barriers could be alleviated (Moore 2015: 51–2). Finally, political history ensures that a people has a history of cooperation that provides a basis for future cooperation and reason to think that such cooperation will be productive.

I use Moore's political conception of a people because its thin and inclusive nature makes it far more important for parties to the original position to be concerned with the capacities of such collectives. Moore is clear that the definition is designed to be 'capacious'. A collective satisfying her conditions could be a cultural nation, an indigenous people, a collective governed by a state or state-like structure, or 'people who have organized into a [*sic*] enduring resistance movement against imperialism' (Moore 2015: 61). It appears the conditions could also characterize what Avery Kolers terms an *ethnogeographic community* ('a group of people marked out by their shared conception of land and their densely and pervasively interacting patterns of land use' (Kolers 2009: 67)); a nomadic people (see Gilbert 2007); what Rawls terms a *decent hierarchical people* (Rawls 1999b: 62ff); or an anti-hierarchical political collect-ive organizing, for example, along communalist lines (see Bookchin 1994).[23]

Whilst these differing group characteristics suggest different stories of how a people came to be formed, facts of geography will tend to play a significant role in these narratives. Living closely alongside others across a common geographical region both facilitates and necessitates political organization. Individuals that share a land-base with one another will be involved in various forms of interaction: both direct and interpersonal, but also indirect (via their impacts on the shared local environment). Over time, these patterns of inter-action may create a community with a shared history of collective organiza-tion in a particular region; and this collective organization creates the potential for the group to become a *political* community—or what I will sometimes refer to as a Moorean people.

6.2.3 *Why collective self-determination is of value to individuals*

The inclusive nature of this Moorean conception of a political people signifi-cantly increases the expectation that parties to the original position will find themselves to be members of such communities. In fact, they may find them-selves to be members of more than one people, since peoples may live alongside and overlap with one another, and individuals with mobile lifestyles or family ties across different communities may identify with, and engage in political cooperation with, more than one group that satisfies Moore's conditions. It thereby becomes apposite to ask whether the parties would accept SD:

SD: The system of natural resource rights must grant every political community [understood as a Moorean people] the entitlements over natural resources that are necessary for engaging in the legitimate exercise of collective self-determination.

---

[23] On the contemporary relevance of this example, see Graeber 2014.

Parties to Contractualist Common Ownership's original position will only accept SD if they have reason to think that it will further the interests of whichever individual they turn out to represent. The strongest arguments in favour of SD will therefore appeal to individual interests that are plausibly universal. In the philosophical literature, arguments along these lines tend to appeal to an individual interest in autonomy, freedom, or non-domination (see Philpott 1995; Nine 2012: 91–2; Banai 2013; Schuppert 2013). In this section, I will appeal to an individual interest in non-domination to make the case that the self-determination of a political community is of value to its members.

Following I M Young, we can take domination roughly speaking to consist in 'institutional conditions which inhibit or prevent people from participating in determining their actions or the conditions of their actions. Persons live within structures of domination if other persons or groups can determine without reciprocation the conditions of their actions' (1990: 38). Young directs us to Philip Pettit for a more precise understanding of freedom as non-domination, which can be contrasted with the idea of freedom as non-interference (Young 2002: 258–9). According to Pettit, to be subject to domination is to have one's choices exposed to *arbitrary* interference by others, where interference is arbitrary 'to the extent that it is not forced to track the interests and ideas of those who suffer the interference' (Pettit 1997: Ch. 2, abstract).[24] An individual can therefore be free in the *non-dominated* sense even though their decisions or actions are interfered with, provided such interference is non-arbitrary or designed to combat domination. On the other hand, an individual can be unfree in the sense of being dominated even when nobody *actually* interferes, if the possibility of arbitrary interference is present.

The dominated individual may have all their basic needs satisfied, or live a life that is otherwise—in material terms—of good quality. Nevertheless, circumstances of domination leave individuals exposed to problematic forms of control. Pettit construes non-domination as a primary good: something that individuals have reason to want 'no matter what they value and pursue' (1997: 90). Freedom from domination, or protection from arbitrary interference, appears to be one of the most fundamental interests of all individuals. Parties to the natural resource rights contract will therefore seek agreement on principles that offer to secure circumstances of non-domination for those they represent.

---

[24] See also Frank Lovett, who describes domination as 'the condition experienced by persons or groups whenever they are dependent on a social relationship in which some other person or group wields arbitrary power over them' (2010: 233).

Why would the system of resource rights mandated by SD promise to serve this individual interest in non-domination? Because non-domination is a social good that must be secured via appropriate collective arrangements and institutions of collective self-determination are well-suited to this task. As explained in §6.2.1, the capacity of collective self-determination has both internal (*self*-rule) and external (presumption against outside interference) aspects. When a collective is successfully engaged in self-determination, these aspects will work together to promote freedom as non-domination for its members.

With respect to the internal aspect, I explained in §6.2.1 that for a group to be truly *self*-determining it seems that it must be democratic, or at least have mechanisms in place to ensure that it operates in accordance with the interests and aims of its members (where this can be assumed to require protections for certain basic rights and freedoms and avenues of political participation). That is, a collective can only be deemed self-determining when its members' basic rights and access to political processes are given sufficient protection to be able to say that the community is *governing itself*, rather than *being governed by* a dictator, faction, or external power. These democratic or protective mechanisms promise to help safeguard individuals from arbitrary interference by co-members of their society, and their political institutions, and thus serve to promote freedom as non-domination.

The internal dimension of self-determination will only be able to do this, however, if these political mechanisms are protected from undue outside interference. This is where the external aspect of self-determination comes in. As Cara Nine points out, powers of self-determination serve to insulate a people from coercion, control, or domination by outside agents (2012: 91–2). This external aspect of self-determination is crucial given that 'domination is a problem which does not respect borders' (Schuppert 2013: 259). Foreign powers, private corporations, and international organizations can occupy a position of dominance with respect to political communities; able to interfere with a community's internal affairs or domestic institutions without regard for the interests of community members.[25] A community's institutions cannot succeed in protecting members from domination whilst such outside interference remains possible. As Cécile Laborde and Miriam Ronzoni put it, 'when citizens live in dominated polities . . . they are themselves exposed to domination' (2016: 279).

---

[25] As Kolers argues, 'The injustice of the contemporary world is not merely a matter of (e.g.) U.S. foreign and fiscal policy affecting outsiders, but of powerful foreign governments and corporations undermining communities' ability to live as, and where, they always have. Impoverished countries have little or no say over transnational institutions such as the IMF and World Bank, let alone U.S. policy, while these institutions have coercive power over the most important decisions of poor countries' (2002: 33). See also Chung & Sager 2005: 327ff.; Laborde 2010: 50; Pettit 2010: 77–9.

The formation of self-determining political communities that can resist the arbitrary exercise of external power thus appears to be an essential means by which to limit global relations of domination, creating a global institutional order in which individuals 'live in the presence of other people and when, by virtue of social design, none of those others dominates them' (Pettit 1997: 67). Within such communities, individuals 'can collectively achieve a status of optimal non-domination' (Laborde 2010: 62). The two aspects of collective self-determination work in tandem here. It is largely *because* the internal aspect of self-determination, when working correctly, helps to create relations of non-domination that the presumption against outside interference also promises to do so. When internal self-determination is absent, for example in cases where a group is living under authoritarian rule, the presumption against outside interference appears to lose a significant part of its value and we may conclude that outsiders have a duty to interfere, *if* this would serve the (non-arbitrary) goal of combatting intra-group relations of domination (see Young 2002: 26).

In sum, collective self-determination offers to protect individuals from domination both by co-members of their political community and their domestic political structures (through its internal dimension); and by outside agents, which may seek to arbitrarily interfere with their lives directly, or via their domestic institutions (through its external dimension). When political communities are truly self-determining, their political institutions are attuned to the will of the people rather than subject to the arbitrary interference of outsiders. Collective self-determination can therefore be defended as a necessary means of promoting individuals' fundamental interest in avoiding domination. This is why parties to Contractualist Common Ownership's original position would accept SD:

SD: The system of natural resource rights must grant every political community the entitlements over natural resources that are necessary for engaging in the legitimate exercise of collective self-determination.

Where, given that collective self-determination has been defended based on its ability to promote the value of non-domination, we can now also conclude that the exercise of this capacity will only be *legitimate* when it does not serve to dominate community members, outsiders, or future generations.

6.3 Collective self-determination and resource rights

In §6.2 I argued that parties to the original position would want resource rights to support the legitimate exercise of collective self-determination, for political communities understood according to Moore's non-statist, political conception of a people. This is because the individuals that the parties represent are likely to be members of such political communities; and because those individuals can be predicted to have a fundamental interest in freedom as non-domination that will be furthered insofar as their communities are successfully self-determining. In this section, I begin my discussion of what a system of natural resource rights must look like, if it is to satisfy principle of SD.

Those seeking to defend resource sovereignty by appeal to collective self-determination seem to view this latter capacity as requiring non-interference and argue on this basis that self-determination demands relatively unlimited rights of jurisdiction over territorial resources. With mind to the distinction between freedom as non-interference and freedom as non-domination, I argue that collective self-determination will be better supported by a system of resource rights under which peoples merely possess a *presumptive* right of exclusive territorial jurisdiction over the land and surface resources of a region. By this I mean that whilst a right of exclusive jurisdiction may be presumed absent certain countervailing considerations, such considerations will frequently be in play, requiring that this right of jurisdiction be moderated or abnegated. Furthermore, such jurisdiction is unlikely to extend as far as proponents of resource sovereignty claim, and may not include underground extractive resources.

6.3.1 *The presumptive right to exclusive territorial jurisdiction*

As explained in §3.1, rights over natural resources may be ones of jurisdiction or ownership, where possessors of jurisdictional rights are entitled to legislate, adjudicate, and enforce ownership rights within a particular domain. I will therefore start by considering how jurisdictional rights over natural resources should be allocated, given acceptance of SD. I assume that jurisdictional rights involve a political form of authority that can only legitimately be possessed by certain collectives.

As explained in §6.2.1, collective self-determination is the capacity of a group to govern its collective way of life by exercising control over certain aspects of its physical, political, social, and economic environment. It is hard to see how a collective can exercise control in these domains without having some measure of control over its *natural* environment. To determine their collective way of life together, it seems that a people must be able to jointly manage their shared *surroundings*: where this will include the land and surface resources—such as soils, vegetation, rocks, and water sources—around which their collective activities revolve.[26] Whether this also includes underground

---

[26] As Kolers points out, 'It is through land use that communities structure their life together...The way a community uses its land significantly shapes how its members eat, work, commute, use leisure time, and participate in public life; land-use decisions affect the public health, life expectancy, and democratic character of communities' (2002: 34–5).

extractive resources, which a community might not even be aware of, is less clear. But certainly, some territorial jurisdiction over a people's surrounding natural resources appears necessary to its collective self-determination.

A right of jurisdiction over land and other natural resources demarcates a territory, within which a people can exercise the internal aspect of self-determination by assigning ownership rights to those resources in a pattern reflecting the interests of its members. This might include individual or group interests in being able to reliably access, manage, use, or control natural resources that are important to personal or cultural identity, or required for engaging in certain valued activities. Members may have different understandings of natural resources and their value, and the resource rights that they claim may conflict with one another; but collective decision-making can be designed with the aim of ensuring that these claims are resolved via mechanisms that represent the conflicting interests of members in a reasonably fair way.

This right of territorial jurisdiction over natural resources must be presumed exclusive for the sake of the external aspect of self-determination. A territory provides a 'zone of control' within which a collective is 'insulated from coercion by others' (Nine 2012: 92). Decisions about the natural resources within a given area tend to have particularly significant implications for those who live there, and a people's control over its collective way of life will be severely impaired if outsiders can arbitrarily interfere with its choices about local land use, energy production (which requires natural resources as inputs), whether resources should be owned privately or in common, and whether foreign companies or investors should be allowed to purchase plots of land or other resources. To be shielded from domination, political communities must be protected from arbitrary outside interference in such decisions.[27]

A significant example of how the self-determination of a people can be devastated by their lack of jurisdiction over local resources is provided by the *international resource privilege*, which has been discussed in the philosophical literature by Thomas Pogge (2008: 119–21, 168–72) and Leif Wenar (2008). The international resource privilege effectively assigns natural resource jurisdiction to whoever can maintain coercive control over the local population; giving authoritarian rulers a de facto entitlement to manage, alienate, and extract income from the resources of the region. This global market rule—which is upheld by wealthy importing states—can have a severe

---

[27] Though Kolers focuses primarily on the value of democracy (and territorial self-determination as necessary for democracy), he similarly defends local jurisdiction in decisions about land use on the basis that such decisions 'have especially grave implications for those who live on the land in question' (2002: 35).

impact on domestic arrangements in regions containing resources that are prized highly by outsiders. In a phenomenon known as the *resource curse*, the problematic incentive and power structures created by this privilege under-mine democracy and economic growth and support authoritarian rule and civil conflict—thus exposing the lives of those in resource-cursed countries to significant and arbitrary interference.

The resource curse might give the impression that there is no necessary link between resource possession and advantage. What it really demonstrates, however, is that resource *proximity* without territorial jurisdiction can con-found the ability of local communities to be self-determining.[28] The possessor of de facto rights over land and extractive resources in resource-cursed countries—namely, the ruling power—does indeed benefit, greatly, from this entitlement. The people suffer because their rights of jurisdiction over their surrounding resources are not recognized and respected, not because resource rights have no link to benefits. What local communities *need* to escape the resource curse is for jurisdiction over the land to be removed from the ruling regime and restored to its rightful place, with the people.

Unaccountable political rulers cannot claim any resource rights on the basis of SD, because such rights will not support the local community's exercise of self-determination. The presumptive right of exclusive territorial jurisdiction over natural resources is possessed by political communities, not political rulers or institutions. And whilst political communities will need some insti-tutional mechanisms by which to administer their resource rights, those institutions must be suitably representative of the people as a whole if they are to succeed in administering resource rights in accordance with the internal dimension of collective self-determination. Where political institutions are not suitably representative, a people may currently lack the ability to *exercise* territorial jurisdiction over natural resources—but this does not mean that it lacks a presumptive right to such jurisdiction.

SD thus supports a people's presumptive right to exclusive territorial jurisdiction over land and natural resources, in support of their legitimate exercise of self-determination, where this includes political communities oppressed by authoritarian rule. And whilst phenomena like the resource curse may make it hard to see how this right can be realized in practice—and what forms of resistance or intervention might be successful or defensible—it is certainly unjustifiable for outsiders to purchase resources from unaccountable regimes. By doing so, they contribute to the oppression of the people and the violation of the peoples' presumptive right to juris-diction over its land.

---

[28] On this point, see also Goldtooth 2004: 10.

6.3.2 *Limits to territorial jurisdiction*

In §6.3.1, I argued that a commitment to SD should lead us to hold that the system of resource rights must grant every political community a presumptive right of exclusive territorial jurisdiction over the land and surface resources of a region where it can engage in the legitimate exercise of self-determination. This right already differs from a statist or nationalist right of resource sovereignty, in the sense that it falls to *political peoples*, which may not be states or nations.

Another major difference, which my terminology of 'presumptive' rights is designed to indicate, is that the right to exclusive territorial jurisdiction that SD supports is strongly defeasible, in the sense that it will often be abnegated or moderated by countervailing considerations. Specifically, it must be abnegated insofar as it conflicts with the satisfaction of basic needs (of either community members or outsiders) and moderated insofar as it conflicts with the self-determination of other peoples (either now, or in the future). The first consideration arises due to the lexical priority of the basic needs principle. The second consideration arises because the importance of collective self-determination both justifies and circumscribes territorial jurisdiction over natural resources; most obviously, because the jurisdiction of one people may undermine the self-determination of another by engendering relations of domination.[29]

The precise scheme of resource rights that will result from application of the two principles can ultimately only be determined by identifying, assessing, and adjudicating between natural resource claims on a case-by-case basis. There are, however, some predictable limits to territorial jurisdiction that the two principles will necessitate. I outline several of these limits in Chapter Seven.

6.4 Conclusion

In this chapter I defended the principle of collective self-determination as a second principle of natural resource justice. This defence emerged from consideration of the principle of natural resource sovereignty, which appears to be

---

[29] One might appeal, here, to what Nine has termed the *Lockean proviso mechanism*: 'an adaptable theoretical/practical tool, [that] can be articulated as the following rule: When the exercise of an exclusive right over goods severely threatens the value(s) that are used to justify the right (or system of rights of which it is a part), then the right should be changed so that it no longer undermines those values' (2010: 362). In this case, the exclusive right over goods is that of jurisdiction over territorial resources and the value that both justifies and is threatened by this right is collective self-determination. As Cécile Fabre also argues, 'if the value of political self-determination is paramount, then one may need to constrain the rights of the resource-rich over their own future for the sake of ensuring that the resource-poor can exercise those very same rights' (2005: 157).

a candidate for agreement from the perspective of Contractualist Common Ownership's original position. I argued that the stewardship defence of resource sovereignty fails. The collective self-determination defence, on the other hand, gets something right. Parties to the original position would indeed accept a principle according to which the system of resource rights must grant every political community the entitlements over natural resources that are necessary for engaging in the legitimate exercise of collective self-determination. But it is a further question whether resource sovereignty is demanded by this principle.

I showed that the principle of collective self-determination supports some system of *exclusive territorial jurisdiction* over natural resources. Jurisdiction over the land and surface resources of a region provides a people with a sphere of control within which it can exercise the internal aspect of self-determination, insulated from arbitrary interference by outside agents. I also argued, however, that this right of territorial jurisdiction can only be *presumptive* in nature, and must be abnegated or moderated if it conflicts with the satisfaction of basic needs, or the self-determination of other collectives. Such conflicts will be discussed further in the next chapter, to demonstrate that this conception of natural resource justice does not support natural resource sovereignty, but instead demands what I will term a system of *limited territorial jurisdiction* over natural resources.

7

Limited Territorial Jurisdiction over Natural Resources

In Chapters Five and Six, I used the Contractualist Common Ownership approach to defend two principles of natural resource justice: a principle of collective self-determination and a (lexically prior) basic needs principle. In this chapter, I further explore and defend the conception of justice composed of these two principles. I discuss the lexical ordering of the principles and the nature and scope of the resource claims that they legitimize (§7.1). Then, I look at how the two principles will work in tandem to justify a system of *limited territorial jurisdiction* over natural resources (§7.2). I also explain how my account of natural resource justice might be integrated into a broader theory of justice concerning other morally significant goods (§7.4). Two important objections to this conception of natural resource justice are addressed along the way: first, that it is too minimal or sufficientarian in nature (§7.3); and second, that it is problematically ideal in the sense that it could not be feasibly implemented (§7.5).

7.1 Two principles of natural resource justice

I have argued that parties representing all human beings in a hypothetical cosmopolitan contract would choose two principles to govern the assignment of natural resource rights. In order of descending lexical priority—reflecting the importance with which the parties would endow them—these are:

1. The Basic Needs Principle (BN): The system of natural resource rights must grant every human being the entitlements over natural resources that are necessary for satisfying their basic needs.

2. The Principle of Collective Self-Determination (SD): The system of natural resource rights must grant every political community the entitlements over natural resources that are necessary for engaging in the legitimate exercise of collective self-determination.

Where the political communities in question are understood in terms of Margaret Moore's political conception of a people and the legitimate exercise of collective self-determination does not serve to dominate community members, outsiders, or future generations.

In this section, I discuss the nature and scope of the resource claims that the two principles will legitimize and the implications of the lexical ordering.

7.1.1 General and particular claims

In §3.3, I made a distinction between general and particular claims to natural resources, where the former constitute claims to some undifferentiated share of certain natural resource types, and the latter constitute claims to certain rights over specific natural resource tokens. Unlike the Equal Division conception of natural resource justice, which only appears able to assess general claims (see §3.7), my conception of natural resource justice can be used to assess and legitimate claims of both kinds.

This conception supports each individual's claim to a *system* of natural resource rights under which they are granted entitlements to natural resources for basic needs satisfaction, and their political community is granted entitlements to natural resources for the legitimate exercise of collective self-determination. This claim is a *general* one, because it is a claim arising from original position reasoning about the correct way to allocate rights to the world's resources, considered as a whole. If the global *distribution* of natural resource rights does not support basic needs satisfaction for all individuals, and collective self-determination for all political communities, then this distribution is unfair.

The entitlements that satisfy such general claims, however, will commonly be to *specific* resources, thus supporting *particular* claims. Basic needs are universal, so one might suppose that they will only ground *general* claims to natural resources: to rights over *some* of the world's water and *some* of its soil, for instance. Reality, however, is such that a significant proportion of these claims will only be satisfied by specific resource rights. People occupy particular locations and thus, rights to natural resources that are out of reach will not serve to satisfy their basic needs, even if respected. The principle of basic needs will therefore frequently ground rights over particular resources: to essential resources that are local to the rights-holder. Over time, institutions may develop that allow basic needs to be satisfied by more distant or imported resources; and in many cases, local resources will not suffice to satisfy basic needs, necessitating redistribution from further afield. But the local resources that individuals use to satisfy basic needs will not always be substitutable with resources from elsewhere. As noted in §5.5: though basic needs are universal, their satisfiers may not be. Those who grow accustomed to satisfying their requirements for food and shelter (for instance) using the natural resources found in a particular region, may not be able to satisfy their basic needs in a different environment with unfamiliar resources.[1]

The self-determination principle will also ground claims to jurisdiction over specific resources, because political communities similarly exercise self-determination in particular places. The way of life that a people develops in the region where it exercises self-determination may not be transplantable to a different natural environment. *Specific* geographical spaces can thus become central to a community's way of life, such that its self-determination will only be protected by a right of jurisdiction over a *particular* region. The region in question will often be that where a people currently resides—but it may also be a region from which that community was forcibly removed, perhaps even a long time ago.[2]

7.1.2 *The scope of claims*

These two principles also restrict the *scope* of entitlements over natural resources that individuals and collectives can legitimately claim. No justification has been given for individuals or collectives to unilaterally appropriate natural resources when this is unnecessary for basic needs satisfaction or the legitimate exercise of self-determination. In other words, resources that are not required for these key activities remain in common; where, according to the Common Ownership conception introduced in Chapter Three, resources in common *belong to everyone* in the very weak sense that each individual has a moral claim to *use* them, but lacks any rights of exclusion.

Amongst the resources remaining in common will be those that no one political community can claim to be specifically essential to its own self-determination, over and above the self-determination of others. This will

[1] As Anna Stilz says, 'Geography and climate may affect the economic and subsistence practices we take up, making it difficult for us to reconstitute these practices in some very different place' (2013: 335). Members of the Penan tribe, protesting the construction of a hydroelectric dam that will displace them from their traditional lands, appear to stake a particular claim of this sort: arguing that if the dam proceeds 'We will be forced to move to an area that we do not know and is not compatible with our life conditions' (Survival International 2009).

[2] This seems to be the case, for example, for the Sioux people, whose lands were unjustly and brutally taken by settlers and remain under US control. Rebecca Tsosie says that (2007b: 46):

for the Sioux people, the wrongdoing continues because the United States still maintains control over the lands that are seen as fundamental to Sioux political and cultural identity and because the United States continues to deny the several bands of the Sioux Nation their sovereign right to protect their land, and the natural and cultural resources comprised within those lands...For the Sioux people, the fight for their land is coextensive with their fight to maintain a separate political and cultural identity.

For the Sioux, then, it appears that collective self-determination is bound up with particular lands and resources, so that their exclusion from these constitutes ongoing, arbitrary interference with their exercise of this capacity.

likely include some resource systems currently perceived to be the Common Heritage of Humankind, such as (parts of) the ocean and its resources, the atmosphere, and the resources of outer space.[3] It will also include tracts of land and resources that are not being used in the legitimate exercise of self-determination, despite being enclosed by internationally recognized state borders.

Though peoples and individuals may have a claim to *use* such common resources, they lack any rights of exclusion (beyond what is necessary for the satisfaction of basic needs) and must render their use compatible with like use by others. In times, like our own, of a large, mobile, and technologically advanced population, it may be necessary to try to establish fair global jurisdiction over common resources, to coordinate use to this end.

7.1.3 *The priority of basic needs*

BN was defended as the minimum that parties to the original position would be willing to accept. It therefore has lexical priority over SD. This means that in cases of conflict, where a choice must be made between an allocation of rights that grants natural resource entitlements for basic needs satisfaction, or else an allocation of rights that grants natural resource entitlements for collective self-determination, this conception of justice favours the former. This is one way in which my account of natural resource justice differs from Moore's, which is otherwise similar in significant respects. Moore agrees that control over and access to natural resources should be allocated with the aim of supporting subsistence and collective self-determination, but thinks that in situations of conflict it is not obvious that the former should trump the latter (2015: 183).

The priority of BN implies that any people's right of jurisdiction over natural resources must be rendered compatible with the basic needs satisfaction of its members, outsiders, and future generations. This places limits on the *exercise* of jurisdiction over natural resources: such jurisdiction must be designed to ensure that members' basic needs are satisfied, and certainly cannot be used to prevent members (or outsiders) from accessing natural resources for basic needs satisfaction. The basic needs principle also constrains the *system* of territorial jurisdiction, because if some political communities lack sufficient territorial resources for their members' basic needs, then the system of resource rights must be adjusted to address this. Such adjustment could comprise rights reallocation (potentially involving the movement of natural resources or people across territorial boundaries), or a redrawing of territorial borders.

---

[3] For discussion of such resources, see Buck 1998; Caney 2012: 269–71.

The preferred option for supporting basic needs satisfaction in any instance should be that which is most compatible with the ongoing exercise of collective self-determination for all peoples concerned. Redrawing of territorial boundaries may score badly on this front. Reallocation of resource rights, on the other hand, might be possible without problematic impacts on capacities for self-determination. In §7.2.4 I will suggest that income rights, in particular, may prove a good candidate for reallocation in pursuit of basic needs satisfaction.

7.2 Limited territorial jurisdiction

The precise scheme of resource rights that will result from application of the two principles can ultimately only be determined by identifying, assessing, and adjudicating between claims to natural resources on a case-by-case basis. SD indicates that each people should be granted a presumptive right of exclusive territorial jurisdiction over the land and surface resources of a region where it can engage in the legitimate exercise of collective self-determination. This is because such jurisdiction provides a people with a sphere of control within which it can exercise the internal aspect of self-determination, insulated from arbitrary interference by outside agents. The two principles also entail, however, that this presumed right must be abnegated if it conflicts with the satisfaction of basic needs; and moderated if it conflicts with other collectives' legitimate exercise of self-determination.

When adjudicating such conflicts, it may—as Chris Armstrong suggests—be helpful to distinguish between the land that a people lives on and any natural resources that are, in principle, removable from that land (2013a: 52–3). A people's self-determination will be served by a *presumption* that its jurisdiction extends to all the surface resources of the region. This presumption makes resource rights more stable and predictable, allowing members to coordinate their resource management in pursuit of collectively determined goals. But in some cases, it will be possible to disperse resource rights outwards, or move resource units to other regions, without undermining basic needs satisfaction or collective self-determination. Any calls for such dispersal must, however, be assessed very cautiously. It can be difficult for outsiders to recognize the ways in which a people is using the resources within its territory; outsiders may, for example, mistake resources that are laying fallow for resources that a people is not using in its exercise of self-determination. And at a more fundamental level, insiders and outsiders may disagree about where the land ends and other resources begin, or what changes or extractions are compatible with the land remaining the same land that it was to begin with.

In this section, I identify several predictable restrictions that any presumptive right of exclusive territorial jurisdiction must be subject to, if it is to satisfy the demands of the two principles of natural resource justice. I conclude that the system of natural resource rights demanded by the two principles will be one of *limited territorial jurisdiction* over natural resources.

7.2.1 Bounded jurisdiction

Each people's presumptive right of exclusive jurisdiction will be bound to the resources of the region where it legitimately exercises self-determination. This raises two important questions: first, how to identify which (if any) people legitimately exercises self-determination in any given location; and second, how to determine the extent of the region over which that community's jurisdiction will range.

I will refer to the first question, of which peoples can legitimately exercise collective self-determination in which places, as the question of just occupancy. In attempting to provide an account of just occupancy, one appears to be pulled in two directions. On the one hand, this account must condemn cases in which a people comes to occupy a region by engaging in dominating interference with pre-existing residents; for example, through expulsion, violence, or subjugation. However, if this account requires a political community to *prove* that their occupation of land cannot ultimately be traced back to such injustice, it seems that few peoples can be deemed to legitimately occupy their land.

This picture is also complicated because the question of how to rectify cases of unjust occupation can become more difficult over time. If people E comes to unjustly occupy land L by wrongfully expelling group I, then justice will demand (at a minimum) that E departs from L so that I can return. However, if this does not happen and new generations come onto the scene, the rectification question becomes more complicated. Whilst members of E who perpetrated the original injustice clearly have no legitimate claim to reside in L, it is not so clear that E's descendants, or those who might later come to reside in the region innocently, similarly lack any claim to remain in the place where they find themselves (although note that a claim to remain in L does not equate to a claim to prevent members of I from returning, or to a claim to privileged political status within that region).

This is a challenging topic that I do not have space to address adequately, so I will merely try to state some minimal parameters for an account of just occupancy. Firstly, I will follow Anna Stilz in holding that a people cannot justly occupy land through expulsion of prior rightful occupants. Such 'wrongful dispossessors' forfeit their rights to be in that place and 'have no justified complaint if they are expelled by way of their victims' reclaiming their place of residence' (Stilz 2013: 352). Secondly, I will borrow from A John Simmons' account of presumptive justification for holdings and apply it to occupancy (1994: 78).[4] Following Simmons, one might think that since occupancy of land is central to a people's ability to satisfy its members' basic needs and exercise collective self-determination, in the absence of (a) 'a complete pedigree' for some contemporary occupancy of land and (b) 'any historical or contemporary evidence' that might be reason for thinking such occupancy unjust, we should presume an entitlement. Clearly, part (b) of this test will not be passed when a people that was expelled from (presumptively) legitimate occupation of that land maintains a desire to return (as is the situation in many real-world cases).

This leads us to the second question, of how to determine the extent of the region over which a people's jurisdiction ranges. Again, I do not have space to address the difficult question of precisely how the bounds of territorial jurisdiction should be delineated. Substantively, this right should only extend over resources that a people has actually incorporated into its legitimate exercise of self-determination. This suggests that many existing states claim jurisdiction over more territory than they are entitled to. Procedurally, where there are conflicts over the boundaries of territorial jurisdiction—with two peoples plausibly claiming the same land for their legitimate exercise of self-determination—this must be settled through a fair political process, with shared jurisdiction as a potential solution (see §7.2.2).[5] This suggests that many, if not most, existing territorial boundaries are not procedurally justified.

It is also important to be clear about the nature of the territorial boundaries under discussion here. To reiterate: I have taken the three dimensions of territorial right—over natural resources, people, and borders—to require separate justification (see §3.1). This means I do not assume that any right of exclusive territorial jurisdiction over *natural resources* comes along with a right of border control. This bounded right of territorial jurisdiction is exclusive in the sense that it is presumed to *exclude others from exercising jurisdiction over the natural resources of the region*; not in the sense that it entitles a people to *exclude individuals from traversing the boundaries of the region* (or becoming members of the community). In the absence of separate justification, the latter entitlement has so far only been implied to exist when cross-border movement will deprive individuals of the natural resource entitlements that they require for

---

[4] Simmons suggests that 'In the absence of both (a) a complete pedigree for some contemporary holding and (b) any historical or contemporary evidence which might count as a reason for denying entitlement to that holding...we should presume entitlement'. This is supported by 'the importance of holdings to persons' projects and life plans and the apparent innocence of the holdings in question' (Simmons 1994: 78). Simmons has suggested that appeals to presumptive justification have a role to play in theories of territorial rights (2016: 157).

[5] On the territorial border as an emergent political phenomenon, see: Walmsley & Nine 2014.

basic needs satisfaction, or collectives of the natural resource entitlements that they require for the legitimate exercise of self-determination. And I believe that such cases will be far rarer than many seem to suppose. In particular, whilst immigration might plausibly threaten disadvantaged or dominated peoples in this way,[6] it does not seem plausible that it will pose a similar threat to wealthy or powerful collectives.

7.2.2 Shared jurisdiction

As noted in §7.2.1, there may be cases in which more than one people possesses a claim to the same land or natural resources on the basis of self-determination. Here, SD may demand that jurisdiction is shared horizontally across political communities.

Cross-region resource systems (like rivers or aquifers) are one example where schemes of shared jurisdiction will likely be necessary for the protection of self-determination. As Cara Nine notes, to be self-determining over the resources of a territory, a collective 'must not be subject to the arbitrary will of another power regarding these resources' (2014: 164). If a downstream people is subject to the arbitrary power of an upstream group who can divert, deplete, or damage shared resources, the former's self-determination will be significantly undermined. In such cases, systems of shared jurisdiction will be required to ensure that the interests of both communities are represented in decision-making regarding how the resource system should be used and managed, how its assimilative capacity should be understood, and how any resource units should be shared.[7]

Shared jurisdiction will also be necessary in cases where peoples, rather than resources, traverse geographical regions; as in the case of nomadic peoples. Though nomadic peoples are mobile, their collective self-determination will still demand a right of territorial jurisdiction over particular regions of land and specific natural resources; since, as Jérémie Gilbert notes, a nomadic people's way of life is 'attached and bound to a specific territory' over which they habitually range. However, nomadic peoples also tend to share land with other groups (which may themselves be nomadic or sedentary) (Gilbert

---

[6] As Moore argues: 'large-scale migration of individuals who happen to be members of a dominant group can lead to the destruction of a (typically, smaller) community's capacity to determine the context in which they live and control the land that they occupy, if they independently arrive in large numbers'. Indigenous peoples, for example, may be justifiably concerned that 'inward migration of non-indigenous people could undermine their capacity to form and maintain their own political societies' (Moore 2015: 200).

[7] For an example of shared jurisdiction, see Nine's (2014) discussion of the *Comisión Administradora del Río Uruguay* (CARU): a joint commission between Argentina and Uruguay over the river that serves as a border between the two countries (also discussed in Mancilla 2016a: 31–2). Alejandra Mancilla's (2016a) discussion of shared jurisdiction over migratory resources is also instructive.

2007: 701–2). Systems of shared jurisdiction will therefore be necessary to ensure that such lands and natural resources are used over time in a way that supports the continued self-determination of the nomadic and other peoples concerned.

In the case of Global Environmental Resources (GERs), which are located within territories but important to the global community, not just shared but *global* jurisdiction may have to be pursued—if the interests of all those for whom the resource holds significance are to be adequately represented in decisions regarding its use and management. Quite *how* global such jurisdiction can feasibly be will depend on the state of international interaction at any given point in history. But as inter-peoples trade and communication expands, it should be possible to make jurisdiction over globally significant resources increasingly inclusive.

Importantly, it appears that various extractive resources should be considered GERs, and thus that rights of jurisdiction over them should be delegated horizontally to shared institutions. This is the case for resources, such as rare earths and oil, that are extremely desirable but distributed very unevenly across the globe, thus possessing geopolitical significance (see Kolers 2012: 274). An exclusive right of jurisdiction over such resources may endow a collective with the power to leverage them in ways that dominate others (Schuppert 2014: 80–1). Furthermore, as noted in §6.1.2, giving peoples full control over extractive resources (as happens under permanent sovereignty) can create serious problems of divergent interests and undermining of responsible stewardship, with potentially severe knock-on effects for the global environment. Globalizing jurisdiction may thus be necessary if extractive resources are to be managed in a way that promotes self-determination for all.

One might worry that shared jurisdiction over extractive resources will undermine the self-determination of the peoples in whose territory those resources are located. As David Miller points out, collectives can be profoundly affected by the decision to exploit such resources, creating worries about this decision being placed out of their hands (2012: 264). This is a very important concern, but one that should be assessed carefully. It is difficult to see why exclusive rights over underground extractive resources *themselves* would be more necessary to the self-determination of one people than another, *provided* the proximate community can veto any exploitation that threatens its land or other resources. Collective self-determination clearly requires a substantial amount of control over the land that a people lives on and the resources that it finds itself surrounded by, but it is not clear why it requires rights over deep underground resources that need to be discovered before they can be exploited. In other words, it is easy to explain why a people has a stronger claim to its surrounding land, vegetation, and water sources (for example) than outsiders, but harder to explain why that people would necessarily have a privileged claim to jurisdiction over any extractive resources beneath the region.

What peoples appear to have a strong claim to, then, is sufficient control over the land above extractive resources, land on which their capacity for self-determination more realistically depends.[8] *If* local communities can veto extraction, then global jurisdiction over the extractive resources themselves (in the sense that a globally representative agency would be charged with distributing the benefits of such resources, *should* a people consent to extraction) does not appear so troubling. Globalized jurisdiction over extractive resources is therefore the ideal, but should only be pursued in circumstances where proximate communities have a strong de facto right of jurisdiction over their land.

SD thus justifies a strong presumptive right of jurisdiction over the land above underground extractive resources, but not exclusive rights over those resources themselves. A people's right to veto extraction is supposed to protect its own capacities for self-determination, compatible with the self-determination of other groups. This veto right does not, therefore, entitle groups to leverage their extractive resources in an attempt to dominate others: it is an entitlement to say yes or no to extraction and to be involved in the extraction process (so as to negotiate any impacts on land and local resources); but grants no privileged entitlement to decide how the extractive resources themselves should be shared. Furthermore, this veto *could* be overridden in cases where resources are required by others for basic needs satisfaction, or their own exercise of self-determination. Such circumstances are likely to be rare, however. Usually, there will be other ways of addressing such deficits that would not interfere so significantly with the self-determination of communities proximate to extractive resources. And in any cases where withdrawal ought to proceed for the sake of outsiders, those with jurisdiction over the land will be entitled to as much control over the extraction process as possible.

7.2.3 Sustainable jurisdiction

I claimed that the two principles of natural resource justice would be chosen on the basis that they promise to serve the interests of all human beings regardless of their time of birth. This means that natural resource rights in the present must not entitle the holders to prevent individuals (or collectives)

---

[8] Nine similarly argues that 'resources located deep underground should not fall within the territorial domain of a collective', but that 'sites of access' should. In her view, this is because 'the scope of territorial rights is limited to only those areas where a collective can establish just institutions'—understood as institutions which provide 'secure access to the objects of members' basic needs' (Nine 2012: 42–4).

from accessing the natural resources that they need to satisfy basic needs (or exercise self-determination) in the future. Any rights of jurisdiction over natural resources—whether held by peoples, shared, or global—will therefore be subject to a sustainability requirement.

Sustainability is a difficult concept to pin down, and there is not space here to discuss precisely what such a requirement should amount to. Broadly speaking, sustainability will require peoples to manage natural resources with the aim of ensuring that their exercise of self-determination can continue in perpetuity; in a way that does not undermine the capacity of future generations of their own, or other, communities to satisfy their basic needs or exercise self-determination.[9] There are bound to be some difficult cases to assess, given that levels of sustainable resource use will vary in line with available technology (recycling technologies, for example). But this does not prevent us from easily identifying some important instances of natural resource use as unsustainable on this basis: soil and groundwater depletion being obvious examples.

As explained in §6.1.2, how resource rights should be arranged if responsible stewardship is to be encouraged will vary from case to case. But concerns for sustainability may require control to be delegated downwards, to smaller groups within a political community; or horizontally, perhaps even to the global level. In the case of fossil fuels, for example, it seems clear that jurisdiction must be globalized if use is to be adequately restricted. The need for jurisdiction to be exercised sustainably may also give some peoples a claim to restrict immigration to the territory, *if* there is a limit to the number of people that can live there sustainably (see Bertram 2018: 67).

7.2.4 Restricted income rights

As Kok-Chor Tan notes, for a political community to control its collective way of life it is not sufficient that it merely have enough resources to satisfy the basic needs of its members; 'differences in power relations between nations, which economic inequality engenders and sustains, obstruct the right to self-determination of the least advantaged' (2004: 117).[10] One might put it this way: similar to how inequalities of property and wealth within a society can undermine the 'fair value' of political liberty (Rawls 1999a: 198–9), economic

---

[9] One could perhaps appeal to Avery Kolers' criterion of 'plenitude', here, according to which peoples can only achieve territorial rights when they are engaged in a lasting project 'of coming better to know and more intelligently to use places' (2009: 134).

[10] Miller also concedes that 'gross inequality between nations makes it difficult if not impossible for those at the bottom end of the inequality to enjoy an adequate measure of self-determination' (2007: 76). In order to promote self-determination 'as a universal value', it will thus be necessary to limit global inequality (Miller 2007: 74, fn.22). See also Hurrell 2001; Laborde 2010: 52–3.

inequality at the global level can prevent some peoples from *realizing the value* of collective self-determination. A people may therefore require more than merely a presumptive right of jurisdiction over the land and natural resources *within its own* territory to exercise collective self-determination. A system of natural resource rights that satisfies SD when global economic wealth is relatively equal will fail to do so if global inequality becomes so great that relations of domination come into play. If the self-determination principle licensed resource rights that resulted in significant inequalities of economic wealth and—thus—power, it would therefore be self-undermining.

As Onora O'Neill argues, 'Power depends on differentials': it is relative lack of 'capabilities and resources', not absolute lack, that results in 'vulnerability to coercion' (2000: 95–6). If some political communities can grow far richer than others due to an entitlement to extract income from more economically valuable natural resources, they will be able to gain a significant advantage in global trade and bargaining relationships. This will enable the rich to increase their economic lead by insisting on terms of trade that see benefits flow disproportionately in their direction. Wealthier collectives can then gain further advantages of development, technology, information, expertise, military might, and political influence—all of which can enable them to interfere with the choices of individuals in poorer countries without regard to their interests or welfare, if left unchecked.[11]

Global economic inequality, *insofar as* it results in domination, must therefore be mitigated if the value of collective self-determination is to be realized for all; and one way to mitigate such inequality is via an appropriately designed natural resource tax. Save in exceptional circumstances, peoples should not be *required* to generate income from their resources. If they choose to do so, however, a portion of that income may be diverted into a global fund and redistributed with the goal of mitigating global inequalities. This scheme could form part of what Tan describes as 'a more egalitarian global structure in which the preconditions for self-determination do in fact obtain universally for all' (Tan 2004: 102), by placing limits on the economic inequality that can result from the use and sale of natural resources.

The idea of an egalitarian tax on natural resources is well established. Such taxes have been proposed by Brian Barry, Paula Casal, Cécile Fabre, Tim Hayward, Avery Kolers, and Hillel Steiner, among others.[12] My own proposal possesses two distinctive characteristics. Firstly, the tax would only be levied

---

[11] Philip Pettit similarly points to 'financial clout' as a resource in virtue of which one agent can exercise power over another (1997: 59). Other theorists who suggest that inequality between political communities can create relationships of domination include Debra Satz (1999: 80–1) and Charles Beitz (2001: 108–9).

[12] See B. Barry 1980: 38; Casal 2011; Fabre 2005: §3; Hayward 2005a; Kolers 2012; and Steiner 1999.

on income that is *actually* generated from the use of natural resources. Steiner's alternative—of taxing the value of resources that are possessed but not used—was seen in §4.2.1 to significantly undermine the self-determination of collectives that do not wish to exploit resources within their territory that are strongly desired (though not necessarily needed) by outsiders.[13] Secondly, the tax will be distributed on a *gap-reducing*[14]—rather than a gap-neutralizing or equal per capita—basis. The aim is to limit global economic inequalities that undermine the self-determination of the less well-off; where, given the metric problem, the gap to be reduced is that between high-income and low-income peoples, rather than a supposed gap in natural resource value. Just how narrow a gap should be aimed for will depend on what level of income inequality is compatible with non-domination between peoples, which will in turn depend on what other checks on power are in play at the global level.

These restrictions on income retention need not be troubling from the perspective of self-determination. As Moore argues, self-determination is not necessarily undermined by restrictions on a collective's entitlement to retain any income extracted from its natural resources, if it is still able to exercise control over them (2012: 95).[15] The economic value of natural resources depends on global market forces and technological progress and can, as a result, vary dramatically and unpredictably over time—enriching and impoverishing those with rights to natural resources 'in seemingly arbitrary ways' (Miller 1997: 105). This instability of market values suggests that income rights over a fixed set of natural resources are a poor means by which to support collective self-determination in the first place.[16] This capacity will be better promoted for all if income rights over natural resources are restricted in line with a gap-reducing tax.

This resource tax may also provide a way of making rights of territorial jurisdiction compatible with the basic needs principle. Peoples that are

---

[13] Kolers similarly defends a restricted tax base (2012); and Armstrong suggests that those concerned to protect self-determination should not be worried about taxes on income that countries have *chosen* to derive from their resources (2013b: 422–3). Such worries about the undermining of self-determination will apply to Casal and Fabre's proposals, since they suggest that a tax be levied on those who possess natural resources—or the land above them—whether or not they exploit them (Casal 2011; Fabre 2005: 158).

[14] This terminology is from Laborde 2010: 60.

[15] One can draw, here, on a distinction that is sometimes made within the concept of ownership between control rights and income rights. It is control rights—rights, for example, of use, possession, management, and exclusion—that generally seem to be most intimately connected to autonomy. See Christman 1994: 166ff.

[16] As John Christman suggests, 'If securing one's autonomy depended on the outcomes of market transactions, that trait would consequently be as fluid, unpredictable, and shifting as are one's prospects in market competition' (1994: 169). Armstrong also notes that for developing countries, being economically dependent on trade in natural resources 'all too often generates vulnerability (to fluctuating prices, to the whims of multinational corporations and arbitrators, to the dictates of international organizations) rather than stability' (2017: 178).

struggling to satisfy their members' basic needs with the natural resources at their disposal could be granted *income rights* to natural resources under the jurisdiction of those with more than enough for their own basic needs. Such rights reallocation could be implemented by designing the tax such that dispersal takes place with a primary goal of securing basic needs satisfaction, and a secondary goal of mitigating global economic inequalities that undermine the self-determination of the less well-off. The primary, sufficientarian, mechanism could help communities struggling to satisfy their basic needs to buy the goods that they require, or to make more productive use of their own territorial resources through investing in technology or restoration.

To sum up this section: the conception of natural resource justice composed of BN and SD can be seen to demand a system of *limited territorial jurisdiction* over natural resources. Whilst each people has a *presumptive* right of exclusive territorial jurisdiction over the land and surface resources of a region where they can engage in the legitimate exercise of self-determination, this right will be *limited* in various respects. Though the exact limits of this right will have to be assessed on a case-by-case basis, it is predictable that a people's right of jurisdiction will be: bound to a site of just occupation; supplanted by systems of shared or even global jurisdiction for resources that are also significant to the self-determination of other political communities; restricted by a sustainability requirement; and subject to a sufficientarian and gap-reducing tax on any income extracted from the region's natural resources.

7.3 The sufficiency objection

There are two major objections to my theory that I will address before applying it to the problem of climate change: the sufficiency objection, which will be dealt with here, and the feasibility objection, which I will consider in §7.5. According to the sufficiency objection, the two principles constitute an unjustifiably minimal—sufficientarian—conception of justice.[17] This can be understood as an objection internal or external to my account. Internally, the complaint would be that I have failed by my own lights, since I claimed to be providing an account of what natural resource egalitarianism amounts to. If my account is instead a sufficientarian one, then I have not made good on this promise, and it is unreasonable of me to reject rival accounts (in particular, Equal Division) for failing to do justice to Equal Original Claims. I will return to this worry towards the end of this section, but first I will address the sufficiency objection understood as external to my account.

---

[17] For critiques of sufficientarianism see, for example, Arneson 2006 and Casal 2007.

7.3.1 *The external objection*

Here, one might be concerned that my conception of natural resource justice appears to condone a world composed of self-determining political communities, where the members of one people (*P*) have rights over only enough natural resources to satisfy their basic needs, whilst members of another people (*W*) possess vast swathes of natural resources. There are two closely related worries about this situation. First, is this outcome not clearly unjust? In which case, the silence of my account regarding inequalities above what might be termed the 'self-determination threshold' appears to make it incomplete. Second, does the principle of collective self-determination really improve the prospects of *P*'s members at all? If not, it seems that this conception of justice would be rejected on the same grounds that I concluded the basic needs principle in isolation would be rejected; parties to the original position will seek to ensure that their interests are better protected than this.

I will start by dealing with the second question. My reply here is that membership in a self-determining political community *does* make individuals better off. There is a significant difference between having one's basic needs provided for by an outside agent—even if that outside agent is acting benevolently at present—and being part of a self-determining (non-dominating) collective that can provide for the basic needs of its members.[18] As Frank Lovett points out, 'being dependent on a person or group who has the power to arbitrarily withhold the goods or services necessary to meet one's basic needs...amounts to domination' (2010: 195). *Ceteris paribus*, members of political communities with *jurisdictional control* over land and natural resources sufficient to satisfy their basic needs will therefore be significantly better off than individuals without collective control over the natural resources on which they depend (even if the latter are provided with natural resources for basic needs satisfaction by outsiders). Parties to the original position would, therefore, agree to the second principle of natural resource justice in addition to the basic needs principle.

The question now, however, is whether the parties would not seek agreement on additional principles—given that the two principles look as though they may permit situations where some peoples end up like *P*, whilst others

---

[18] In Nine's view, it does not appear possible for basic needs to be satisfied in the absence of collective self-determination, because she takes the latter to be *necessary* to the former (2012: 39). However, Nine considers political control over one's environment to be a basic need (2012: 32–3), whilst I have only taken basic needs to include physical health and a less expansive form of autonomy. On my view, an individual could have their basic needs provided for without being a member of a self-determining political community—the objects of their needs could, for instance, be provided by a benevolent external power. My claim is that this individual would be significantly better off as a member of a self-determining collective with control over its own territory, even if their level of basic needs satisfaction were no different.

end up like *W*. We are going to have to flesh out this example, however, to determine whether it is so problematic.

First, note that I have not taken the right of territorial jurisdiction over natural resources to go hand in hand with a right to restrict entry to (or exit from) that region. The right of territorial jurisdiction is presumed exclusive in the sense that it rules out other collectives exercising *jurisdiction* over the land and resources in question; not in the sense that it permits a people to exclude individuals from *entering* the region. A people must offer good justification for any supposed right to exclude individuals from immigrating or becoming members. Such justification may well be possible in *P*'s case: Firstly, given that *P* is only just able to satisfy the basic needs of its members with the resources at its disposal, immigration could pose a threat to basic needs satisfaction. Secondly, there may be reason to worry that high levels of migration from *W* to *P* could create a situation in which the former can dominate the latter, undermining *P*'s exercise of collective self-determination. This line of justification does not appear reversible, however. Unless flows of migration from *P* to *W* will threaten basic needs or undermine either community's capacity for self-determination, it is not clear why any restrictions on movement would be justified. Unless a case can be made for exclusion on other grounds, then, members of *P* can justifiably move and become members of *W* instead, should they have the desire and the wherewithal.

Second, note that *W*'s territorial claims are not only justified, but also limited, by the principle of collective self-determination. Provided *W* has territory sufficient to exercise collective self-determination, it has no claim to unilaterally expand its realm of exclusive jurisdiction outwards. The principles do not justify the exclusive appropriation of resources that peoples cannot claim to be specifically necessary to their own exercise of self-determination (where this will include many valuable underground extractive resources, which I have argued should generally be subject to shared jurisdiction). They also do not justify the expansive appropriation of territory due to unsustainable resource use. This may allay the sufficiency objection somewhat, because it suggests that uneven possession of natural resources will be subject to practical constraints.

Peoples *will* develop different ways of life, however, resulting in some requiring larger territories or different resources to exercise sustainable self-determination than others—so the worry behind the sufficiency objection remains. One thing to note about the example, though, is that it says nothing about the other resources at *P* and *W*'s disposal. Though poor in natural resources, *P* could be much richer than *W*, or better off in terms of infrastructure and other human-produced goods. It is questionable whether greater natural resource possession (on whatever metric one chooses) necessarily translates into greater economic wealth. As many have observed, it certainly does not appear to in our world.[19]

The proponent of the sufficiency objection might plausibly reply, however, that larger possession of natural resources *would* translate into greater economic wealth if rights of possession were respected. The connection between natural resource rights and prosperity has arguably been severed in our world due to injustices such as colonialism and the resource curse. Since these are cases in which a peoples' moral or legal rights over their resources go unrealized, they do not serve to undermine the claim that more expansive resource rights *would* result in greater economic power *if respected*; making it the case that W will not only possess more natural resources than P, but also greater economic wealth.

But on the contrary, the link between natural resource wealth and economic wealth remains contingent even in a hypothetical world where resource rights are respected, because self-determining collectives may decide not to translate the former into the latter. If W is one of these collectives, whilst P is a country that succeeds economically despite being poorly endowed with natural resources, then this may again allay any worries about this discrepancy in their natural resource possession.

Nevertheless, the proponent of the sufficiency objection might still object that W's greater *opportunity* for economic wealth is unfair. What if we are comparing two communities that *do* wish to convert their natural resources into economic benefits? Well, in this case any economic inequality between them is supposed to be limited by the gap-reducing natural resource income tax defended in §7.2.4. Ultimately, the principle of self-determination *does not* specify a sufficiency threshold for natural resource rights, beyond which we need not be troubled by any inequalities. As I have argued, how one political community fares and what it can do with the natural resources within its jurisdiction depends in part on the resource use of other peoples. If a people is to exercise self-determination, it is not sufficient that the community be provided with enough natural resources to satisfy the basic needs of its members: not in the presence of significant global inequalities of economic wealth and power.

Therefore, if W's exploitation of territorial resources enables it to become significantly richer than P, a redistributive tax on W's natural resource income is called for—insofar as this is necessary to prevent such enrichment from facilitating W's domination of P. This measure will not result in an *equal*

---

[19] Joseph Heath goes as far as to claim that 'There is essentially no correlation between the domestic supply of natural resources and the wealth of a nation, simply because the two have nothing to do with one another' (Heath 2005: 215). See also Fabre 2005: 142–3; Rawls 1999b: 108, 117; Risse 2012: §6.10.

distribution of natural resources (by any metric), but it will help to create global circumstances in which political communities are equal in the sense that their resource rights do not support relations of domination.

7.3.2 The internal objection

This line of reasoning also suggests a way for me to respond to the *internal* sufficiency objection, according to which it is misleading for me to construe my account as a form of global egalitarianism regarding natural resources. A first, easy response to this objection would be to point out that I am at the very least an egalitarian about natural resources at a fundamental level, because I am committed to a bedrock principle of Equal Original Claims. However, this response is too fast. Equal Division theorists are also likely to accept this as a bedrock principle and yet in Chapter Four, I rejected their view as being insufficiently impartial to *do justice to* Equal Original Claims. Given that my own view appears somewhat *sufficientarian* in nature, am I not open to similar critique?

Here, it is important to recall why natural resource egalitarians should reject Equal Division. The reason is that although any view of this form will indeed advocate a scheme of natural resource rights that is *distributively* equal, no such distribution can succeed in respecting Equal Original Claims. I have argued that any substantively equal distribution of natural resources will in fact be *inegalitarian* in the sense that it privileges and imposes a singular understanding of the value of natural resources; an understanding that can reasonably be rejected by some of those with an equal original claim to this good. This is why proponents of Equal Division cannot do justice to Equal Original Claims. Attempting to equalize natural resource rights in accordance with any single metric would be similarly problematic to aiming to equalize human-produced goods in accordance with a metric like prestige. This might be how some people understand the value of such goods, and moves in the direction of greater equality by this measure might be feasible. But this is not what egalitarian justice demands. Not every equal distribution is supported by principles of egalitarian justice. Some equal distributions will be irrelevant to global egalitarianism whilst others may even run counter to it.[20]

But if global egalitarianism concerning natural resources cannot be cashed out distributively, what other options are there? I have suggested that we enshrine Equal Original Claims procedurally: these claims can be respected

---

[20] For example, Satz suggests that 'When distributive inequality in resources does not lead to domination, marginalization, or status hierarchy, it is unclear that egalitarians should be concerned with it' (1999: 73); and Armstrong, who is a global egalitarian, nevertheless suggests that stipulating an equal distribution of fresh water shares would be 'perverse' (2017: 74).

by defending principles of natural resource justice from an original position in which all claimants are represented as equals. And I argued that the principles selected from this perspective will not be principles of distributive equality, but will instead be principles that serve to protect basic needs and combat domination by supporting the self-determination of peoples. As Elizabeth Anderson points out, opposing relationships of domination and other forms of oppression is a key goal of egalitarian political movements (1999: 312). She terms theories that align with this goal, by viewing equality as a social relationship, 'relational' theories of equality (Anderson 1999: 313). Another view of this form can be found in Samuel Scheffler's account of equality 'as a social and political ideal that governs the relations in which people stand to one another' (2003: 31). I suggest that my own account can indeed be viewed as a form of egalitarianism concerning natural resources, then—when such egalitarianism is understood relationally.[21]

A relational egalitarian about natural resources will ask how resource rights should be arranged in pursuit of egalitarianism's political aim: 'to create a community'—in this case, a global community—'in which people stand in relations of equality to others' (Anderson 1999: 289). My answer is that this aim will be served when resource rights protect basic needs and shield individuals from domination; and that this is what it means to treat all individuals as equal claimants of the world's resources. My Contractualist Common Ownership approach also embodies equality in the sense that it takes individuals to treat one another as equals by restricting their appropriation of natural resources in line with principles that can be justified to all others as equal claimants. I argued that the principle of equal division cannot be justified in this way, but the principles of basic needs and collective self-determination can be.

As Anderson also notes, relational theories of equality may well mandate certain distributions of goods as instrumental to, or a part of, securing egalitarian social relationships (1999: 313–4). In my case, I have defended a sufficientarian distribution of resource rights in support of basic needs; territorial jurisdiction (albeit limited) for each political community, over the region that it legitimately occupies; greater sharing of control rights over resources that are important to the self-determination of more than one people; and a more egalitarian distribution of natural resource income, in the form of a gap-reducing global tax.

It is again clear that these features will not serve to ensure that peoples have equal natural resource shares on any metric. However, they *are* designed to help secure individuals worldwide with a safety net of basic resource

---

[21] For an account of relational equality at the global level, see Brock 2009: Ch. 12.

entitlements; provide political communities with an arena in which to exercise self-determination by assigning local resource rights in accordance with the interests of their members; reduce the vulnerability of those communities in the face of fluctuating natural resource values; and mitigate inequalities that can subject peoples and their members to domination. Scheffler, who also notes that promoting the ideal of social and political equality will entail the pursuit of certain distributive arrangements, similarly suggests that these will be along the lines of protecting basic needs, reducing dependency on market forces, and avoiding 'excessive variation' in income and wealth that generates 'inequalities of power and status that are incompatible with relations among equals' (2003: 23).

To conclude this section: I have argued that my theory can legitimately be described as an account of global egalitarianism concerning natural resources; where egalitarianism is construed relationally, as a social and political ideal. Natural resource egalitarianism of this form need not insist on distributive equality. Returning to my imagined example: it could still be the case that W possesses both more natural resources than P (on some given metric) *and* greater economic wealth, even once the gap-reducing natural resource tax has been implemented with the goal of ensuring that W and P stand in relations of non-domination. Will this remaining distributive inequality not be troubling? In response to this, I can merely say that I only attempt here to give an account of what global justice requires with respect to natural resources. The acquisition and use of natural resources is a very important human practice, but clearly not the only one. The conception of natural resource justice that I have defended could be combined with other principles of justice for other—human-produced—goods; and other principles of justice regarding practices, exchanges, relations, and institutions at the global level. If any inequalities remaining after satisfaction of the two principles are unfair, I claim that is likely because they violate other principles of global justice.

7.4 Beyond natural resources

As just explained, the conception of justice defended in this work only directly concerns natural resources and thus would need to be combined with principles of justice for other goods, and other human practices and relations, to establish a full theory of global justice. This is not an exercise that I attempt here. Instead, the subsequent chapters will proceed to draw normative conclusions about the problem of climate change using this conception of natural resource justice alone. I defend this method of partial integrationism in Chapter Eight.

In §5.3.2 I defended my Contractualist Common Ownership approach from the objection that it constitutes an unjustifiably restricted account of global justice, because it does not consider other important goods (economic goods, for example). I concluded that my conception of natural resource justice should ultimately be combined with principles of justice concerning other goods and that the resulting theory of global justice could well be a pluralistic one; where principles pertain for different reasons, take different forms, apply to different sets of people, and relate to different goods, institutions, and practices. I am not going to expound in much more detail on what the resulting theory of global justice might look like, because this is a much bigger project than that which I undertake here. However, with the conception of natural resource justice derived from Contractualist Common Ownership now specified, it is possible to note some constraints on what an acceptable complete theory could look like.

There will likely be many sets of principles consistent with the two defended here, that could be combined with them to yield a more complete theory of global justice. However, principles for human-produced goods that do not similarly protect basic needs satisfaction (for all human beings) and collective self-determination (for all peoples), even if technically consistent, are not going to function very effectively alongside these principles of natural resource justice. This is because the demand for a *system* of natural resource rights that grants each individual entitlements over natural resources for basic needs satisfaction, and their people entitlements over natural resources for the legitimate exercise of collective self-determination, is prior in two senses. Firstly, by setting restraints on what human beings can do with natural resources, it also constrains what goods and societies they can construct *using* those resources. Secondly, it is operative regardless of the other goods that humans produce or the practices that they engage in. This is because individual rights to use natural resources for basic needs satisfaction, and collective rights to use natural resources in the legitimate exercise of self-determination, cannot be extinguished by changes that others make to the natural world.

Regarding the first point: The principles of justice entail that it is unjust for humans to use natural resources in ways that prevent the satisfaction of basic needs or the legitimate exercise of self-determination—and since one unavoidably uses natural resources in the production or implementation of other goods, this prohibition is simply going to carry over to the production and use of other goods. Regarding the second point: Even where individual violations of the two principles of natural resource justice do not take place, processes of invention and production can accumulate in ways that, over time, result in a situation where individuals and collectives that could once satisfy basic needs and exercise self-determination with the natural resources at their disposal are no longer able to do so. For example, material inequalities may accumulate and thereby expose some peoples to domination, or global circumstances may change in ways that alter the satisfiers of basic needs (or the ability of individuals to access those satisfiers). Because the principles of natural resource justice remain operative when these consequences occur, they will then demand a reordering of the system of natural resource rights, with the goal of restoring capacities for basic needs satisfaction and collective self-determination.

The principle of collective self-determination also, however, gives strong reason to minimize any significant changes to the system of natural resource rights, since stable resource rights are more conducive to the exercise of this capacity. It will thus be much more in keeping with the spirit of this principle if it is combined with principles for human-produced goods and relations that likewise demand that basic needs be guaranteed and self-determination supported, in part by placing restrictions on permissible inequalities of wealth and power at the global level, and demanding that global institutions and practices be designed to support every political community in the legitimate exercise of collective self-determination.

7.5 The feasibility objection

The middle section of this work—from Chapter Three to the current chapter—pursues a project in (relatively) ideal theory. Some might worry that the resulting conception of natural resource justice is *problematically* ideal, in that it is hopelessly utopian and pays insufficient concern to matters of political feasibility. In a world where many individuals are excluded from the natural resources that they require for their basic needs, and many political communities lack a sphere of robust territorial jurisdiction over land and natural resources in support of their self-determination, one could reasonably doubt that such demands of justice would ever generally be acknowledged—let alone met. But if principles of justice are simply infeasible to implement, then what real use are they?

I do not want to grant too much weight to the feasibility objection, because I believe that principles of justice can play an important role even when they seem utopian. First, and perhaps most obviously, they can serve as a 'yardstick' by which to measure how far short of justice the world is falling (see Valentini 2012: 660). This enables us to identify injustices and, potentially, corresponding duties of rectification. Second, principles of ideal justice can be used to identify actions and policies that will perpetuate old, or create new, injustices. In the third and final section of this work, I return to the problem of climate change in a world where the principles of justice here defended are frequently—and have frequently been—disregarded and suggest that these principles can play both roles. I intend for this exercise to serve as some justification of the relatively ideal theorizing engaged in here, by showing how this theory can be applied to yield conclusions about a real-world problem.

But whilst I do not wish to grant too much weight to the feasibility objection, I also do not want to dismiss it too quickly. In this section, I will therefore attempt to defuse the objection somewhat. Feasibility worries seem impossible to allay entirely, particularly when lengthy discussion is not possible. What I will do here, then, is provide some reasons for optimism, with the aim of shifting the burden of proof towards those who would object that the principles here defended are problematically infeasible to implement.

7.5.1 *Understanding feasibility*

Drawing on Pablo Gilabert and Holly Lawford-Smith's exploration of the concept of political feasibility (Gilabert & Lawford-Smith 2012; see also Lawford-Smith 2013), the feasibility objection can be made more precise by construing it in three different ways: namely, as a challenge concerning *categorical feasibility*, *stability*, or *accessibility*. Starting with categorical feasibility, the question is whether a theory could be implemented without violating certain hard constraints that set permanent or absolute limits on what can be done. Such constraints could be logical, nomological, conceptual, or biological. They could also concern technological capacity or resource availability (see Gilabert & Lawford-Smith 2012: 813–16; Lawford-Smith 2013: 252–3). If implementing a theory would violate such constraints, it is categorically infeasible.

According to the view I have defended, a just world is one in which respect is given to every individual's rights to natural resources for basic needs satisfaction, and every political community's entitlements to natural resources for the legitimate exercise of collective self-determination. The construction of such a world does not appear to defy constraints of logical, nomological, or conceptual possibility. Certain hard constraints of resource availability might be a more reasonable concern, the question being whether the world, as it is now, possesses sufficient natural resources for everyone's basic needs and sufficient land for all political communities to have an adequate sphere of territorial jurisdiction. Resource scarcity is a serious problem of increasing severity. But in a world in which there is currently a huge degree of waste, overconsumption, and inefficiency; there is reason to be optimistic that there would indeed be enough to go around if only natural resources were used and shared more justly.

My theory therefore does not look particularly vulnerable to the feasibility objection understood categorically. Feasibility worries may remain, however, with respect to softer constraints on what is possible: psychological, economic, institutional, or cultural constraints, for example. Soft constraints are malleable and can be transformed or dissolved altogether. They do not *rule out* the implementation of principles, but instead make implementation comparatively less probable. Such constraints can nevertheless provide reason to think that implementing a theory would be relatively infeasible along two dimensions. First, the stability dimension: in the face of soft constraints, could the arrangements or institutions necessary for implementing the theory be sustained? Second, the accessibility dimension: given soft constraints, is there a path that can be taken from the world as it is now, to a state of affairs in which the theory is implemented? (Gilabert & Lawford-Smith 2012: 811–16. See also Buchanan 2004: 38; Cohen 2009: 56–7). I will address the stability and accessibility worries in turn.

7.5.2 *Stability*

Considering the feasibility challenge as a charge of instability, the question is whether a theory, if implemented, could be expected to last for any reasonable length of time. To score well on this test, it must be possible to implement the theory via arrangements that are compatible with certain soft constraints regarding what human beings are (or can be) like; and the kind of institutions they are able to support and sustain.

If a system of limited territorial jurisdiction satisfying the two principles could be established, it is not clear why it would be condemned to unravel. One key threat to the stability of this system will be processes of resource development that expand economic inequalities between peoples and, thereby, support relations of domination between the rich and the poor. The gap-reducing tax is supposed to prevent resource use from contributing to such inequalities, but one might worry whether this arrangement is one that human beings can reasonably be expected to uphold. Picture a political community, R, that uses its natural resources to generate high levels of income. Can R reasonably be expected to cooperate with institutions that will tax that income and redistribute it to countries that have not been able, or willing, to use their own natural resources to create comparable levels of economic wealth?

Similar worries might arise regarding the institutions of global jurisdiction that I suggest should be pursued for certain significant resources, including many underground extractive resources. Here, one might fear it is unrealistic to think that communities living above sites rich in oil or precious minerals, say, would ever cooperate with such institutions. Would such collectives not reject shared jurisdiction, instead aiming to keep the benefits of the resources beneath their territory to themselves?

These are serious worries, but I do not think they are insurmountable. One might note first that all political communities will have at least some reason to support these global institutions. This is because there is something of a veil of uncertainty effect at play for natural resources, in the sense that it is not always possible to predict where important resources will be discovered in the future; or whether natural resources that are presently of little economic value may later become extremely sought after due to technological innovations. All political communities are therefore in a situation of some uncertainty regarding the comparative value of the resources within or under their own territory and their relative ability either to convert resources into wealth, or to access specific resources that may turn out to be significant in the future.

A system in which the income generated from resources is taxed and redistributed to reduce the gap between the rich and the poor, and where globally significant resources are placed under global jurisdiction, to be used in a way that takes everyone's interests into account, thereby offers even the most powerful political communities some benefit, and a reason not to defect. The global tax provides a safety net for those who lack marketable or otherwise valuable resources, or who have resources that are highly prized now, but may turn out to lack competitive value in the future. Global jurisdiction reduces the possibility that significant resources could be placed beyond a community's reach, but within the reach of others. Arguments in favour of limited territorial jurisdiction over natural resources do not have to appeal solely to justice, then, but can also appeal to each community's interest. One might also appeal to each community's interest by pointing out that global jurisdiction over certain key natural resources can help solve collective action problems that would otherwise make it difficult to protect the global environment.

Another reason to think that this system need not be unstable is that there appears to be some straightforward ways of enforcing it. Imagine a political community, N, that desires to enrich itself by retaining all the income that can be extracted from the resources of its territory, and all the benefits of the resources beneath its territory, for itself. N therefore refuses to cooperate with the gap-reducing tax, or to share jurisdiction over the globally significant resources beneath its territory. In this situation, other peoples can sanction N by ceasing to engage in any trade of natural resources with that collective. This will curtail N's ability to generate income from its resources. It may also make it very difficult for N to make good use of the globally significant resources beneath its territory, if such use requires technology composed of natural resources not found in N's territory. Such sanctions thus provide another avenue for endowing a system of limited territorial jurisdiction over natural resources with stability.

7.5.3 *Accessibility*

The accessibility worry concerns whether there is a path of action from where we are now, to a state of affairs in which the demands of this theory of natural resource justice are met. Regarding the basic needs principle: Can we get from our current situation, where many lack secure access—or any access—to the natural resources necessary to their basic needs, to a world in which assured resource entitlements and, where necessary, redistributive schemes make this no longer the case? Regarding the principle of collective self-determination: Can we get from a world in which permanent sovereignty constitutes a central organizing principle, to one in which far more limited territorial jurisdiction is paired with shared or even global jurisdiction over certain significant resources—including various water sources, fossil fuels, and rare minerals? From circumstances in which many peoples are denied adequate control over—or even access to—the land on which their self-determination depends, to a situation in which all peoples (which, recall, includes non-state political communities) have their rights of territorial jurisdiction recognized and respected by international agents and corporations—including a right to veto the extraction of resources from under their lands? From a situation where patterns of income extraction from natural resources are extremely inequitable, to one in which a gap-reducing natural resource tax mitigates relations of international domination?

Addressing the accessibility challenge adequately would require lengthy discussion of potential pathways to a just state of affairs. These pathways would also have to be subjected to intense scrutiny concerning potential negative side effects of reform efforts, to show that this state of affairs is not only accessible, but *morally* accessible. For a theory to be morally accessible, 'the transition from where we are to the ideal state of affairs should be achievable without unacceptable moral costs' (Buchanan 2004: 38). In making assessments of moral accessibility, input from those who stand to be most affected, and who are therefore in a good position to anticipate some of these dangers, will be crucial.

I do not have the space or the expertise to provide a detailed response to the accessibility challenge. It is hard to predict what changes in the global order could be achieved through political processes, legal methods, campaigning, activism, or experiments in living; or what combination of forces could ultimately realize the system of limited territorial jurisdiction over natural resources that I have defended as presenting the ideal. However, I will again attempt to defuse this challenge somewhat, by briefly suggesting that one obvious soft constraint on accessibility—namely, broad international support for the principle of permanent sovereignty over natural resources—does not pose an insurmountable barrier to implementing the alternative system of resource rights demanded by the two principles.

As Lawford-Smith points out, 'facts about entrenched political institutions make outcomes clashing with those institutions unlikely to succeed' (2013: 255). Though permanent sovereignty has only been an international norm since around the 1960s, support for it has been strong and repeatedly confirmed (see §6.1.1). Nico Schrijver goes so far as to claim that 'it is obvious' this institution will not 'totally wither away' (1997: 395). This makes permanent sovereignty an important institutional soft constraint on political reform. This existing norm grants states strong and comprehensive rights over all surface and subsurface resources in their recognized territories, presenting a barrier to the limiting and dispersing of jurisdiction over natural resources that I have defended as a demand of justice. Furthermore, Schrijver suggests that one can discern 'a clear tendency ... to confine the circle of direct permanent sovereignty subjects solely to *States*' (1997: 390; emphasis added);[22] clashing with my claim that rights of territorial jurisdiction should fall to political peoples, which need not be governed by state-like structures.

However, though sceptical that permanent sovereignty will wither away completely, Schrijver does think that what this principle *'represent[s]* in a changing world' is open to question, and that interpretations of permanent sovereignty may change as international law continues to evolve (1997: 395; emphasis added). In fact, Schrijver is quite optimistic here, suggesting that:

> a trend can be discerned towards a law which is humankind-oriented, under which both States and (groups of) individuals can be held responsible for environmental degradation and under which sustainable development and environmental preservation are approached from a global perspective. Furthermore, there is also a trend towards co-operation for the implementation of everybody's right to development, the proper management of natural wealth and resources, equitable sharing of transboundary natural resources and the global commons, and preservation for future generations.

If Schrijver is correct about this trend, then there is hope that global efforts might eventually succeed in moving the world away from a system of permanent sovereignty altogether, and towards a system of limited territorial jurisdiction.

Some existing international documents, including the UN Declaration on the Rights of Indigenous Peoples (UN 2007) and various other human rights agreements, provide additional reasons to think that such change is feasible. The former declaration demonstrates the power of non-state peoples to command acknowledgement of their rights on the global stage and gain international recognition that control over territory and natural resources is not the sole prerogative of states (see also Daes 2004: 17–18). Numerous other

---

[22] See also Armstrong 2017: 162.

human rights documents suggest that there already exists some international, cross-cultural agreement on what might be deemed basic needs, along with acceptance that such needs are a matter of global concern.[23] If it is recognized that the satisfaction of human rights will often depend on secure entitlements over natural resources, this might be a route via which the basic needs principle could be implemented.[24] One key soft constraint on accessibility, then—in the form of current international acceptance of permanent sovereignty over natural resources—may well prove to be amenable to transformation or dissolution in pursuit of justice.

7.6 Conclusion

The aim of this chapter was to expand on, and further defend, the theory of natural resource justice that I have formulated in the middle section of this work. This concludes Part II. In Part III, I return to the matter of climate change equipped with this theory as a tool for addressing and understanding this problem.

---

[23] The Universal Declaration of Human Rights, for example, enshrines a right to 'a standard of living adequate for the health and well-being of [oneself] and of [one's] family, including food, clothing, housing and medical care and necessary social services' (UN 1948: Art. 25).

[24] Some progress on this was made in 2012, when the UN appointed a Special Rapporteur on human rights and the environment, in recognition of the fact that 'A safe, clean, healthy and sustainable environment is integral to the full enjoyment of a wide range of human rights, including the rights to life, health, food, water and sanitation' (UN n.d.).

Part III
Natural Resources and Climate Justice

Part III
Natural Resources and
Climate Justice

8

Revisiting the Global Emissions Budget

In this final section of the work, I use the theory of natural resource justice that I have formulated to reconsider the problem of climate change. In Chapter Two I criticized a popular argument for the equal per capita emissions view (EPC), according to which the global emissions budget should be allocated on an equal per capita basis. The atmospheric commons argument claims that since rights to the atmosphere should be distributed to all human beings globally on an equal per capita basis, so should emission quotas. I identified two related problems with this argument.

Firstly, by focusing on the atmosphere rather than climate sinks as a whole, the atmospheric commons argument misidentifies the global commons that assimilates anthropogenic greenhouse gas (GHG) emissions. Carbon dioxide (CO_2), in particular, simply pools in the atmosphere until it is removed and assimilated by the climate system's oceanic and terrestrial sinks. Secondly, the argument neglects to consider whether the territorial location of some of these sinks could entail that certain individuals or collectives have a privileged claim to them. I also argued that it is unclear whether the principle of equal division, invoked by Steve Vanderheiden in his atmospheric commons argument, could be used to save EPC. This principle states that each individual is entitled to an equally valuable *bundle* of natural resource rights. It would take further work to defend any claim that these equally valuable bundles must contain equal per capita shares of GHG assimilative capacity.

I concluded that our engagement with concerns of natural resource justice must be much deeper, if it is to be informative regarding the problem of sharing the global emissions budget. Having devoted the middle section of the work to these concerns, I have now identified a more fundamental problem for those who might hope to defend EPC using the principle of equal division. Namely, that we should reject this principle and instead adopt the approach that I termed 'Contractualist Common Ownership'.

I used Contractualist Common Ownership to defend two alternative principles of natural resource justice: a principle of collective self-determination and a (lexically prior) basic needs principle. These principles do not obviously mandate equal per capita shares of (all or any) natural resources (on any metric). To defend EPC now, theorists would have to argue that equal per capita emissions are necessary for ensuring the universal satisfaction of basic needs, or for enabling all peoples to engage in the legitimate exercise of self-determination. In this chapter, I argue that these principles instead suggest a different solution to this important allocation problem. This discussion spans two of the three climate question categories identified in §1.3.2: the atmospheric target and mitigation. In the two chapters following, I turn to the third and final category—that of unavoided impacts—with a discussion of climate change and historical accountability.

I start by providing a brief defence of the method of *partial integrationism* adopted in this section of the work, noting that my approach in this chapter is at least relatively *holist* in nature (§8.1). It is holist in the sense that the two principles of natural resource justice can be applied not only to the problem of *sharing* the global emissions budget, but also the prior matter of *setting* the budget. I explain the problem of setting the budget in more detail (§8.2), before using the basic needs principle (§8.3), followed by the principle of collective self-determination (§8.4), to draw conclusions about these two problems. Applying the principle of collective self-determination is more difficult, because it grounds many conflicting claims regarding the emissions budget (§8.4.1). I address this difficulty by formulating some guidelines for adjudicating between self-determination claims (§8.4.2). I conclude that the emissions budget should be set within the parameters of enabling basic needs satisfaction for current and future individuals and—if this does not determine a unique budget—protecting collectives from climate impacts that threaten their legitimate exercise of self-determination through territorial displacement. If this emissions budget allows for what we might term 'secondary emissions' (emissions beyond what is required for basic needs), fair international negotiations will be needed to determine the just distribution of any secondary emissions budget (§8.5).

8.1 Integrationism and holism

In this and the remaining chapters, I proceed to draw normative conclusions about the problem of climate change using my conception of natural resource justice. In terms of the integrationism–isolationism distinction introduced in §1.2.3: this means that though I reject isolationism about climate justice (because I hold that climate change is not an issue that can be addressed fairly in abstraction from other matters of global justice); the theory of climate justice that I present instead is only a partially integrated one. I do not attempt to draw normative conclusions about climate change by reference to what purports to be a comprehensive theory of global justice, but rather by reference to a more limited conception of the demands of justice at the global level.

Is such partial integrationism open to critique? The concern with isolationist accounts of climate justice is that they leave too much out and therefore risk making recommendations that might appear just when climate change is considered on its own, whilst in fact being detrimental from the perspective of global justice more broadly. Could my account not similarly make climate recommendations that are good from the perspective of natural resource justice, but bad from the perspective of a more comprehensive theory of global justice? This is certainly a worry. However, I think it is a reasonable method to proceed by isolating issues where this helps to reduce complexity, then subjecting the resulting conclusions to examination to see if they do indeed conflict with other requirements of global justice. Because I only attempt the former step in this work, the latter is an important task that remains to be completed. The partially integrated approach taken here will nevertheless be a worthwhile contribution to reasoning about climate justice insofar as it is illuminating, as I hope to prove it is in this final section of the work.

The approach that I adopt here is certainly more integrationist and holist than the versions of EPC that I have sought to reject. As explained in §2.1, EPC is a very atomist-isolationist approach to climate justice, insofar as it treats allocation of the emissions budget as a standalone problem. Defenders of EPC appear to assume that the question of how to *set* the emissions budget (that is, to establish the permissible human use—or assimilative capacity[1]—of the global climate sink); will be dealt with separately from the question of how to *share* that budget (by allocating use-rights to that sink capacity). The principle of equal shares invoked by defenders of EPC is only taken as relevant to this posterior question—and it is difficult to see how it could help solve the prior problem of setting the budget. A principle stating that a certain natural resource should be shared on an equal per capita basis does not tell you how to determine the capacity of that resource. Thus, whilst defenders of EPC may note that setting the emissions budget is a moral problem—one raising, in particular, questions of what the current generation owes to future generations[2]—they seem to view it as a somewhat separate moral problem; one that will be solved using different normative principles.

In contrast, the principles of natural resource justice that I have defended are not only relevant to the question of how to *share* the emissions budget.

---

[1] As explained in §2.2, assimilative capacity should be understood as the capacity of a resource system to receive waste without being subject to overuse, where what counts as overuse depends on the features of the resource system that humans wish to—or are obliged to—maintain (the feature in this case being some level of climatic stability).

[2] See, for example, Agarwal 2002: 378; Vanderheiden 2008a: 111–12.

In requiring that any allocation of natural resource rights be consistent with the satisfaction of basic needs and the legitimate exercise of collective self-determination, they are also informative about *setting* the budget (in line with these requirements). This chapter therefore considers both *mitigation* (sharing the budget) and the *atmospheric target* (setting the budget). The problem of sharing the emissions budget has already been discussed at length in Chapter Two. In §8.2, I explain the problem of setting the budget in more detail, before using the principles to address both issues.

8.2 The atmospheric target

To estimate the global emissions budget, it is first necessary to determine what changes in the climate our policies should aim to prevent. At the international negotiations, the stated objective is prevention of 'dangerous anthropogenic interference with the climate system' (UN 1992: Art. 2); and efforts to prevent such interference have been framed as identifying—and then aiming to stay below—a 'safe' limit to global average temperature rise. The nature of this limit has been debated repeatedly at United Nations Framework Convention on Climate Change (UNFCCC) meetings, with the alternatives generally taken as 1.5 and 2°C.[3] I do not mean to imply that this framing of alternatives has any principled basis. As Sheila Watt-Cloutier (2004) pointed out over a decade ago, dangerous changes in the climate are already taking place ('Climate change is dangerous in the Arctic *now*' (emphasis in the original)). Once a temperature limit is selected, scientists can estimate what atmospheric concentration of GHGs is consistent with ensuring, to a certain probability, that the limit will not be breached; and, correspondingly, what quantity of GHGs can be emitted if atmospheric concentrations are to be kept below this level. This provides an emissions budget, several of which can be estimated for any given temperature limit (with each budget assigned a different probability of keeping to that limit).[4]

The choice of a temperature limit—and a corresponding emissions budget—has several implications regarding natural resources. The setting of a budget effectively places constraints on the current generation's permissible use of

[3] This was a significant topic of debate at COP15 in Copenhagen (2009), and again at COP21 in Paris (2015), having been returned to many times in the interim.

[4] Carbon Tracker, for example, calculate two budgets for each of four temperature limits (1.5, 2, 2.5, and 3°C); one budget giving a 50 per cent chance of keeping within that limit, and one giving an 80 per cent chance. They estimate that it is already too late to have an 80 per cent chance of limiting global average temperature rise to 1.5°C. To have a 50 per cent chance of keeping to this limit, only $550GtCO_2$ (gigatonnes of CO_2) can be emitted between 2013 and 2100. To have an 80 per cent chance of limiting temperature rise to 2°C, the budget increases to $975GtCO_2$ (Carbon Tracker 2013: 10–11). The gravity of these restrictions can be appreciated once it is noted that total reserves of fossil fuels are estimated to be equivalent to $2,860GtCO_2$ (Carbon Tracker 2013: 14). See also IPCC 2013: 103.

climate sinks: both in terms of employing them to assimilate GHG emissions, and with respect to interacting with them in other ways (for example, by requiring parties to refrain from deforestation or implement new soil management techniques).[5] Constrained use of the assimilative capacity of climate sinks entails constrained combustion of fossil fuels. These constraints must be severe, perhaps allowing only 20 per cent of total fossil fuel reserves to be exploited by 2050 (Carbon Tracker 2013: 4). Both climate sinks and fossil fuels are currently employed by human beings in satisfying basic needs (for food and adequate shelter, for example) and exercising collective self-determination, among other things. Restricting use of these resources is essential, however, in part because climate impacts are already negatively affecting natural resource systems that human beings depend upon to satisfy their basic needs; through drought and biodiversity loss, for example. Similarly—as residents of low-lying islands are all too aware—in the absence of significant restrictions on fossil fuel and climate sink consumption, climate impacts will displace political communities from the land where they exercise self-determination.

The decision regarding a target limit to global average temperature rise should therefore be informed by the two principles of natural resource justice that I have defended; first and foremost, by the lexically prior basic needs principle.

8.3 The emissions budget and basic needs

The basic needs principle (BN) demands that the existing generation restricts its use of climate sinks in line with ensuring that climate change does not prevent future generations from accessing the natural resources necessary for their basic needs, implying an upper bound to the emissions budget. Many decision-makers in wealthier industrialized states appear confident that future members of their community will be able to adapt to a world that is 2°C warmer (assuming they are genuinely concerned for these future people, that is). Representatives of other peoples (certain members of the Alliance of Small Island States (AOSIS), for example) have argued that their very 'survival' depends on 'keeping global warming well below 1.5 degrees' (AOSIS 2012), and have long campaigned for a lower temperature target. These campaigns finally seemed to be heeded at COP21 in Paris (2015), where the Parties—though employing unfortunately vague terms—emphasized a target not only

---

[5] Scientists recognize this by incorporating assumptions about sink preservation and emissions from land use change into their budget estimates. Carbon Tracker, for example, assumes that '7.3% of total CO_2 emissions are generated by land use, land-use change and forestry for carbon budgets up to 2050' (Carbon Tracker 2013: 13).

of 'Holding the increase in the global average temperature to well below 2°C above pre-industrial levels', but also of 'pursuing efforts to limit the temperature increase to 1.5°C above pre-industrial levels' (UNFCCC 2015: Art. 2). BN tells in favour of a lower target and a correspondingly restricted budget; to reduce future climate impacts on water sources, resources essential for food production, and other natural supports for basic needs satisfaction.[6]

On the other hand, the basic needs principle also suggests a *lower* bound to the emissions budget, grounding what one might term an inviolable right to *subsistence emissions* for all individuals (see Caney 2009: 138–9; Vanderheiden 2008a: 243–7).[7] A subsistence emissions budget can be estimated by considering how much consumption of climate sink capacity is currently necessary for the global satisfaction of basic needs: what quantity of emissions are necessary, for example, to ensure that all human beings have access to goods such as food and water, shelter, and appropriate healthcare and education. Given that many people do not have access to such things at present, some may be entitled to emit more GHGs than they do currently (at least in the absence of alternative means of provision).

Simon Caney suggests that it should be possible to calculate the budget for subsistence emissions on a need-by-need basis, 'working back from each basic need to determine what greenhouse gas distribution is needed to meet this'. He outlines how such distributions might be derived for the basic need for food and the basic need for 'minimally acceptable' healthcare, suggesting this process could be 'reiterated for other key needs, such as housing, heating, and education' (Caney 2012: 296–7). Such calculations can provide estimates of 'bottom-up, country-specific energy and emissions requirements' (Rao & Baer 2012: 656); thus providing an estimate both of the total subsistence emissions budget currently required, and its distribution.[8]

---

[6] See, for example, Maúre et al., who conclude from climate model simulations that 'The implication of keeping the Paris Agreement for the [southern African] region cannot be overemphasized as impacts on the region's agricultural systems and water resources can be substantially reduced by limiting the global average temperatures well below 2.0°C and particularly under 1.5°C' (2018: 8).

[7] The notion that individuals have an inviolable right to subsistence emissions is often discussed by reference to Henry Shue's 1993 paper 'Subsistence Emissions and Luxury Emissions'. However, Shue here claims that 'inalienable [emissions] allowances' for 'the poor in the developing world' should provide for more than mere subsistence. Reflecting what appears to be a concern for self-determination, Shue suggests that these populations be guaranteed 'a certain quantity of protected emissions' to use however they wish, so as to have 'some measure of control over their lives rather than leaving their fates at the mercy of distant strangers' (1993: 58). Following criticism by Hayward (2007: 440–3), Shue later concedes that what really needs to be guaranteed for subsistence is energy; which may currently require emissions as a means, but need not do so indefinitely (Shue 2013: 392).

[8] In this paper (cited by Caney), Narasimha D Rao and Paul Baer attempt to specify a methodology for the calculation of 'decent living' emissions; those required for the consumption of 'a set of basic goods including adequate nutrition, shelter, health care, education, transport, refrigeration, television and mobile phones' (Rao & Baer 2012: 656). Such calculations would be

It is important to note that human efforts can shrink the subsistence emissions budget. As Henry Shue states, GHG emissions are in large part an 'avoidable necessity' (2014: 9). Humans only need to emit significant quantities of GHGs in satisfying their basic needs because they live in societies dependent on fossil fuels. Whilst this remains the case, the current generation must be granted a considerable budget for subsistence emissions; but this entitlement comes hand in hand with an obligation to rapidly shrink this budget through efforts to reduce fossil fuel dependency. Subsistence emissions can be reduced by modifying agricultural practices and switching to renewable energy to power homes, schools, and healthcare centres. Some political communities will, however, find avoiding this necessity easier than others. Collectives should not be required to restrict their use of fossil fuels if this will threaten their members' basic needs satisfaction. Measures to reduce the emissions required for basic needs should therefore be put in place wherever possible, but may have to be funded by those whose capacity to satisfy basic needs will not be undermined by such obligations.

The subsistence emissions budget may be too large to ensure that climate change does not prevent future generations from accessing the natural resources necessary for their own basic needs. If so, the basic needs principle suggests that the global emissions budget will consist solely of subsistence emissions and, furthermore, that attempts to shrink the subsistence emissions budget will have to be combined with greater efforts to enhance climate sinks; develop ways to capture and store carbon;[9] and implement strong pre-emptive adaptation measures designed to protect the resources that future generations require for their basic needs.

Alternatively, it may be that protecting the natural resources that future generations require for their basic needs is compatible not only with subsistence emissions, but also with what one might term *secondary emissions*; emissions, that is, which are not necessary to the satisfaction of basic needs.[10] In this case, the basic needs principle does not determine a unique emissions budget. The principle of collective self-determination will therefore have to be deployed to determine where—between the lower bound set by the subsistence emissions of those existing, and the upper bound determined by

---

done on a country-specific basis because variation in the determinants of living standards and energy efficiency means that members of different societies will require unequal levels of decent living emissions (Rao & Baer 2012: 666, 676).

[9] Carbon capture and storage may not be much help here: some claim that it will only extend the emissions budget for a 2°C target by 12–14 per cent, even given various optimistic assumptions (Carbon Tracker 2013: 12–13).

[10] These emissions—often termed 'luxury emissions' (see Shue 1993)—are those which Vanderheiden claims should be distributed on an equal per capita basis (Vanderheiden 2008a: 226–7). Given that the basic needs threshold is relatively modest, many secondary emissions will not actually result from luxurious activities; but rather from transport, industry, and non-basic healthcare, for example.

protection of resources for the future satisfaction of basic needs—the limit to global emissions should be.

8.4 The emissions budget and collective self-determination

As explained in §1.1.3, mitigation and adaptation are linked in that the amount of mitigation pursued now will influence how much adaptation is necessary in the future. This link can be utilized by those seeking to defend a more generous emissions budget; who may argue that by committing to more adaptation, we reduce the need for mitigation.

Thom Brooks, for example, claims that instead of restricting the emissions budget, emitters could ensure that their actions do no harm by paying for adaptation—in the form of flood defences, inoculation against disease, and new technologies that make crops more resilient, say (2012: 5–7). Similarly, some might claim that if reducing emissions would be more expensive than *compensating* peoples for any damages they suffer from resulting changes in the climate, then compensation is the best policy. Wilfred Beckerman, for example, considering a possible future in which Bangladesh loses *20* per cent *of its territory* due to sea level rise, states that if the cost of

> *taking draconian action to reduce CO_2 emissions* . . . turned out to be far greater than the cost to Bangladesh of the sea level rise, it would *obviously* be in everybody's interests to abstain from this drastic action and to compensate Bangladesh gener-ously out of the savings that would be made. (1992: 486; second emphasis added)

These arguments appear to suggest that due to the alternatives of adaptation and compensation, future protection of basic needs is consistent not only with subsistence emissions, but also with significant amounts of secondary emissions.

However, *even if* compensation and adaptation measures can ensure that basic needs are protected—and this is a big if, given the severe and unpredictable nature of many climate impacts—they are unlikely to successfully address the significant threat that climate change poses to the self-determination of vulnerable collect-ives. One should note, first, that if climate impacts cause loss or damage to the land and resources that a community is using to support its collective way of life (through, say, agriculture, housing, important infrastructure, or governmental activities), financial compensation is unlikely to succeed in preventing capacities for self-determination from being severely compromised.[11]

---

[11] Avner De-Shalit (who offers an alternative argument against the possibility of compensating for displacement by climate change, based on the importance of having a 'sense of place' (2011: 321)) claims one reason we might worry that 'compensation is inappropriate in the case of environmental injustice', is that 'in most cases the ones causing the harm (and usually benefiting from it) are those who define the terms of compensation' (2011: 327, fn.22). The

Adaptation measures may also threaten to significantly undermine the self-determination of the collectives that require them, unless implemented with extreme care. These measures may force political communities into relations of dependence with outsiders responsible for maintaining sea walls, or on new technologies that presumably cannot promise to prevent problems such as crop failure and that may not be made freely available. Such adaptations would thereby leave those communities open to new forms of domination, which could have been avoided through mitigation. More importantly, however: adopting compensation or adaptation in place of a smaller emissions budget, without consulting the peoples whose lands and resources will bear the most significant impacts of that choice, arbitrarily interferes with the basic territorial decision-making of those communities. Expanding the emissions budget on this basis would thus constitute a significant violation of the principle of self-determination.

The principle of collective self-determination also appears to demand a more restricted emissions budget because, *ceteris paribus*, adaptation schemes are plagued with more uncertainty than mitigation schemes. The actions required to mitigate climate change—reducing emissions and enhancing sinks—are known and relatively well understood. If the necessary economic and technical resources are available (or made available, as they should be to those in need), then collectives can implement these measures in an careful manner. Adaptation measures, on the other hand, may have to be implemented at short notice, with little planning, in reaction to unexpected climate impacts.

This is not to say that mitigation does not pose a threat to self-determination; many current mitigation efforts certainly do. There is money to be made from climate mitigation, so those with vested interests may attempt to push through lucrative sink enhancement or emissions reduction projects in ways that bypass local decision-making, perhaps even threatening local communities with displacement or dispossession. Take renewable energy schemes. As the IPCC notes, though 'Renewable energies are often seen as environmentally benign by nature...no technology—particularly in large scale application—comes without environmental impacts' (IPCC 2014c: 546). Even when energy production utilizes renewable resources such as wind, water, geothermal heat, or sunshine, the technologies that convert these resources into energy tend to require *non*-renewable extractive resources for their manufacture. The World Bank suggests that transitioning to a low-carbon future will likely increase demands for numerous mineral and metal

financial compensation offered by the US to the Sioux people for the wrongful seizure of the Black Hills (which the Sioux consider sacred and inalienable), is an example of such injustice in compensation (see the discussion in Tsosie 2007b).

resources, including 'aluminum (including its key constituent, bauxite), cobalt, copper, iron ore, lead, lithium, nickel, manganese, the platinum group of metals, rare earth metals including cadmium, molybdenum, neodymium, and indium—silver, steel, titanium and zinc' (Arrobas et al. 2017: xii). Renewable facilities can also take up large tracts of land in their implementation, potentially commandeering resources that local communities were using for other purposes.

Increased renewable energy production thus threatens to have negative environmental impacts through mining, transportation, manufacture, and siting; and these environmental impacts will have knock-on political effects. The new material demands of renewable technology, and the increased economic value that these demands will endow certain natural resources with, also presents a risk in the form of the resource curse—the danger being that the stream of benefits from such resources could be co-opted by, and used to sustain, regimes that thwart the self-determination of the people.

These concerns highlight how crucial it is for climate mitigation to involve the reduction of energy use alongside a switch from carbon-based energy to renewables.[12] It is important to note, however, that these threats are at least relatively foreseeable and potentially addressable. It is *possible* to choose between mitigation policies with the aim of inhibiting arbitrary interference with capacities of self-determination. For example, it is possible to reject mitigation policies that threaten to displace local communities; to deploy measures designed to prevent new demands for extractive resources from fuelling conflict or supporting authoritarian rulers; and to prioritize renewable energy schemes that enhance opportunities for local decision-making. The threats to self-determination from climate impacts, on the other hand, may be foreseeable but extremely hard to address, or hard to foresee in the first place.

For example, though it is foreseeable that sea level rise of a certain magnitude will result in some peoples losing their entire territory, it is very hard to address the severe obstacle that this poses to a people's self-determination. Loss of territory perhaps even, as Cara Nine suggests, presents an *existential threat* to capacities for self-determination (2010: 360). And sea level rise is at least relatively easy to predict. Other climate impacts—and their knock-on socio-economic effects—could be very hard to foresee, presenting a serious challenge for communities seeking to maintain control over their collective way of life. Some of these hard to predict climate impacts may also be

---

[12] Winona LaDuke puts this problem in stark terms, when discussing the negative impacts of hydroelectric dams on indigenous communities: 'So long as the issue of consumption is not addressed, someone's land and lives will be traded for someone else's cappuccino machine' (1994: 139).

impossible to adapt to in such a way that nobody's basic needs go unmet; whilst it should be possible to implement mitigation policies in ways consistent with the satisfaction of basic needs. Thus, other things being equal, the principles provide several reasons to favour mitigation over adaptation.

However, arguments appealing to collective self-determination have also been deployed by parties seeking to reject restrictions on their use of climate sinks and fossil fuels. Some have claimed that their collective's lifestyle will be destabilized by constraints on emissions;[13] some have claimed that their collective economic life will be jeopardized by losses of fossil fuel revenue;[14] and some have claimed that duties to preserve and enhance terrestrial sinks may place problematic restrictions on development options.[15]

Protecting self-determination therefore appears to be a difficult goal in the context of climate change—one raising considerations that tell both for and against a more austere emissions budget; and both for and against certain mitigation measures. One might worry, therefore, that rather than helping to solve this problem, the principle of collective self-determination seems to complicate matters by engendering conflicting claims. How can this principle adjudicate, for example, between the Inuit's claim to territory on which they can continue to pursue their traditional way of life, and the United States' claim to prolong the use of fossil fuels that underlies its high-emission lifestyle?[16] How can it adjudicate between the claims of oil-producing nations to maintain economies dependent on income extraction from fossil fuels, and the claims of those who fear their development will be arrested if they cannot engage in deforestation?[17]

In what remains of this section, I will first provide some general guidelines for adjudicating between conflicting claims to natural resources that appeal to collective self-determination; and then use these guidelines to assess the claims to land, fossil fuels, and climate sinks that arise in disputes over the emissions budget.

[13] Then US President George H W Bush, for example, famously opposed climate commitments at the Rio Earth Summit in 1992 by stating that 'the American way of life is not up for negotiation' (Goodman 2011).

[14] OPEC claims that oil-producing developing countries are 'Especially vulnerable' to mitigation measures, which would reduce fossil fuel revenue, 'wreak havoc with their economies', and thereby do serious damage to their 'economic and social fabric' (OPEC 1998).

[15] See Narain 2011.

[16] The Inuit are already struggling to maintain their way of life because of changes to the Arctic environment, as outlined in the Inuit Circumpolar Conference's petition to the Inter-American Commission on Human Rights, ('seeking relief from violations resulting from global warming caused by acts and omissions of the United States' (http://www.inuitcircumpolar.com/uploads/3/0/5/4/30542564/finalpetitionicc.pdf)).

[17] OPEC has argued that within our mitigation efforts, the need to reduce fossil fuel consumption should be offset by increasing sink capacity (Barnett & Dessai 2002: 234).

8.4.1 *Assessing self-determination claims*

The two principles of natural resource justice that I have defended must be applied on a case-by-case basis to identify and adjudicate between claims to natural resources. There is significant potential for self-determination claims to come into conflict, here; but there are also ways to assess such claims and weigh them against one another.

Self-determination claims can first be assessed on grounds of *legitimacy*. According to the view defended in this work, any right of jurisdiction over natural resources must be bound to the region where a people engages in the legitimate exercise of collective self-determination; where the legitimate exercise of this capacity does not serve to dominate community members, outsiders, or future generations. This constraint blocks states' claims to jurisdiction over lands that they occupy unjustly (over the territories of indigenous peoples, for example). It also invalidates the natural resource claims of authoritarian governments (though this does not, of course, entail that *the people* of the country in question lacks a claim to territorial jurisdiction in support of its self-determination). Legitimacy in addition demands that jurisdiction be sustainable, in the sense that resource management is designed to support the ongoing exercise of self-determination.

Secondly, one must be careful to determine the *scope* of self-determination claims. Whenever communities stake claims to natural resources on grounds of self-determination, it is important to consider precisely which resource rights are necessary for the exercise of this capacity. It should not be assumed that self-determination justifies exclusive jurisdiction over underground extractive resources or resources with cross-territory significance—or full rights of income retention. One must also consider whether the natural resource rights that communities lay claim to can be substituted by other goods.

Third, when considerations of legitimacy and scope do not settle the matter of conflicting claims, one must remember that the principle of collective self-determination was defended as a means for protecting individuals from domination (understood as exposure to outside interference that is arbitrary in the sense that it is not forced to track their interests). *Opposing domination* should therefore be a key aim in adjudicating between self-determination claims. This suggests two further guidelines. First, that it will be most important to ensure that resource rights support the self-determination of political communities that are exposed or vulnerable to domination; and second, that international negotiations concerning natural resources must be designed to protect these collectives, and their members, from arbitrary interference by more powerful others.

These two guidelines relate to the fact that in our nonideal world, many peoples already struggle to exercise self-determination, and are subject to domination by various international agents. Some political communities are far richer and more powerful than others, and in possession of sufficient resources to successfully adapt to various changes in their circumstances (greater economic power in general providing a collective with a broader set of choices). Other communities are poor, marginalized from international decision-making, and already unable to exercise self-determination in a very meaningful sense; perhaps struggling to even satisfy the basic needs of their members—thus being possessed of a very narrow set of options—and vulnerable to domination by a range of outside agents. If natural resource rights are to support self-determination for *all* peoples, then the interests of those exposed or vulnerable to domination should carry the most weight when adjudicating between resource claims; and in global decision-making concerning natural resources.

8.4.2 *Weighing claims to fossil fuels, climate sinks, and land*

I will begin with an assessment of claims to engage in the extraction, transportation, and sale of fossil fuels; as made, for example, by the United States, Canada, the United Kingdom, Norway, and members of OPEC. Claims to exploit fossil fuels start on a weak footing in terms of *scope* since, as argued in §7.2, exclusive jurisdiction over underground resources and incidents of income retention are particularly hard to defend on the basis of self-determination. The scope problem is especially pronounced in cases where collectives claim an entitlement to extract resources from beneath land over which they have no particular claim in the first place (such as the sea floor). Many fossil fuel claims are also of questionable *legitimacy*. The decision to pursue exploitation may not have been sufficiently collective, for example, with governments ignoring protests from the local communities that will be impacted by extraction. Worse still, in many cases exploitation is pursued by authoritarian regimes, or utilizes land (whether for extraction or transportation) that is unjustly occupied. In these cases, satisfaction of fossil fuel claims will undermine rather than promote the legitimate exercise of collective self-determination.[18]

Political actors from regions rich in fossil fuels may object that their economies are dependent upon the right to extract income from these resources. However, whilst all political communities are entitled to resource rights in

---

[18] As Leif Wenar points out, the ruling regimes of many oil-rich states—including members of OPEC—are very oppressive, failing to accord their citizens even minimal civil liberties or political rights (2008: 22–5). An example of injustice in fossil fuel transportation is provided by the Dakota Access Pipeline. Led by Standing Rock Sioux Tribal members, thousands of people gathered at camps in 2016 to oppose this pipeline, which is planned to be constructed 'on lands and through waters the tribe never ceded consensually to the U.S. and that remain environmentally and culturally significant for tribal members' safety and wellness' (Whyte 2017c: 155).

support of their self-determination, they do not have a right to support their own economies through resource use that threatens the self-determination of others. When natural resources are valued on the basis of income extraction alone they are entirely substitutable by other goods. Furthermore, it is hard to see why some political communities have more of a right to the income that can be extracted from fossil fuels than others, purely due to the geographical location of such resources. In fact, rights of income retention over fossil fuels would better promote the value of collective self-determination if allocated to poor or disadvantaged peoples, making it particularly difficult for relatively wealthy countries to justify their exploitation of such resources. The legitimacy of claims over fossil fuels is also undermined by considerations of sustainability, given that global use of such fuels must be phased out rapidly to prevent dangerous climate change.

Considerations of scope, and the potential substitutability of natural resources that are valued purely as economic goods, also undermine many use-rights that are claimed to the *assimilative capacity* of climate sinks on grounds of self-determination. Where collectives claim such rights for energy production or agriculture (a major source of GHGs), surrogate goods are often available, at least to some extent. Reducing consumption, increasing efficiency, and switching to renewable technology or different agricultural practices that reduce demand on these sinks need not involve problematic changes to a collective's way of life;[19] provided that the implementation of such measures is forced to track the interests of those impacted by them. Claims to use climate sinks for the assimilation of anthropogenic emissions again score poorly in terms of sustainability (undermining their legitimacy), and are particularly weak when made by wealthy and powerful states like the United States—which have the capacity to pursue their way of life by other means whilst remaining free from domination.

What about the claims of peoples with significant terrestrial climate sinks within their territories? In particular, might these collectives lay claim to a larger share of the global emissions budget? (the possibility discussed at length in Chapter Two). According to the view I have defended, peoples do indeed have a strong presumptive right to exclusive *jurisdiction* over the forests and soils of the region where they legitimately exercise self-determination. Since self-determination is not exercised legitimately when it is used to dominate, concerns of legitimacy will block states' claims to jurisdiction over forests in cases where the state arbitrarily interferes with the lives of local communities, and in cases where local communities are unjustly marginalized from state decision-making. But where this is the case, local peoples—insofar as they are

---

[19] See Caney 2012: §7.

not similarly engaged in dominating their members or outsiders—will be the possessors of a presumptive right to exclusive jurisdiction over forests.

However, the GHG assimilative capacity of these resource systems is a Global Environmental Resource (GER). Jurisdiction over this assimilative capacity should therefore be shared and globalized insofar as this is necessary to support the self-determination of outsiders, *provided* such global governance can shield local interests from undue interference by the global majority. To determine which decisions about forests should be taken at the local level, and which should be delegated to a global institution, it is important to consider what system of governance will best support the self-determination of political communities with and without significant territorial climate sinks. As noted in §8.4.1, it is the interests of those exposed or vulnerable to domination that should carry the most weight in the design of such institutions, which in this case will include communities that are at risk of climate disaster and forest peoples with insecure land tenure.

In designing just governing institutions for resources that act as terrestrial sinks, one might start by considering precisely which rights over these resources any given people can legitimately claim on the basis of self-determination (a question of *scope*). Rights to access forests, manage forests and soils, and withdraw material units from these resource systems— vegetation and wood, for instance—will tend to be of greatest importance for local communities. Use-rights to the *GHG assimilative capacity* of forests and soils, on the other hand, do not necessarily appear more essential to the self-determination of those in whose territory they are located, over other peoples with similar energy and agriculture needs and alternatives (in terms of their potential for renewable energy production, for example). Where sink-rich peoples lack other means of energy production—perhaps *because* forest preservation limits the amount of land available for renewables—this may be reflected in a claim to a greater share of the emissions budget; but otherwise their claims should be considered in the same way as peoples that are similarly situated with respect to their energy and agriculture needs.

This gives rise to an initial suggestion that just governance for resources that act as terrestrial climate sinks will incorporate local control over access, management, and withdrawal of material resource units, whilst a global institution should legislate, adjudicate, and enforce rights to withdraw units of GHG assimilative capacity from those resources.[20] Serious potential for conflict remains, however, over matters of sink preservation. If decisions about sink preservation are made at the global level, this could result in significant outside interference with local use (resident communities may, for example,

---

[20] See also Alejandra Mancilla (2016b: 139–40), who suggests that the use of carbon sinks should ideally be regulated by a 'multi-lateral authority'.

find that they are prevented from cutting down trees or making decisions about soil management). If this decision is instead left to local communities, some might decide to pursue policies that reduce the assimilative capacity of those resources, thereby undermining global governance of the emissions budget.

Special decision-making procedures must therefore be put in place to ensure that local and global interests receive adequate representation in decisions about where and how terrestrial sink capacity will be preserved. It is essential that local peoples participate in these decisions because sink preservation targets and mechanisms can have a severe impact on the environment that surrounds them and the parameters of their lives there. As well as threatening outside interference with local decision-making, sink preservation could lock in severe global inequalities of income and development that threaten the self-determination of some currently disadvantaged peoples.

I explained in §8.4 that considerations of self-determination tell—other things being equal—in favour of mitigation rather than adaptation, and thus the aim should be to ensure as much sink preservation as possible, consistent with the ongoing self-determination of local peoples. Where the decision is to preserve, local communities should be given as much control as possible over managing, monitoring, and enforcement; and if necessary provided with the resources by which to implement these measures. For preservation duties to be fair it is also of vital importance that global institutions with jurisdiction over the emissions budget are just—and can be perceived as such by local peoples. For example, political communities with development needs should not have their capacities for self-determination impacted by preservation duties so that richer collectives can continue to engage in luxury activities that are not necessary to their own self-determination. As parties that contribute to the maintenance of a vital global good, forest peoples must have a significant role in decisions concerning how forests should be protected, and to what end.

One important end of sink preservation is the protection of land. As argued in §6.3.1, a people's jurisdiction over land appears to be a fundamental enabling condition of its legitimate exercise of self-determination. When communities stake claims to land for this purpose, their claims will be strong in terms of both legitimacy and scope. And as explained in §7.1.1, self-determination will usually ground claims over *particular*, non-substitutable, geographical regions. For the islanders of Tuvalu or the Inuit, for example, collective way of life is strongly attached to particular lands and resources. Climate change-induced displacement could thus make the continued exercise of self-determination near impossible. Restrictions on the exploitation of fossil fuels and consumption of climate sink capacity do not pose a comparable threat to this capacity. Claims over land to be used in the legitimate exercise of self-determination therefore have a privileged status in conflicts over the emissions budget, telling in favour of a budget that promises to respect such claims by averting climate impacts that threaten territorial displacement.[21] Where efforts fail in this regard, local communities should have most say concerning at what point relocation becomes the best option; and what such a move should look like.

Those with economies based on the extraction and sale of fossil fuels or high per capita GHG emissions might complain that this necessitates an ambitious atmospheric target that is biased in favour of vulnerable groups including indigenous peoples and small island nations. Why must the United States and members of OPEC, for example, make significant changes to their way of life through the adoption of more stringent mitigation measures in order to ensure that these communities are protected from displacement; especially if it might be cheaper—as Beckerman suggests—to financially compensate those whose territory is lost?

There is an important difference, however, between the claim to exercise collective self-determination through the sustainable use of local land and resources, and the claim to continue a way of life based on the unilateral appropriation of GERs such as fossil fuels and climate sink capacity. Peoples like the Inuit and Tuvaluans do not dominate outsiders through use of their territorial resources; but those who unilaterally exploit fossil fuels and climate sinks *do* arbitrarily interfere with the choices of other collectives, who are thereby excluded from having a similar say over resources that are of significance to everyone.

Thus, whilst use of fossil fuels and climate sink capacity must be governed by global institutions to limit such arbitrary interference, global governance should be designed to respect local rights over land to be used in the legitimate exercise of self-determination. In other words, to ensure that the world's resources are not used by some collectives in a way that dominates outsiders and future generations, entitlements to use fossil fuels and climate sinks *must be* up for global negotiation; whilst a people's presumptive right of exclusive territorial jurisdiction over land where it can engage in the legitimate exercise of self-determination must be respected and protected as far as possible.

So far, I have mostly been using considerations of the legitimacy and scope of self-determination claims to adjudicate between the conflicting claims to fossil fuels, climate sinks, and land that arise in debates concerning the global emissions budget. I suggested that claims to exploit fossil fuels will frequently be weak on grounds of both scope and legitimacy. There may be legitimate

---

[21] See Rebecca Tsosie (2007a) for a discussion of the grave harm that can be done by relocating indigenous groups from their traditional lands, and the importance of the right to self-determination for protecting indigenous peoples from such harm. See also Heyward 2014.

claims to extract income from fossil fuels, but these will be strongest for poorer political communities (regardless of where those resources are located) and are weakened because as an economic good, the right to exploit these resources is both unsustainable and substitutable. Similar considerations apply when use-rights are claimed to the assimilative capacity of climate sinks on economic grounds. Fossil fuels and climate sink capacity are GERs, and thus should be subject to global jurisdiction designed to ensure that their use is constrained to sustainable limits and serves to promote the self-determination of all political communities. Such global jurisdiction must be designed to preserve as much local control over forests and soils as possible, compatible with a privileged goal of protecting political communities from displacement from the land that they need for their legitimate exercise of self-determination. This privileged goal should determine the upper bound of any secondary emissions budget, and emitters, fossil fuel developers, and groups pursuing deforestation have a duty to change their economic practices in support of this budget.

Alongside considerations of legitimacy and scope, I offered a third method for adjudicating between self-determination claims: namely, to choose options that best oppose domination. This can be done in two ways: first, by prioritizing the claims of those who are currently vulnerable or exposed to domination; and second, through careful design of international institutions. For some communities, climate change poses a near-absolute threat to self-determination due to pre-existing socio-economic disadvantage and political marginalization. To retain any modicum of control over their collective existence, the self-determination claims of such peoples must be given priority in cases where they conflict with the claims of more powerful collectives. Vulnerable peoples must also have strong representation in decisions regarding the emissions budget (such as whether, for example, a budget that gives only a 50 per cent probability of staying below the temperature target is satisfactory).

International negotiations will also be an important means by which to allocate any secondary emissions budget. This is in part due to the complex nature of mitigation: support for self-determination can be pursued in a number of ways and there is unlikely to be any unique budget allocation that will best serve this end. Putting it in Caney's terms, the just distribution of the secondary emissions budget is thus 'epiphenomenal' (2012: 299). Given the lack of a uniquely just solution, the only way to determine a specific allocation will be 'to have political processes in which the relevant parties decide what particular combination of natural resources will be employed in order to realize people's entitlements' (Caney 2012: 298). Such processes are of more than practical importance, however. They are also a crucial means by which to promote self-determination, by ensuring that the interests of all peoples are given adequate representation in a decision that will significantly shape their way of life.

8.5 Conclusion

In setting the emissions budget, first and foremost the global community should seek to calculate each society's subsistence emissions needs, and how far and how quickly they can be reduced. If the subsistence emissions of those existing threaten to engender climate impacts that will prevent future generations from accessing the natural resources necessary for their own basic needs, then attempts to rapidly reduce dependence on GHG emissions must be combined with increased sink-enhancement and adaptation efforts. If, on the other hand, protecting the natural resources that future generations require for their basic needs is compatible not only with subsistence emissions, but also with some secondary emissions (those that are not necessary to the satisfaction of basic needs), the size and distribution of this secondary emissions budget should be decided in accordance with the principle of collective self-determination.

The principle of collective self-determination tells in favour of a more restricted secondary emissions budget for two main reasons. First, mitigation techniques can be implemented in a relatively predictable way and such measures are therefore, *ceteris paribus*, more compatible with the ongoing exercise of collective self-determination than adaptation or compensation. Second, the claims of political communities over the lands on which they can engage in the legitimate exercise of self-determination appear to be stronger, in several respects, than the claims of collectives to use fossil fuels and climate sinks for economic purposes. Any secondary emissions budget should therefore be set at a level that protects peoples from climate impacts that threaten to displace them from the lands on which they can engage in the legitimate exercise of self-determination. The allocation of secondary emission quotas within this budget must be determined by fair international agreement, via negotiations that effectively place the Earth's GHG assimilative capacity under global jurisdiction. These negotiations must be designed to ensure that communities who live on or near resources that act as climate sinks, and other disadvantaged or vulnerable political communities, are protected from domination.

9

Historical Emissions Debt

In this chapter and Chapter Ten, I conclude my discussion by examining a topic within the third and final category of climate justice questions: that of unavoided impacts.[1] My focus is theories of climate debt, which I take to be distinguished by their commitment to the core claim that certain wealthy or industrialized parties owe a debt of compensation to some of those suffering from the unavoided impacts of climate change; where the notion of a *debt* is used to indicate that the obligation in question is rectificatory in nature— owed as a result of historical wrongdoing—rather than a matter of charity or beneficence. Climate debt claims might be vindicated on multiple bases, because there could be several reasons why the wealthy or industrialized possess duties to rectify the unavoided impacts of climate change. One particularly common way that claims of climate debt have been defended, however, takes such debts to derive from historical wrongdoing concerning natural resources; in particular, the wrong of consuming more than a fair share of global climate sink capacity. I term this the Historical Emissions Debt view.

In this chapter, I aim to reject this popular method for defending the climate debt claim. The argument runs as follows. I start by introducing the problem of unavoided climate impacts (§9.1). I then present the Historical Emissions Debt view, according to which at least some of the cost of such impacts should be borne by those who have historically emitted more than their fair share of GHGs (historical polluters); or else, those who are appropriately related to historical polluters. I explain the appeal of such a view and note how it may also be framed as a beneficiary pays approach to climate change, at least when the beneficiary pays principle (BPP) is given a rectificatory reading (§9.2). I then argue, however, that the Historical Emissions Debt view (and the rectificatory BPP) face a seemingly insurmountable challenge, in that they cannot succeed in identifying the acts of overuse through which

---

[1] The other categories identified in §1.3.2 were that of the atmospheric target and that of mitigation—both of which were discussed in Chapter Eight.

emission debts or duties of rectification are supposed to be incurred (§9.3.1). I consider whether a redistributive reading of the BPP could do better, but argue that it faces a similar problem (§9.3.2). I conclude that since none of these accounts appear defensible, those seeking to substantiate the climate debt claim would do better to attempt this by other means (§9.4). This is the task of Chapter Ten, in which I argue that climate debts may yet be shown to derive from historical wrongdoing concerning natural resources, once we take a broader perspective on this form of injustice.

9.1 Unavoided impacts

As explained in the introduction, this chapter and the next concern normative questions arising in the context of unavoided climate impacts. Such impacts most obviously include the various environmental disturbances discussed in §1.1.2, such as sea level rise and coastal flooding, storm surges, extreme weather events, heatwaves, drought, flooding, ecosystem and biodiversity loss, and water scarcity. These disturbances threaten severe knock-on socio-economic and health impacts. Reducing the risk of such negative consequences will require communities to engage in anticipatory adaptation, which is often costly.

The need for anticipatory adaptive measures highlights how threatened climate impacts can create costs whether or not they are actualized. Many of the consequences of climate change are uncertain in the sense that whilst climate scientists can confidently predict that there will be an increase in extreme weather events, the location, direction, and magnitude of such events tends to be much harder to foresee. Thus, unavoided impacts should also be taken to include the *risk* that different individuals and communities are subjected to because of climate change. Whether or not these risks end up ripening into physical harms, they constitute a negative impact in virtue of the uncertainty that they impose and the anticipatory adaptive costs that they call for.

Where climate risks materialize into harms, the question of compensation arises. This was a live topic at the 2013 Conference of the Parties (COP) in Warsaw (COP19), which took place under the shadow of the destruction wrought on the Philippines by Typhoon Yolanda (Haiyan). One dispute at this conference centred on the question of whether measures to help countries suffering 'loss and damage' from climate change (that is, impacts that cannot be adapted to) should be couched in terms of compensation at all. Parties such as the members of AOSIS (the Alliance of Small Island States) had long pressed for the UNFCCC to incorporate a loss and damage mechanism with an explicit compensatory component, and for this mechanism to be governed under a separate institution to that of adaptation.[2] But at COP19, wealthier countries including Australia, the United States, and members of the European Union resisted such demands. Disagreement over the issue resulted in the G77 and China bloc walking out of the negotiations (Vidal 2013). In the end, the Warsaw International Mechanism (WIM) for loss and damage associated with climate change impacts was established, but placed under the pre-existing Cancun *Adaptation* Framework—with no reference to compensation appearing in the decision (UNFCCC 2014: Decision 2/CP.19).

The question of loss and damage, and where it should be situated within the structure of the UNFCCC, was returned to at the 2015 COP in Paris (COP21). It was decided that the WIM would continue and, significantly, the resulting agreement addresses loss and damage in its own Article, separate to the issue of adaptation, where it is agreed that the WIM 'may be enhanced and strengthened' (UNFCCC 2015: Art. 8.2). In the accompanying decision text, however, it is explicitly stated that Article 8 'does not involve or provide a basis for any liability or compensation' (UNFCCC 2015: paragraph 52).

This chapter and Chapter Ten will consider the normative issues raised by unavoided climate impacts, understood to encompass both risks and harms, with their attendant costs. If the climate debt claim can be substantiated, this will show that compensation certainly is owed to some of those who are burdened by these unavoided impacts. In §9.2, I present a theory of climate debt according to which it is owed, more specifically, by historical high-emitters.

9.2 The Historical Emissions Debt view

The notion of climate debt is closely related to the notion of a broader, *ecological* debt that is sometimes claimed to be owed by the Global North to the Global South due to the former's unjust and excessive consumption of the world's natural resources. Environmental economist Joan Martinez-Alier, for example, construes the climate debt (in his words, the 'carbon debt') as one of the most significant components of this broader ecological debt (2002: 229–33).[3] These concepts have entered the international climate debate due to the efforts of indigenous peoples, campaigners, non-governmental

[2] See, for example, AOSIS 2008. As far back as 1991, an AOSIS representative from Vanuatu proposed to the UNFCCC that 'The financial burden of loss and damage suffered by the most vulnerable small island and low-lying developing countries...as a result of sea level rise shall be distributed in an equitable manner amongst the industrialized developed countries' (UNFCCC 1991. Art. 3.1).

[3] The concept of ecological debt has been discussed and developed by non-governmental organizations and environmental economists including Martinez-Alier since at least the early 1990s. See, for example: Martinez-Alier 1993. For a historical overview and analysis of the concept, see Martinez-Alier 2002: Ch. 10; Goeminne and Paredis 2010.

organizations, the media, and representatives of states such as Bolivia;[4] and are increasingly drawing the attention of theorists concerned with the normative dimensions of climate change.[5]

As perhaps indicated by the varying terminology that is used in discussion of climate debts—with theorists talking variously in terms of CO_2 debt, carbon debt, emissions debt, atmospheric debt, ecological debt, or natural debt[6]— there does not appear to be a settled understanding of precisely how such debt claims should be understood. Furthermore, there are numerous different ways that one might fill out the details of such accounts. For one thing, different theorists might take different historical injustices to have given rise to climate debts. In addition, as Tim Hayward suggests in his discussion of the closely related concept of *ecological* debt, one might ask 'how literally the idea of debt should be taken in this context, and how it might be quantified and attributed' (2005b: 197). In this chapter I critique a rather literal understanding of climate debt, common in the academic literature, which aspires toward a precise quantification and attribution of such obligations. To distinguish this conception, I refer to it as *the Historical Emissions Debt view* (HED).[7]

9.2.1 Characterizing the view

Climate debts are often defended by reference to theories of natural resource justice, being claimed to arise on occasions of *overuse*, or *excessive use*, of certain natural resources. We should take these allegations to be staking a normative claim, because the limits beyond which overuse is said to take place are not given by nature, but are instead supposed to be determined by requirements of justice.[8] Thus, in order to identify such climate debts, we first need to

---

[4] See, for example, the Anchorage Declaration (2009); the People's Agreement of Cochabamba (2010); the list of 254 organizations endorsing the Third World Network's 'Repay the climate debt' letter (Third World Network 2009); the joint report by the World Development Movement and Jubilee Debt Campaign (Jones and Edwards 2009); Naomi Klein's 2009 *Rolling Stone* article; and the statement by Bolivia (Navarro 2009).

[5] Though these discussions often use different terminology—talking variously in terms of 'CO$_2$ debt', 'carbon debt', 'emissions debt', 'atmospheric debt', 'ecological debt', 'natural debt', or simply 'debt'—they appear to be latching onto roughly the same concept. See Agarwal 2002: 377; Baer 2002: 402; Beckerman & Pasek 1995: 410; Caney 2006a: 464; Cripps 2011a: 126; Duus-Otterström 2014: 450; Grubb et al. 1992: 312; Halme 2007; Hayward 2007: 445; Kartha 2011: 508–9; Knight 2011: 535; Martinez-Alier & Naron 2004: 18–19; Meyer & Roser 2006: 238; Miller 2008: 133; Page 2007: 460; Pickering & Barry 2012; Sinden 2010; Smith 1991 and H P Young 1990: 8. Some theorists *equate* such debt with the idea of historical responsibility (Athanasiou & Baer 2002: 121) or historical accountability (Neumayer 2000: 186; Risse 2012: 394, fn.16).

[6] See fn.5.

[7] Though Eric Neumayer also uses the term 'Historical Emission Debt' (2000: 186), we define this concept in different ways.

[8] For example, Tom Athanasiou and Paul Baer state that 'The historical and continuing *overuse* of the atmosphere by the North can be seen to be the accrual of a massive ecological debt' (2002: 82; emphasis added); Göran Duus-Otterström talks in terms of 'uncompensated overuse of the atmospheric commons' (2014: 456); and Joan Martinez-Alier and Stephen Naron describe the

be in possession of principles specifying limits on the just use of natural resources; limits beyond which one can conclude that debts are incurred. In other words, we need to identify a background theory of rights, or entitlements, to natural resources. Different accounts of climate debt can then be distinguished by the *kind* of natural resources that they claim to have been subject to unjust use and the background theory of natural resource justice that they assume. According to the Historical Emissions Debt view that I will be assessing here, the natural resource that has been subject to unjust use is global climate sink capacity, and the background principle of justice is one specifying fair shares of this resource.

Jonathan Pickering and Christian Barry's paper 'On the concept of climate debt' is illustrative of the prominence of HED in the philosophical literature. Here, Barry and Pickering focus only on views that incorporate a 'core' proposition that climate debts are incurred by 'Countries that have emitted *more than their fair share* of the Earth's capacity to safely absorb emissions' (2012: 670; emphasis added). A principle specifying fair shares of the Earth's ability to assimilate GHGs is thus supposed to enable us to identify emission debtors and creditors as—in the first instance—those who have consumed more than their fair share of climate sink capacity and those at whose expense this excess use took place, respectively. The identity of the (original) debtors according to HED is thus quite clear: it is those who, via their emission of GHGs, have consumed in excess of their fair share of climate sink capacity.

The corresponding climate creditors (those at whose expense this overuse has taken place) could be either of two groups: those who are left with a smaller share of natural resources than that to which they were entitled as a result;[9] or, those who bear the costs of the climate impacts to which such overuse has contributed. The reasoning in both cases is roughly speaking the same, with the idea being that if only debtors had refrained from consuming more than their fair share of this resource, then: 1) nobody would have been left with a smaller share than that to which they were entitled; and 2) total

---

carbon debt as 'the damage caused by rich countries through their *excessive* emissions, past and present, of greenhouse gases' (2004: 19; emphasis added). Theorists may not be explicit about the normative nature of such claims, but as explained in §2.2: the notion of resource overuse appears to be a human one, with any restraints being set by the features of a resource system that we wish to—or are obliged to—maintain. Some of these restraints will be determined by considerations of justice and then, as Hayward says: 'If we assume that there is a determinate limit to the amount of ecological space that anyone might *justly* use, then it is intelligible also to say that anyone who uses more than their just share incurs an "ecological debt"' (2007: 445; emphasis added). Gert Goeminne and Erik Paredis similarly talk of ecological debts arising from 'use at the expense of *equitable* rights' (2010: 703; emphasis added).

[9] Usually, this is understood as those who must emit less than a fair share of GHGs due to the excessive emissions of others (see, for example, Baer 2002: 402), but presumably this could be expanded to also include those that must engage in more demanding forest preservation and enhancement schemes in order to mitigate these excessive emissions.

emissions would not have exceeded the assimilative capacity of the climate sink, leading to dangerous climate impacts (on the assumption that the fair shares principle divides a 'safe' budget of emissions).

Due to the present focus on unavoided *climate* impacts, I will be taking HED to adopt the latter interpretation of climate creditors (it should be possible to see, however, that the problem I raise for this view is a fortiori a problem for those adopting the alternative construal of climate creditors). With this account of historical emission debts in hand, one can then argue that they are like financial debts in that they can be passed on to third parties in certain ways (perhaps through the transfer of goods to which those debts are attached). And when emission debts are accrued by collective entities such as companies and states, they may be claimed to persist through time despite changes in the membership of those entities.

Summing up, then, the view under discussion can be characterized more precisely as follows: (1) historical emission debts are incurred by emitting GHGs in excess of one's fair share of climate sink capacity; (2) the debtors are individuals or collectives that either (a) historically emitted beyond a fair share themselves (historical polluters), or (b) are related to historical polluters in an appropriate way; and (3) the creditors are individuals or collectives on whom the unavoided impacts of climate change impose costs (where, as indicated in §9.1, these encompass costs associated with both adaptation and loss and damage). I leave the question of what is owed by the debtors to the creditors open, but note that part of the appeal of HED appears to be that historical emissions can be relatively easily attributed, quantified, and then converted into financial obligations.[10]

9.2.2 Motivating the view

HED might appear to hold promise for those who wish to defend what I will term the *strong thesis* of historical accountability for climate change, according to which some parties have duties to address the unavoided impacts of climate change that are A) *rectificatory* in nature; and B) owed due to activities *dating back over a significant period of time* (perhaps ideally, even, to the industrial revolution).[11] HED's picture of accountability possesses several attractive features. If defensible, one might hope to use estimates of cumulative

---

[10] As H Damon Matthews puts it, 'Fossil fuel carbon debts are easy to calculate . . . and could also potentially be monetized using estimates of the economic cost of climate damages from CO_2 emissions' (2016: 63). Environmental justice project EJOLT notes some might worry that the employment of such methodology means that the notion of climate or ecological debt 'implies monetisation of nature's services' (EJOLT 2013).

[11] See, for example, Alexa Zellentin; who aims to defend rectificatory climate duties on the basis of 'all emissions produced by states since the Industrial Revolution', considered 'as a whole' (2015b: 261).

emissions—the estimates of total emissions per country dating back to 1850 provided by the World Resources Institute, for example (Baumert et al. 2005: 32)—to quantify corresponding responsibilities to rectify the problem of climate change proportionally, country-by-country, and then monetize them. The question, however, is whether this is a defensible understanding of historical accountability for climate change.

It seems that duties to bear the costs of climate change can only be given a rectificatory rationale when they are 'based on the wrongfulness of what was done' (L. Meyer 2013: 610). As Alexa Zellentin puts it, 'rectificatory justice requires both responsibility for causing the problem at hand in a morally significant way *and wrongdoing*' (2015b: 269; emphasis added). However, it is hard to identify any *general* element of wrongdoing in historical acts of GHG emission. The problem here is that, as David Miller says, climate change does not appear to be like more familiar instances of historical injustice—cases like transatlantic slavery, for example—'where there was a clear historic wrong that required, and may still require, redress' (2008: 136). The very thing that makes the climate sink so prone to overuse—namely, the difficulty of preventing anybody, anywhere from accessing it—also means that many of the injustices that tend to plague natural resources have not (yet) been a problem in its case. Nobody has fought wars over climate sink capacity, drawn borders around it to unjustly exclude others, or forcibly taken control of it.

The elusive *wrongful factor*[12] in historical use of the climate sink cannot reliably be located in the intentions of historical emitters since—as has often been pointed out—many of them were excusably ignorant that their actions were contributing to climate change.[13] One might instead seek to pinpoint the wrong in the harm done to the victims of climate impacts, but this is not a straightforward connection to make. The actions of a significant proportion of historical emitters would not have subjected anybody to harmful climate impacts *at all* had climate change been addressed effectively—because such impacts would then have been avoided. In the case of many historical emitters, then, whether we can even *consider* them to have wronged any victims of climate change depends on events taking place *after* their actions. If emissions had stayed at a sufficiently low level,[14] or renewables had replaced carbon-based energy production in time, or international action to mitigate climate change had succeeded—historical emitters could have used the same amount

[12] Edward Page uses this terminology in his discussion of a beneficiary pays principle closely related to HED (2012: 311).

[13] See, for example: Bell 2010: 437–8; Caney 2005c: 761–2; Moellendorf 2012: 140.

[14] Page claims that annual emissions prior to 1950 could have been 'sustained indefinitely' without resulting in dangerous climate impacts (2012: 312). Whether or not this is correct, presumably there is *some* date prior to which anthropogenic GHG emissions were sufficiently low to be successfully assimilated by the climate system.

of climate sink capacity, but there would have been no victims of climate impacts for them to have wronged.[15] Thus, it is not clear how pointing to harmful climate impacts alone can enable us to deem as wrongful any anthropogenic emissions that took place prior to that harm becoming an inevitable consequence.

The promise of HED is that it appears to offer a way around this problem. Here—to borrow an analogy from Axel Gosseries—we can view the Earth's assimilative capacity for GHGs as a 'bin' into which anthropogenic emissions are dumped (2005: 282). Until the top of the bin is reached, no dangerous interference occurs with the climate system and there are no victims of anthropogenic climate change. Once this capacity is breached, however, dangerous interference results—and then we are faced with the question of who is responsible for this problem, and how the costs of dealing with it should be allocated.[16] HED makes the seemingly plausible suggestion that we should figure out what a fair distribution of emissions within the *safe* amount would have been and then count emissions exceeding a fair share as wrongful emissions, which incur a debt to those impacted by climate change. When historical accountability is construed this way, the ignorance of historical polluters is supposed to become irrelevant because we can say that they committed a wrong unknowingly and thus should be held (at least partly) *liable* for the resulting costs of their excess emissions, even if they cannot be morally blamed for them.[17]

At this point, it is essential to be clear that the notion of an historical emissions debt (even if defensible) could only provide a partial picture of accountability for the costs of unavoided climate impacts. This is because there are various other, very important grounds on which such accountability should be allocated. It is crucial to remember that many of those who have contributed—and most of those who are now contributing—to the problem of climate change cannot claim to be excusably ignorant. As Jeremy Moss and Robyn Kath state, the excusable ignorance objection has limited plausibility for emissions taking place after the publication of the IPCC's first report in 1990,[18] but these emissions 'in fact constitute a large and rapidly increasing proportion of emissions since 1750—approximately half of the carbon

---

[15] See also Moellendorf 2014: 172.

[16] This is an oversimplified model in two respects. Firstly, as Gosseries says, it implies the existence of a 'clear threshold' beyond which negative impacts occur—something that is likely lacking in reality (2005: 282). Furthermore, the Earth's assimilative capacity for GHGs is not fixed in this way; it can be reduced by deforestation, for example, and increased by afforestation.

[17] See Bell 2011b: 407–8; Neumayer 2000: 188; Shue 1994: 363.

[18] There is some debate about at which point the excusable ignorance objection loses its force. By saying that the objection has limited plausibility post-1990 I do not intend to imply that it is plausible prior to this. Stephen Gardiner, for example, presents evidence indicating that 'by 1965 there was high-level political awareness (and concern) about the existence, magnitude, and timing of the climate threat' (Gardiner & Weisbach 2016: 113).

emissions due to fossil fuel use and cement production, at the time of writing' (2018: 12). Thus, faulty intentions come into the picture as a significant ground of rectificatory duties. One might claim, for example, that individuals, collectives, and corporations that have avoidably (in some sense to be specified) continued to exploit fossil fuels, emit GHGs, and deplete forests when they knew, or should (in some sense to be specified) have known, that they were contributing to a significant environmental problem are both morally culpable and significantly accountable for dealing with the resulting impacts. The same holds for those who have sought to obstruct action on climate change by spreading misinformation and undermining international cooperation, and political agents that have failed in their duties to support and implement fair and effective climate policies.

HED is thus best understood as claiming that liability can be attributed on *additional* grounds to these (rather than claiming that it should be attributed on *alternative* grounds). The idea is that regardless of whether their intentions were faulty, some parties can be deemed liable for climate costs because they consumed climate sink capacity in violation of a principle of fair shares. It is this core claim that I will be assessing in what follows, and to simplify matters, I will be focusing on examples in which these other grounds of accountability do not appear to apply. The question, then, will be whether excusably ignorant historical polluters can be said to have incurred a debt to those impacted by climate change purely in virtue of the excessiveness of their emissions.

It is also vital to understand that if the answer to this question is no (as I shall argue), that does not entail that the climate debt claim collapses. The other grounds of rectificatory responsibility that I have just outlined will still support the claim that certain wealthy or industrialized parties owe debts of compensation to some of those suffering from the impacts of climate change; for example, because those parties have knowingly continued to engage in activities contributing to this problem when they were well equipped to do otherwise. I seek to reject HED, then, not because I think this will lead to significantly different conclusions about *where* rectificatory climate duties fall, but rather because I think it gives the incorrect answer about *why* they fall there.

Before I move on to critique HED, it is also important to note that those who defend accounts of historical accountability for climate change along these lines do not always talk in terms of debt. Some theorists advocating the *beneficiary pays principle* (BPP) also assign the financial costs of climate action to individuals and collectives that are appropriately related to historical polluters (again understood as those who historically used more than a 'fair share' of the Earth's assimilative capacity for GHGs). In this case, specifically, the relevant relation is taken to be the receipt of benefits derived from those allegedly unjust, excess emissions (see, e.g., Bell 2010: 437–8; Page 2011: 421–2).

On this understanding of the BPP—which I will refer to as the *rectificatory* reading—the beneficiaries of wrongfully excessive historical emissions must bear climate costs so as to rectify this injustice.

An alternative, *redistributive* reading of the BPP is also available. This reading departs from HED because it no longer grounds climate duties in the supposed *wrongfulness* of the historical emissions from which some present-day individuals benefit. Instead, the redistributive BPP demands that we redistribute from beneficiaries to those impacted by climate change in order to realize a fair overall distribution of the benefits and burdens of GHG emissions. In what remains of this chapter, I present a key problem for HED and both formulations of the BPP. With the ground thus cleared, I then present an alternative picture of historical accountability in Chapter Ten.

9.3 Rejecting the Historical Emissions Debt view

It should be clear from the exposition of HED in §9.2 that this account of historical responsibility for climate change is incomplete without stating what fair shares of climate sink capacity would have amounted to historically. It is here we find the most fundamental challenge for HED: defending a principle of justice that can be applied retroactively to identify fair shares of this resource. In this section I will argue that the lack of such a principle means that this 'fair emission shares' interpretation of climate debt cannot be rendered complete.

9.3.1 *Fair shares of the climate sink*

To identify the acts of overuse through which historical emission debts are originally supposed to be incurred, a principle of justice specifying limits on permissible use of the climate sink is essential. Here, many theorists appear to believe that 'The principles of historical responsibility and equal entitlements come together naturally in calculations of "natural debt"' (Grubb et al. 1992: 313), claiming such debts to accrue to those who have appropriated more than an *equal per capita* share of climate sink capacity.[19] However, the two principles of natural resource justice that I have defended do not support the claim that climate sink capacity should have been shared throughout history on an equal per capita basis. This way of specifying when GHG emissions incur a debt is therefore lacking in justification. One obvious alternative to this equal per capita approach would take historical emission debts to be incurred

[19] See Athanasiou and Baer 2002: 82; Baer 2002: 402; Kartha 2011: 508–9; Martinez-Alier and Naron 2004: 18; Matthews 2016; Neumayer 2000: 185–6; and Sinden 2010: 343–5.

through use of the climate sink in violation of the principle of resource sovereignty.[20] This option is also ruled out, however, because I have shown the principle of resource sovereignty to be likewise indefensible.

In the face of this challenge, the HED theorist could attempt to save their view by proposing an alternative account of what fair shares of climate sink capacity would have amounted to historically.[21] However, the theory of natural resource justice defended in the middle section of this work suggests that no such account will be forthcoming. To defend any particular historical principle of fair shares for the climate sink, theorists would have to argue that this allocation of natural resource entitlements was required for the satisfaction of basic needs, or necessary for political communities to be able to engage in the legitimate exercise of self-determination. Recall, however, that when looking forward and thinking about how to distribute the *remaining* emissions budget (in Chapter Eight), there did not seem to be a uniquely just solution to this allocation problem. This is because self-determination can be promoted in many different ways, involving different divisions of the emissions budget. But this reasoning also applies when looking back to ask how shares of climate sink capacity *should* have been distributed globally. Again, there does not seem to be any unique distribution of climate sink capacity that would have best supported basic needs satisfaction and collective self-determination.

As also explained in Chapter Eight: as a forward-looking distribution problem, there are ways to address this challenge. Namely, by designing a fair political process via which the secondary emissions budget can be allocated, taking broader concerns of global justice into account. But the problem remains that with no such process having taken place in the past, the question what a fair share of climate sink capacity *would* have been seems to have no determinate answer.[22] Thus HED and the rectificatory BPP (which, recall, also relies on a notion of wrongfully excessive emissions) appear hopelessly incomplete. They are unable to identify the acts of overuse that are supposed to underwrite the rectificatory climate duties that they aim to defend.

---

[20] The broader concept of ecological debt is sometimes construed this way, for example in a Global Footprint Network campaign that identifies ecological debtors as those who fail to live within the ecological means of the resources available 'within their own borders' (GFN 2012b). Hayward also identifies (and critiques) this way of construing ecological debt (2005b: Ch. 6, fn.5).

[21] This is a move made by Duus-Otterström (2014: 457) and Derek Bell (2010: 429). Neither is very specific about what fair shares would amount to if not equal shares (in Bell's case, this is because he doubts that we need to have a particularly detailed account to identify historical polluters).

[22] Caney agrees that when we (rightly, he thinks) take a more integrated approach, which does not consider the just distribution of emission shares taken in isolation, we will find that 'It does not make sense to refer to *the* fair distribution of greenhouse gases'. This is because on an integrated approach, concerned with fair shares of a ' "total package" of goods . . . we have *no* reason to endorse a principle that applies solely to one particular item, such as greenhouse gas emissions' (Caney 2012: 271). There is simply 'no such thing as a fair distribution of greenhouse gas emissions per se' (Caney 2009: 137).

HED theorist Göran Duus-Otterström appears to recognize this problem. He concedes that his account of 'atmospheric debt' assumes, but does not defend, a form of isolationism according to which one can identify fair shares of 'the atmosphere' (read climate sink capacity), in the absence of a broader theory of global justice. In the terminology introduced in §1.2.3, this is a form of *atomist* isolationism. If such isolationism is not defensible, Duus-Otterström accepts that his approach 'must either be abandoned or its conception of debt must be considerably widened' (2014: 462). I am arguing here that such atomist isolationism is *not* defensible. In Chapter Ten, I provide a wider notion of climate debt designed to avoid this problem.

9.3.2 *Fair distribution of the benefits*

Without a principle of fair shares to rely on there are resulting difficulties in determining which currently existing agents—if any—should be held accountable for historical use of the climate sink. It is sometimes claimed that current members of wealthy or industrialized states inherit the historical emission debts of their predecessors because they are in receipt of benefits or holdings derived from these past, excess emissions (see Duus-Otterström 2014: 456–61; Neumayer 2000: 189).[23] The problems just raised obviously create difficulties for this view, however, because unless one can show that unfair shares of climate sink capacity were used in the creation of any particular benefits, then it is unclear why we should think that there are debts attached to these assets—or that such debts are inherited along with them.

By shifting to focus on the *benefits* of historical emissions one may, however, think we have a means by which to formulate a view rather like HED, but which might more easily be rendered complete. In the absence of a principle identifying fair shares of climate sink capacity itself, that is, we might instead invoke a redistributive version of the BPP, considering what would be a fair distribution of the *benefits and burdens* created by historical use of climate sinks. On this beneficiary pays view, one might argue that those who have on balance benefited from the use of this resource owe a debt of compensation to those who are overall burdened by the climate impacts to which such use has causally contributed.

On this *redistributive* reading of the BPP, the problem of historical emissions is no longer claimed to reside in the fact that they consumed more than a fair share of climate sink capacity. Instead, injustice is located in the resulting distribution of costs and benefits. What appears to be demanded on this view,

---

[23] HED theorists might support this claim by suggesting, as Hayward does in his discussion of ecological debt, that when one inherits an asset, one must also assume any liabilities that are attached to it; because otherwise the 'legitimate interests' of creditors would be harmed (2008: 15).

then, is not rectification for wrongdoing, but rather redistribution in pursuit of fairness. Thus, this picture of accountability does not seem able to construe present-day duties to address climate change as rectificatory (thus abandoning claim A of the strong thesis of historical accountability for climate change, identified in §9.2.2). It does, however, succeed in identifying duties that appear to be *compensatory* in nature, rather than duties of beneficence. And it appears to support claim B of the strong thesis, because it retains the ability to take emissions-producing activities dating back over a significant period of time to be relevant to the present-day assignment of these compensatory duties. The redistributive BPP may thus be an attractive option for those aiming to defend a relatively strong thesis of historical accountability for climate change, given the failure of HED and the rectificatory BPP.

The problem, however, is that it is not clear why those in receipt of benefits derived from historical use of climate sinks should be held accountable for dealing with any corresponding climate costs. Presumably the enjoyment of some of these benefits is justified—benefits necessary to the satisfaction of basic needs, for example. This beneficiary pays approach also appears to have some troubling implications. Imagine two societies, prior to the discovery of climate change, one of which (G) developed using geothermal energy, whilst the other (C) only had access to coal. Furthermore, imagine that although C's wealth places it safely over any threshold identified by one's general theory of global justice—and that it could contribute to the costs of climate impacts without being pushed under this threshold—it is significantly poorer than G. Perhaps G grew rich through its abundant access to geothermal energy and other valuable natural resources (perhaps, even, fossil fuels that it sold for profit because it did not have much need for them itself), whilst C only possessed very inefficient technology that created high emissions in the production of its lesser benefits.

The redistributive BPP suggests that current members of C owe a greater debt to those burdened by climate change than current members of G, because they have received more benefits from historical exploitation of the climate sink. But this does not seem fair—at least if we assume that C's benefits were, otherwise, innocently acquired. The redistributive BPP appears to impose greater burdens on current members of C purely due to the bad luck of being descended from a previous generation which only had access to a form of energy production that, unbeknownst to them, contributed to a problem that all countries are now exposed to—but which G is much better placed to deal with than C (due to its higher income and superior access to renewable energy sources).

Note that this worry is somewhat different to one raised by Caney, which may appear similar on the surface. Caney points out that the polluter pays principle (PPP)—according to which those who emit more than a fair share of

GHG emissions should be held accountable for the costs of climate change—may impose burdens on the impoverished. As Caney points out, this worry could be obviated by combining the PPP with a rule that 'the poor should not pay' (2005c: 763). But in my imagined case, the worry is not that C is impoverished—I have stipulated that it is not. The concern is instead that although present members of C have inherited more economic benefits from historical use of the climate sink than G, it seems hard to say that C has benefited more in an *unjust* way. It appears to be merely a matter of bad luck that the natural resources available to the earlier generation of C turn out to have contributed causally to negative climate impacts; and thus, C's receipt of these benefits does not appear to be the right kind of feature on which to base special rectificatory duties.

The idea behind the redistributive reading of the BPP appears to be that the benefits and burdens of historical use of climate sinks should be distributed in a compensatory manner purely because they 'share common origins' (Page 2012: 313); but this proposal instantiates an strangely *resource-specific* breed of egalitarianism.[24] As I have argued, although there is good reason to think that rights to the Earth's natural resources as a whole should be allocated in a way that does justice to Equal Original Claims, there is no obvious reason to think that the benefits and burdens derived from use of the global climate sink *in particular* should be distributed in a specific way. Some individuals and collectives may be unproblematically in receipt of greater benefits of historical use of climate sinks (in particular, those who do not occupy a position of dominance internationally); and those burdened by threatened or resultant climate impacts could be compensated with the benefits of other natural resources.

To conclude: problematically for proponents of HED and the rectificatory BPP, there is no fair shares principle for historical use of the climate sink considered in isolation; and problematically for proponents of the redistributive BPP, there is no fair shares principle for the benefits and burdens derived from such use considered on their own either. This means that none of these accounts of historical responsibility for climate change can be rendered complete.

---

[24] This terminology is adapted from Gosseries who, in his own discussion of historical emissions, describes 'an *action-specific* redistributive approach' as one having a logic 'akin to the rejection of arbitrariness present in egalitarian theories', but with its scope restricted to deal only 'with benefits and harms that are causally related' (2004: 50). Bell argues that this approach should be rejected because 'We should not focus on the distribution of the benefits and burdens resulting from particular actions (or sets of actions)', but should instead 'focus on the overall distribution of benefits and burdens' (2010: 437). I claim that we should reject the resource-specific redistributive BPP for a similar reason: because we should focus on the overall pattern of benefits and burdens derived from use of the Earth's resources, rather than any one resource in isolation.

9.4 Conclusion

I have argued that, unfortunately for proponents of HED or the BPP, one cannot look in isolation at mere inequalities in consumption of climate sink capacity, or the resulting distribution of burdens and benefits, and claim to be able to identify injustice in human interactions with this resource. To be clear, this does not mean that duties of rectification cannot be grounded in acts of GHG emission. As I said in §9.2.2, it seems clear that those who have avoidably continued to exploit fossil fuels, emit GHGs, and deplete forests when they knew, or should have known, that they were contributing to a significant environmental problem are both morally culpable and significantly accountable for dealing with the resulting impacts—along with those who have sought to obstruct action on climate change, and political agents that have failed in their duties to promote fair and effective climate policies.

What I have rejected, however, is the notion that historical climate debts can be identified by retroactively deploying some supposed fair shares principle for historical consumption of the climate sink, or the benefits thereof. This notion thus cannot be used to support the core climate debt claim that certain wealthy or industrialized parties owe duties of rectification—duties grounded in historical wrongdoing—to some of those suffering from the impacts of climate change. I am nevertheless confident that the climate debt claim can be vindicated by various other means. For one thing, I believe this claim may be substantiated from a wider perspective; one that considers broader historical patterns of natural resource use, by reference to a more comprehensive theory of justice for the Earth's resources. This is the task that I embark on in the next, penultimate, chapter.

10

The Significance of Historical Injustice Concerning Natural Resources

In Chapter Nine I began my discussion of theories of climate debt, which I took to be characterized by the core claim that many wealthy or industrialized parties possess duties to address the unavoided impacts of climate change that are rectificatory in nature, owed as a result of historical injustices. I considered and rejected one way that reasoning about natural resource justice has been deployed in defence of the climate debt claim: what I termed *the Historical Emissions Debt view* (HED). HED might seem attractive in that it attempts to ground climate debts in an historical injustice that can be clearly identified, quantified, and monetized (namely, historical overuse of climate sink capacity). According to the theory of natural resource justice defended in this work, however, HED cannot provide an accurate account of historical responsibility for climate change.

In this chapter, I develop an alternative defence of the climate debt claim, via a broader discussion of how historical wrongdoing concerning natural resources could be relevant to climate justice. Closely examining climate change as a problem of global justice, I argue that theorists should ask why some groups are more *vulnerable* to climate impacts than others; and, in particular, to what extent unequal vulnerability could be a result of historical injustice (§10.1). Given the subject of this work, I focus on historical injustice concerning natural resources and, more specifically, colonial resource exploitation as a significant instance of such injustice (§10.2). I argue that legacies of colonial resource exploitation are likely to be a significant contributor to present-day vulnerability in countries that have since gained formal independence (§10.3). Such legacies have important implications for our understanding of climate vulnerability (§10.4.1). They also render some climate duties rectificatory in nature, thus supporting the climate debt claim and vindicating the strong thesis of historical accountability, by showing that some parties have duties to address the unavoided impacts of climate change that are: A) rectificatory in nature; and B) owed due to activities dating back over a significant period of time (more specifically, activities involving the unjust use of natural resources) (§10.4.2). Finally, I argue that by recognizing climate change's historical roots in natural resource injustice, we can learn important lessons about how similar wrongs could be perpetrated through climate policies (§10.4.3).

I conclude that there is good reason to think that historical injustices concerning natural resources have made a significant contribution to the problem of climate change; and that they must be recognized and rectified if we are to address this problem fairly (§10.5). These injustices can be identified, and rectification attempted, without the level of precision that HED aspires to. But fully understanding and rectifying these wrongs will not be a straightforward task. As a problem of global justice, climate change has a more complex history than HED might be taken to imply.

10.1 Climate change as a problem of global justice

As explained in Chapter Nine, proponents of HED attempt to construe some obligations to assist those subjected to unavoided climate impacts as duties of rectification for historical wrongdoing; specifically, the wrong of consuming more than a fair share of climate sink capacity. This enables HED to support what some claim to be a 'common normative belief...that bearing an appropriate share of the global climate response burden is a matter of rectificatory justice, of "making amends", rather than behaving beneficently to disadvantaged states or seeking to realize a preferred global pattern of resource distribution' (Page 2012: 307).

However, theorists face a problem in rendering HED complete because although they attribute debts to agents that are *causally* implicated in climate change (debts being said to accrue to those who emit more than a certain amount), they face a significant challenge in explaining why we should take *merely* emitting beyond a certain amount to constitute wrongdoing.[1] But without wrongdoing in the picture, it is hard to support the claim that rectificatory duties are in play. In this chapter I argue that on a better understanding of climate change as a problem of global justice, historical wrongdoing certainly is a big part of the picture—one just needs to look elsewhere to see this.

---

[1] Of course, emitting beyond a certain amount *could* constitute wrongdoing if the emitter *knows* (or should have known) that they thereby contribute (avoidably) to climate change, because then faulty intentions may be identified—but this is not the claim that HED makes. HED locates wrongdoing in the supposed excessiveness of the emissions *themselves*, not the intentions of the emitter.

10.1.1 *Disaster risk: exposure and vulnerability*

To think carefully about historical responsibility for climate change, it is first important to try to better comprehend the nature of climate change as a problem of global justice. Stephen Gardiner suggests that one of the key features characterizing this problem is that of *'skewed vulnerabilities'* (2011a: 119). He refers here to how those who have emitted the most tend to be least at risk of climate impacts, whilst those who have emitted the least face the greatest threat from climate change. HED picks up on one dimension of this skewed risk, by examining the normative implications of unequal emissions. I submit that there is something to learn by looking at things from the other direction, examining more closely the phenomenon of unequal risk.

One can better understand *why* climate change places some human beings at greater risk of disaster than others by drawing on the IPCC's Special Report on Managing the Risks of Extreme Events and Disasters (IPCC 2012). Roughly speaking, the IPCC understands a disaster to be an adverse impact which 'produce[s] widespread damage and cause[s] severe alterations in the normal functioning of communities or societies' (IPCC 2012: 4). What the special report highlights is that the risk of such disaster emerges not from the threat of climate events alone, but from 'the interaction of weather or climate events, the physical contributors to disaster risk, with exposure and vulnerability, the contributors to risk from the human side' (IPCC 2012: ix). I will follow the IPCC in referring to climate events as the *physical* determinants of disaster risk, and vulnerability and exposure as the *social* determinants. This is somewhat misleading, since climate events are also socially determined insofar as they derive from anthropogenic activities (of GHG emission and sink depletion); and because vulnerability and exposure will have physical contributors and manifestations. But provided this is borne in mind, the distinction should prove a helpful one.

The first social contributor to disaster risk—exposure—describes the extent to which a given element (e.g. a population, its livelihood, or other assets) is present in a place that could be adversely affected by climate events. The second—vulnerability—'refers to the propensity of exposed elements ... to suffer adverse effects when impacted by hazard events'. Exposure is a *necessary determinant* of disaster risk; if a population or system is not exposed to climate events, then it is not at risk of climate disaster. Exposure is not, however, a *sufficient* determinant of disaster risk. This is because it is possible to be exposed to climate events but not vulnerable—for example, by being located in a floodplain but having the capacity to deploy defences that will prevent a climate change-induced flood from creating significant losses (IPCC 2012: 69).

Vulnerability is thus a very important driver of disaster risk, but one that is often overlooked in discussions about climate change and historical responsibility. When theorists focus only on determining who can be taken to have emitted (or benefited) beyond their fair share of GHGs, for example, they effectively restrict their concern to the question of who should be held responsible for the *physical* determinant of disaster risk (the physical determinant, recall, being the climate events to which GHG emissions have causally contributed). But as the IPCC explains, 'climate change is not a risk per se'. Rather, the risk to which communities are subject arises from the interaction of climate changes with vulnerability and exposure (IPCC 2014a: 1050). So why not also consider historical responsibility for these necessary *social* determinants of disaster risk—and in particular, for vulnerability?

10.1.2 *Vulnerability and responsibility*

I have been trying to make it more apparent that climate change, as a problem of *global justice*, is not just a problem of climate events, but also of the underlying social situations that those climate events interact with. HED looks to the historical consumption of climate sink capacity in an attempt to assign some moral responsibility for the *physical* drivers of climate change. I will instead be looking at use and control of natural resources more broadly, in an attempt to assign moral responsibility for some of the *social* drivers that make climate change such a challenging problem of global justice.

One potential reason why many theorists do not attend to the question of who should be held responsible for the vulnerability component of disaster risk is that this propensity to suffer adverse effects derives from a very complex set of influences. Whilst the anthropogenic drivers of climate events are relatively easy to identify—namely, human activities that lead to increased atmospheric concentrations of GHGs, such as deforestation and the burning of fossil fuels—vulnerability is 'a result of diverse historical, social, economic, political, cultural, institutional, natural resource, and environmental conditions and processes' (IPCC 2012: 32). Several factors can, however, be singled out as major contributors to vulnerability.

High vulnerability, the IPCC suggests, is 'mainly an outcome of skewed development processes, including those associated with environmental mismanagement, demographic changes, rapid and unplanned urbanization, and the scarcity of livelihood options for the poor'. Other contributing factors identified are 'poverty, and the lack of social networks and social support mechanisms' and 'global processes' including 'international financial pressures, increases in socioeconomic inequalities, trends and failures in governance (e.g., corruption, mismanagement), and environmental degradation' (IPCC 2012: 70–1). Vulnerability can also result from land tenure arrangements that create insecurity, or that leave certain groups marginalized (IPCC 2012: 306; 2014d: 1051).

It will be impossible to explain *precisely* why any given human community is characterized by factors that render it more or less vulnerable in the face of climate events. This presents a challenge for determining which parties should be held responsible for the fact that climate change poses much greater risk to some communities than others. Nonetheless, I will argue that any adequate explanation of the social inequalities that engender the uneven distribution of vulnerability to climate change must acknowledge that numerous historical injustices have played a role in creating this state of affairs, including significant injustices concerning natural resources.

10.2 Historical injustice and natural resources

In order to make progress towards understanding who might be held responsible for the fact that some human populations are particularly vulnerable to climate change, it seems that we must explain why it is that some communities are burdened by problems of underdevelopment; environmental degradation and mismanagement; poverty, inequality, and scarcity of livelihood options; institutional weakness and failed governance; vulnerability to international financial pressures; or land tenure arrangements that engender insecurity and marginalization. Such explanations will take work and will necessarily differ for each community. But we can be certain that various historical injustices will play a role in these accounts.

World history is significantly characterized by injustices including war, imperialism, colonialism, exploitation, and slavery; all of which have helped to bring us to our present circumstances. Each of these forms of injustice will have played a role in rendering some communities particularly vulnerable to climate events; for example, through legacies of environmental degradation, failed governance, or poverty and inequality. Attempting to more fully comprehend these wrongs and their enduring significance is a vast undertaking that must be steered by those who bear the weight of these legacies. In what follows, I attempt to make some contribution to this discussion, by examining a set of injustices that align with the subject of this work: injustices concerning natural resources.

I have defended two principles of natural resource justice:

1. The Basic Needs Principle (BN): The system of natural resource rights must grant every human being the entitlements over natural resources that are necessary for satisfying their basic needs.

2. The Principle of Collective Self-Determination (SD): The system of natural resource rights must grant every political community the entitlements over natural resources that are necessary for engaging in the legitimate exercise of collective self-determination.

These principles identify natural resource injustice as taking two central forms: first, use of natural resources that prevents others from satisfying their basic needs; and second, use of natural resources that prevents political communities from engaging in the legitimate exercise of self-determination. The first form of natural resource injustice will be the most important to address, given the priority of BN. Such injustice could involve damaging, destroying, or blocking access to natural resources that individuals require for basic needs satisfaction. The second form of natural resource injustice could involve a community being denied sufficient control over natural resources to exercise the internal aspect of self-determination (whether by external powers or their own government); a people being physically excluded from the land where it had been engaged in the legitimate exercise of self-determination; or a people being placed at such disadvantage by international inequalities that they are no longer able to realize the value of their territory as a site of self-determination.

To give some more specific examples: Individuals, companies, and collectives commit an injustice when they prevent others from satisfying their basic needs by damaging the natural resources on which those others depend—for example, by pollution, the dumping of waste or destructive acts of war. Injustices are perpetrated through the expropriation of land and natural resources that others are (justifiably) using in order to satisfy their basic needs or exercise self-determination, say through forced displacement or the withdrawal of resource units against the will of the people. Injustice takes place when members of a political community are thwarted in their satisfaction of basic needs, and barred from the exercise of self-determination, because they are prevented from exercising control over the land on which they live, and the natural resources that surround them—as takes place under colonialism or authoritarian rule. And natural resources are used unjustly by those who ensure that access to them is determined in accordance with the international resource privilege—the unjust global rule, introduced in §6.3.1, that undermines collective self-determination by engendering the problems associated with the resource curse.

How natural resource injustice might be rectified will vary from case to case. In some instances, return or restoration of the natural resources in question will be possible; in other cases, matters of reparation will be much more difficult to resolve. It seems clear, however, both that human history is replete with violations of natural resource entitlements, and that sincere attempts at rectification are rare. To simplify the discussion that follows, I will narrow my focus by looking at one significant form of historical injustice concerning natural resources in more depth, with the goal of showing that the ongoing failure to rectify this injustice constitutes part of the problem of climate change.

The example in question is that of colonial resource exploitation. This choice should not be taken to imply that colonialism is the only instance of historical injustice in natural resource use that holds contemporary significance, or that this is a form of injustice that has been successfully resigned to the past. Nor should it be taken to suggest that the wrong of colonialism can be reduced to the violation of natural resource entitlements. Colonialism is a vast wrong that encompasses, in Aimé Césaire's words (2000: 42–3):

> force, brutality, cruelty, sadism, conflict...forced labor, intimidation...theft, rape...relations of domination and submission...'thingification'...societies drained of their essence, cultures trampled underfoot, institutions undermined, lands confiscated, religions smashed, magnificent artistic creations destroyed, extraordinary *possibilities* wiped out...millions of men torn from their gods, their land, their habits, their life...millions of men in whom fear has been cunningly instilled, who have been taught to have an inferiority complex, to tremble, kneel, despair...natural *economies* that have been disrupted...food crops destroyed, malnutrition permanently introduced, agricultural development oriented solely toward the benefit of the metropolitan countries;...the looting of products, the looting of raw materials.

Wrongful confiscation of land, unjust interference with local land-use, and the looting of raw materials are thus only some aspects of colonialism.[2] Nevertheless, the widespread and long-standing practice of using and controlling land and other natural resources in ways that thwart the basic needs satisfaction and self-determination of colonized communities makes colonialism a very important example of injustice concerning natural resources. In other words, whilst injustices concerning natural resources are but one element of colonial wrongdoing, colonial resource exploitation is a very significant form that natural resource injustice has taken throughout history. In §10.3, I will identify ways in which such wrongdoing may have contributed to present-day climate vulnerability.

10.3 Climate change and colonialism

The suggestion that colonialism holds relevance for climate justice is not novel. It is a particularly common theme in the emerging field that Kyle Whyte (2017b) terms *Indigenous Climate Change Studies*, but also recurs in the broader philosophical literature. Henry Shue, for example, suggested in a

---

[2] Although a significant aspect, insofar as the drive to amass natural resources was a motivating factor for other atrocities. Frantz Fanon suggests that: 'Deportation, massacres, forced labor, and slavery were the primary methods *used by capitalism to increase its gold and diamond reserves*, and establish its wealth and power' (2004: 57; emphasis added).

1992 paper that 'colonial exploitation' may have contributed to what he terms the 'background injustice' of the climate negotiations. As Shue notes, poverty can make parties vulnerable both to climate events and to political manipulation. Many poorer countries do not have the resources to cope with even moderate levels of climate change, leaving them in such desperate need of *some* international agreement on climate action that they might have no alternative than to concede to 'unconscionable terms' (Shue 2014: 38–9). Insofar as colonial exploitation has engendered such poverty and vulnerability, it has therefore also helped to place certain parties at an unfair disadvantage in the climate negotiations. Gardiner—referencing Shue—similarly suggests that 'the history of colonialism' may have contributed to the serious injustice of the present world system; injustice that will undermine fair climate governance by enabling the powerful to take 'further advantage of those already exploited under the current structure' (Gardiner 2011a: 119).[3]

Another theorist who suggests that colonialism has contributed to the problem of climate change is Robert Melchior Figueroa, who also uses the terminology of *background injustice*. Focusing on indigenous peoples in particular, Figueroa argues that colonial practices and their legacies—including 'resource exploitation, relocation, land appropriation... persistent economic exploitation... historical under-representation in environmental decision making', gross distributive inequities and struggles over self-determination—'capture the causal roots of precisely why indigenous groups are the most vulnerable and impacted by climate change' (2011: 235–6).[4] More recently, Whyte has argued that 'The same colonial practices and policies that opened up Indigenous territories for deforestation and extractive industries are the ones that make adaptation difficult for Indigenous peoples today' (2017b: 156–7). This means that for many indigenous peoples, climate change is less a new phenomenon than a continuation of the same environmental change that has long been imposed upon them through colonialism (see also Whyte 2017a).

Despite these suggestions, however, the causal contribution of colonialism to the problem of climate change—and the present moral significance of such contribution—remains underexplored in the philosophical literature on climate justice and responsibility.[5] Shue may provide some explanation of this

---

[3] Gardiner claims that our present circumstances of global injustice are also a result of 'currently pronounced global poverty and inequality, and the role of rich nations in structuring existing transnational institutions' (2011a: 119)—factors that seem difficult to separate from colonialism.

[4] Support for Figueroa's claims can be found in the latest IPCC report, where it is noted that indigenous communities in North America are vulnerable in part because 'The legacy of their colonial history' has stripped them 'of land and many sources of social and human capital' (IPCC 2014b: 1471).

[5] Whyte similarly suggests that: 'While ongoing, cyclical colonialism is a major issue taken up by the Indigenous climate justice movement, it is rarely considered in the governmental and academic literatures that can be and often are used to understand Indigenous vulnerability to climate change and justice' (2017a: 97).

lacuna when he offers his own reasons for not pursuing the matter further: though the vulnerability of some parties to the climate negotiations is clearly enhanced by factors such as poverty, the extent to which such poverty results from colonialism depends on what Shue takes to be 'important but intractable debates about causal mechanisms' (2014: 41). The causal mechanism in the case of GHG emissions, on the other hand, is much harder to dispute: historical contributions to increased atmospheric concentration of GHGs—and, therefore, to the physical drivers of climate risk—can be identified and quantified relatively easily. This could be a major reason why many discussions of historical responsibility for the problem of climate change focus on the contribution of past emissions rather than injustices such as colonialism.

Nevertheless, as Shue also points out, 'causal responsibility does not translate smoothly into moral responsibility' (2014: 41, fn.11). It could therefore be the case, so far as climate change is concerned, that though a charge of *causal* responsibility may be made more easily with respect to past emissions, a charge of some form of *moral* responsibility could be on stronger ground in instances where it can be shown that clear historical wrongs are causally implicated in this problem. If colonialism has contributed to present-day vulnerabilities to climate change, then there is a case to be made that some of the moral responsibility for this problem falls to the perpetrators of colonial injustice. Furthermore, one might then be able to show that some present-day parties possess duties of rectification for colonial injustice that are owed to those who have been left vulnerable. In other words, this might provide one way of supporting the core climate debt claim that certain wealthy or industrialized parties possess duties to combat climate change that are rectificatory in nature, owed as a result of historical injustices.

In the rest of this section I try to show that colonialism has indeed contributed to climate vulnerability. I start by narrowing my focus further, to cases in which previously colonized groups have now gained formal independence as sovereign nations. I then examine some of the lasting effects of histories of colonial resource exploitation. Finally, I explain how such legacies are likely to have contributed to climate vulnerability.

10.3.1 *Different forms of colonialism*

As Avery Kolers notes, 'It would be a mistake to think that there is a single phenomenon—"European Colonialism," "imperialism," etc.—that is the same thing always and everywhere, from 16th-century Peru to 19th-century Oklahoma to 21st-century Queensland' (2017: 738). Colonialism has taken varied forms throughout history. In some cases, local communities were completely devastated; in others, they were displaced and dispossessed, or exploited as a source of labour. In places like North America, Australia, and

New Zealand, colonizers settled in the territory and attempted to set up political institutions resembling those of Europe; elsewhere, very little settlement occurred and colonies were essentially exploited as a source of income, wealth, and natural resources.

This latter form of economic colonialism took place across 'much of Africa, Central America, the Caribbean, and South Asia' (Acemoglu 2003: 29), where colonial powers established what Daron Acemoglu, Simon Johnson, and James Robinson term *'extractive institutions'*. They refer here to 'bad and dysfunctional institutions' designed to allow one group to extract resources 'at the expense of the rest of the society' (Acemoglu, Johnson, and Robinson 2006: 21). In extractive colonial states, the main purpose of such institutions was of course to exploit the resources of the colonized region for the benefit of the metropole, the so-called 'resources' in question including not only natural resources such as precious minerals, but also *people*.

My focus in what follows will be economic colonialism rather than settler colonialism. More specifically, I will be restricting my attention to cases of economic colonialism that are historical in the sense that there has since been a formal withdrawal of colonial power, with the previously colonized population gaining independence as an internationally recognized sovereign nation (what I will refer to as a 'post-independence country'). My discussion will concern the contemporary significance of the unjust exploitation of natural resources that took place during these historical periods of formal, economic colonialism.

The reason I focus on these cases is *not* because they are the most relevant to the problem of climate change. As others have made clear, many non-state indigenous peoples have been—and remain—subjected to colonial (or neo-colonial) resource policies and practices, in ways that hold great significance for climate justice (see, for example, Goldtooth 2004; Whyte 2017a). The question of climate justice for indigenous peoples should in fact be deemed particularly pressing due to the nature of the losses that indigenous peoples are threatened with, and indigenous peoples' significant marginalization in international climate negotiations.[6] Considerations of justice for indigenous peoples also hold important lessons for our thinking about climate justice more broadly. As will become clear, my discussion of climate justice concerning post-independence countries has been greatly informed by work by and about indigenous peoples.

The reason I do not include indigenous peoples and settler colonialism in the discussion that follows is that I here retain a focus on the relationship between climate change and *historical* injustice, and therefore need a way to

---

[6] On this, see, for example, the Anchorage Declaration 2009; Figueroa 2011; Heyward 2014; Tsosie 2007a.

individuate between injustices that can or cannot be taken as consigned to the past in some sense. In the case of post-independence countries, colonial resource policies are an injustice that can—in some sense at least—be understood as historical; in that there has been a formal end to colonialism in the countries in question (though this is not to say that newly independent countries have not continued to be subject to international relations and resource policies that may accurately be described as *neo*-colonial in nature).[7] In the case of indigenous peoples for whom colonialism was never formally (let alone actually) ended, the question of the relationship between climate change and colonial resource exploitation is more complicated. I am not able to do justice to this matter here, so will instead focus my argument on post-independence countries.[8] My discussion can be read as an attempt to pick up where Shue left off, by addressing the question of whether prior colonial relationships between parties to the UNFCCC negotiations—between France and Haiti, the Netherlands and Indonesia, or Britain and Jamaica, say—shape the climate claims and duties that those nations possess (see Shue 2014: 41).

10.3.2 *Legacies of colonial resource exploitation*

There are numerous reasons to think that historical practices of colonial resource exploitation will have a continuing and pernicious legacy in many post-independence countries. Powers of self-determination, once devastated or suppressed, are not easily realized even when formally protected by international law;[9] and various colonial or neo-colonial policies will have made the exercise of this collective capacity even more difficult for newly independent peoples.

One problem is that of path dependence, which refers to how institutions established by colonial powers are likely to be structured in ways that are difficult for previously colonized peoples to alter. Frantz Fanon suggests that a colonial preoccupation with the extraction of natural resources will have contributed to this problem. Colonial powers, insofar as they were interested solely in extracting certain resources from the region, made no attempt to investigate whether the local population could support itself by alternative economic means—through use of renewable resources such as the rivers and

---

[7] See Nkrumah 1965.

[8] A further complication that I cannot address adequately here is that problems of climate justice for indigenous peoples obviously arise in post-independence countries also. As Bonita Lawrence notes, indigenous peoples in postcolonial states and those in settler states will confront some common injustices (for example, both are likely to find their lands 'targeted as a source of exploitable resources'). Other of their struggles, however, will be distinct and unique to their particular circumstances (Lawrence 2010: 512–13).

[9] The UN Declaration on the Granting of Independence to Colonial Countries and Peoples only dates back to 1960.

sun, for example. This means that 'the young independent nation is obliged to keep the economic channels established by the colonial regime', and to continue supporting the economy by exporting raw resources: 'The colonial regime has hammered its channels into place and the risk of not maintaining them would be catastrophic' (Fanon 2004: 56–7).

Acemoglu, Johnson, and Robinson also suggest that path dependence is likely to be strong in countries where colonizers set up or took over extractive institutions. In general, very few constraints were placed on political power in these extractive colonies. Rather, colonizers intentionally created 'authoritarian and absolutist states with the purpose of solidifying their control and facilitating the extraction of resources' (Acemoglu, Johnson, and Robinson 2001: 1375), placing 'a high concentration of political power in the hands of a few who extracted resources from the rest of the population' (Acemoglu, Johnson, and Robinson 2002: 1264). Such institutions will tend to have significant staying power because even after independence, elites in extractive societies—who can benefit by using the state's power to expropriate from the people—will have much to lose from a change in governance, and may therefore resist any attempts at reform. Quoting Crawford Young, Acemoglu, Johnson, and Robinson suggest that the supposedly 'new states' that emerged on independence were often really 'successors to the colonial regime, inheriting its structures, its quotidian routines and practices, and its more hidden normative theories of governance' (Acemoglu, Johnson, and Robinson 2001: 1376; quoting C. Young 1994: 283).

Significantly in the context of climate change, Acemoglu, Johnson, and Robinson claim that the most serious long-term economic effects of extractive colonial institutions result from the role that they played during the Industrial Revolution. Elites in extractive states had a reason to block industrialization due to fears that it would undermine their position of power (Acemoglu, Johnson, and Robinson 2002: 1273). Thus, while colonial powers 'sowed the seeds of underdevelopment in many diverse corners of the world by imposing, or further strengthening existing, extractive institutions' (Acemoglu and Robinson 2012: 250), they also—through those same institutions—contributed to current global inequalities by ensuring that some, but not others, were able to take advantage of the Industrial Revolution (Acemoglu and Robinson 2012: 271). This suggests that even if—as I have argued—gross disparity in GHG emissions across countries is not unjust *in itself*, this disparity does appear to be a symptom of an underlying injustice.

Colonialism thereby 'not only explains why industrialization passed by large parts of the world but also encapsulates how economic development may sometimes feed on, and even create, the underdevelopment in some other part of the domestic or the world economy' (Acemoglu and Robinson 2012: 273). Colonial resource exploitation will not only have negatively impacted local groups in absolute material terms—through environmental degradation and the imposition of problematic land tenure arrangements, for example—but also in relative terms. In relative terms, colonial rule served to create severe underdevelopment and economic disadvantage locally, whilst enriching the metropole. Colonial policies of resource exploitation thereby engendered significant global inequalities of wealth and power. As Fanon puts it (2004: 53–8):

> European opulence is literally a scandal for it was built on the backs of slaves, it fed on the blood of slaves, and owes its very existence to the soil and subsoil of the underdeveloped world...The wealth of the imperialist nations is also our wealth...In concrete terms Europe has been bloated out of all proportions by the gold and raw materials from such colonial countries as Latin America, China, and Africa. Today Europe's tower of opulence faces these continents, for centuries the point of departure of their shipments of diamonds, oil, silk and cotton, timber, and exotic produce to this very same Europe. Europe is literally the creation of the Third World. The riches which are choking it are those plundered from under-developed peoples.

These material inequalities would be difficult to counter even after independence since, as Daniel Butt points out, 'it is hard to acquire alternative entitlements once one has been unjustly deprived of large quantities of one's natural resources and/or is at a competitive trading disadvantage relative to other nations' (2009a: 113). This difficulty was reinforced by the global order that emerged from imperialism; one dominated by rich and powerful agents, where unjust inequalities could be sustained and enhanced. Today, the global order continues to be governed by structures that were 'developed on the terms of the affluent states, and shaped in their interests' (Butt 2009b: 171), and the same Western powers that were responsible for colonialism have been able to mould international law 'so as to secure and legitimate...advantages which were often improperly obtained' (Butt 2009b: 163–4). These global structures help to explain why it remains the case that 'some of the poorest countries in the world are former colonies of some of the richest' (Butt 2012: 230).[10]

Rules concerning resource concessions provide one example of the way in which external interference has served to undermine local control over land and resources post-independence. Armstrong explains that a key goal for newly independent countries was to be able to cancel resource concessions that had been granted to foreign investors by colonial powers and, crucially, to decide what compensation would be owed for such cancellation. The hope was that newfound control over territorial resources would provide a means of

---

[10] Acemoglu, Johnson, and Robinson take economic data to suggest that colonialism created a 'reversal of fortune', in the sense that 'Among countries colonized by European powers during the past 500 years, those that were relatively rich in 1500 are now relatively poor' (2002: 1231).

reducing global economic inequalities. However, powers including France and Britain insisted on maintaining many resource concessions, claiming that they retained legal force despite being signed by colonial powers. Colonial powers also ensured that international law would determine appropriate compensation in the event of resource concessions being cancelled—not newly independent countries. Contemporary rules regarding resource concessions continue to place serious constraints on the self-determination of the post-independence countries that are party to them (Armstrong 2017: 166–7).

The international resource privilege is another example of an international rule that has served as a barrier to self-determination in post-independence countries (the focus of critiques by Thomas Pogge (2008: 119–21, 168–72) and Leif Wenar (2008; 2016)). This rule exacerbates the already challenging task of establishing meaningful forms of self-determination following colonial rule, by creating ongoing barriers to local jurisdiction over territorial resources. The international resource privilege has already been discussed in §6.3.1, so I will not go over it in much detail here except to note that Wenar explicitly suggests it is very plausibly viewed as 'a holdover from an earlier era of expansive sovereignty and colonial rule' (2008: 14). By upholding the international resource privilege, powerful and wealthy countries help to ensure that elites who succeed in capturing extractive colonial institutions after independence can cement their power and exploit a territory's resources at the expense of local self-determination.

The resource privilege is a clear illustration of the way in which the global system of natural resource governance remains—to a large extent—an exploitative system, reminiscent of earlier periods of colonialism. This is a system in which various structures (including laws, incentives, and markets) serve to ensure that the rich and powerful can access and control the resources that they want, whilst disadvantaged collectives are often unable to make decisions about the very resources on which they live and depend—or to resist displacement, destruction, and expropriation. There is ample reason to think, then, that many post-independence countries remain burdened by the pernicious legacies of historical practices of colonial resource exploitation.

10.3.3 *Colonial legacies and present-day vulnerability*

Section 10.3.2 hopefully makes clear that there are many ways in which histories of colonial resource exploitation will be causally implicated in present-day climate vulnerability. Colonial resource policies plausibly have continuing legacies including environmental degradation and mismanagement resulting from the overexploitation of land and natural resources; persisting land tenure arrangements that breed marginalization and insecurity; self-determination struggles, institutional weakness, authoritarian governance and elite capture; underdevelopment; enduring problems of poverty, social inequality and lack of diversity in livelihood options; and vulnerability to global economic and political pressures in an international order structured by rich and powerful (and often ex-colonizing) states.

Drawing on empirical data, J. Timmons Roberts and Bradley Parks reach a similar conclusion. Referring in particular to cases where colonial powers structured economies around the 'extraction of raw materials', they argue that 'many of the most important causal forces driving hydrometeorological risk—from declining terms of trade and deteriorating infrastructure to degraded natural environments and weak and corrupted political institutions—are a *direct consequence* of extractive colonial legacies' (Roberts & Parks 2007: 104–5; emphasis added). Elsewhere, they draw on three case studies to argue that 'The "root causes" of climate disasters lie in colonial histories and current relations with the global economy that keep these nations vulnerable' (Parks & Roberts 2006: 351). Jon Barnett and John Campbell likewise conclude that colonialism has served to increase vulnerability in Pacific Island communities through land-use policies that reduced agricultural diversity, introduced less resistant crops, and replaced land that was used for local food production with commercial agriculture (Barnett & Campbell 2010: 34–5).[11]

Thus, whilst historical GHG emissions are an undeniably significant contributor to the problem of climate change (being, as they are, the major anthropogenic cause of physical climate events), it is important not to overlook the fact that colonial histories of resource exploitation are also causally implicated in this problem. Colonialism has helped to create a world characterized by severe inequalities in vulnerability to climate events (and, thus, disaster risk), and in doing so it has also helped to make climate change a particularly significant problem of global justice. In cases where the risks to which colonial resource exploitation has contributed are realized in actual disasters, both historical emissions and colonial practices will have some share of causal responsibility for the resulting harms.

Against this historical background, climate change appears less like a totally new problem, and more like an enhancement of pre-existing, unrectified, or ongoing injustices, many of which derive from the same historical system of control over the natural world that created such high and unequal rates of fossil fuel exploitation and GHG emission in the first place. Thus, as Whyte points out in discussion of climate justice for indigenous peoples, it would be a mistake to take the view that 'Climate change impacts are like new problems that exacerbate old problems...(e.g. colonialism) [that] are themselves

---

[11] In this case, furthermore, colonial powers (and missionaries) also helped to increase climate *exposure*, by encouraging communities—many of which had traditionally been situated inland, on higher ground—to settle in coastal villages (Barnett & Campbell 2010: 35).

unrelated to climate change' (2017a: 99). Our present circumstances may be notable in that the threats resulting from global patterns of natural resource exploitation have become, fairly quickly, unprecedented in scope and magnitude. However, many of the underlying vulnerabilities that the physical phenomenon of climate change interacts with in producing harm have been present for far longer, and derive from similar practices of exploiting natural resources at the expense of important human interests. Taking this view, global climate change appears as a new and particularly aggressive symptom of a much older form of injustice.

10.4 Present normative significance

The picture of causal responsibility for climate disasters that emerges from §10.3 is a complicated one. When communities are subject to climate impacts, it appears that causal responsibility for this harm will be shared not only between those who engaged in activities (such as deforestation and the burning of fossil fuels) that enhanced atmospheric concentrations of GHGs, but also those who contributed to that community's vulnerability and exposure to climate events. This latter category will include both domestic and international agents and, in many cases (as I argued in §10.3), colonial powers.

The moral significance of such causal responsibility nevertheless remains to be determined. For a start, the relative causal efficacy of any given factor that has contributed to climate risk will be difficult to determine. Then, we must note again that 'causal responsibility does not translate smoothly into moral responsibility' (Shue 2014: 41, fn.11). For example, some of those causally implicated in climate risk may not be morally culpable (for example, individuals and collectives that have contributed to exposure through faultless decisions to form settlements in coastal areas). On the other hand, some of those morally culpable may not have an obvious causal link to climate harms (for example, political actors that have failed to do enough to tackle the problem, and those who have undermined climate action through political lobbying and misinformation campaigns).

To add further complication, both causal and moral responsibility for climate risk may fail to ground any present liabilities to bear the costs of climate adaptation or compensation for loss and damage. Those whom we judge to be morally or causally responsible may turn out to no longer be alive, or there may be reasons to excuse them from bearing the costs (because they are now impoverished, for example). The problem of how to attribute responsibility for the emissions of those no longer alive is sometimes addressed by appealing to a beneficiary pays principle (BPP), but on the current—more complex— picture it is not clear which beneficiaries we would even assign liability to:

how would we share costs between the beneficiaries of GHG emissions, defor-estation, fossil fuel extraction and sale, misinformation campaigns, political inaction, or colonial practices and other activities that contribute to vulner-ability and exposure?[12]

In this section I will argue that despite this complexity, there are at least three ways in which histories of colonial resource exploitation can be seen to have significance for climate justice. First, they are important for our under-standing of climate vulnerability; second, and relatedly, they suggest that certain parties possess duties towards the vulnerable that are rectificatory in nature, owed as a result of colonial injustice; and finally, they reveal patterns of resource injustice that could be perpetuated by future climate policies.

10.4.1 Understanding vulnerability

In §10.3, I argued that there are various ways in which histories of colonial resource exploitation will be causally implicated in the current vulnerability of some human communities to climate change. In this section I draw on literature about climate vulnerability in indigenous communities, to highlight two reasons why it is important to recognize when vulnerability in post-independence countries is a result of colonial injustice.

First, efforts to reduce vulnerability may backfire if its underlying causes are misidentified. Discussing Inuit vulnerability to climate change, Emilie Cam-eron objects that it is a failing for research identifying 'rapid social, cultural, political, and economic change over the past decades' as important contribu-tors, not to 'explicitly name these changes as tied to colonialism' (2012: 109). This failing can result in vulnerability being framed 'as a matter of enhancing *local capacities*, rather than attending to the structural and systemic processes by which those capacities are continually undermined' (Cameron 2012: 110). For post-independence countries also, if external influences or unrectified legacies of colonial exploitation are the problem, then seeking to reduce vulnerability by enhancing internal capacities may be suboptimal or even counterproductive. As Leon Sealey-Huggins argues with respect to Caribbean societies, though vulnerability here 'has geophysical dimensions, it is largely

---

[12] Shue notes that the problem of complexity also plagues approaches like HED and the BPP, citing H P Young's argument that: 'not only did producers benefit from unregulated past emissions, so did consumers and investors...For example, the rents to oil-producing countries over the past half-century would surely have been less if CO_2 emissions had been taxed or restricted during the period. Indeed, the entire economic order has been based on a regime of free CO_2 disposal. The accumulated benefits and blame are both so widely diffused that *past emissions are not a reliable measure of cumulative liability. In fact, the true extent of each country's liability is probably impossible to estimate*' (Young 1990: 8; emphasis added; cited in Shue 2014: 41, fn.11). Even if we take a narrow view, then—focusing only on historical responsibility for climate events but not exposure or vulnerability—the focus on emissions is deceptive in its simplicity.

structured by unequal social relations which are imperialist in character' (2017: 10). Insofar as they fail to acknowledge this, ahistorical responses to vulnerability will be undermined because they misidentify the cause of the problem.

Second, such misidentification may constitute disrespect towards the community in question. This point has again been made forcefully in the case of indigenous peoples. As Whyte notes, for many indigenous peoples 'the concept of societies having to adapt constantly to environmental change is not new' and the suggestion that indigenous peoples are more vulnerable to climate change because their way of life is somehow 'more' dependent on the environment than others is problematic (2017a: 89, 98). Richard Howitt et al. make a similar point. Describing colonization and marginalization as slower, underlying, 'unnatural disasters' that wreak havoc in indigenous communities, they argue that a just and sustainable response to climate change 'requires acknowledgement that the outcome of natural disasters is often mediated by the unnatural disaster of colonial and post-colonial state policies and practices' (Howitt et al. 2012: 48). When parties fail to acknowledge this, they appear to 'blame the victim' by suggesting that 'the problem rests in the inherent vulnerabilities and lack of capacity of indigenous people and their culture' (Howitt et al. 2012: 57). The same concerns apply in the case of post-independence countries that are vulnerable partly due to histories of colonial resource exploitation. If vulnerability is a result of the legacies of colonialism, it seems not just misleading but disrespectful to suggest that it is instead a problem inhering in the community.

10.4.2 *The nature of climate duties*

In §10.4.1, I suggested that one reason why colonial histories of resource exploitation have current normative significance is that they have contributed to present-day climate vulnerability. One might add that insofar as injustice *has* produced vulnerability, this situation should be rectified by those responsible for repairing the injustice. Thus, histories of colonial resource injustice also have normative significance because they suggest that some present-day parties may owe duties of rectification, to post-independence countries that have been left more vulnerable to climate change by the legacies of such wrongs.

A failure to rectify such injustice would then constitute part of the reason why some countries retain a high level of vulnerability to climate impacts. Those in possession of such rectificatory duties would be the perpetrators of colonial injustice, or others appropriately related to the perpetrators—who are likely, in many cases, to be presently wealthy states, individuals, or corporations. Thus, this would offer a way to support a claim of climate debt and, with it, the strong thesis of historical accountability for climate change: a way to show that various wealthy or industrialized parties do indeed possess duties to combat climate change (duties to address the colonial legacies that leave some communities more vulnerable) that are *rectificatory* in nature, owed due to colonial histories of natural resource injustice *dating back over a significant period of time*.

One way to support this idea would be to draw on an illustrative model proposed by Butt (2013: §61.3). Butt asks us to imagine a case in which one nation—let us call it Nation *E*—commits an environmental injustice against another—call it Nation *S*—and refuses to honour the duties of rectification that it rightfully owes. One hundred and fifty years down the line, *S* is still suffering from the effects of this environmental injustice, though *E* is no longer benefiting. Current members of *E* claim that they do not have duties to rectify the original injustice because it resulted from the actions of a past generation.

Butt argues that *E* can still be held to have duties of rectification if three assumptions hold: 1) that 'the failure to rectify an injustice for which one is responsible itself constitutes an act of injustice'; 2) that nations can be held collectively responsible for the actions of their political leaders; and 3) that the identity of a nation persists despite changes to its membership over time, through overlapping generations. Then, it appears that 'responsibility for failing to rectify injustice can persist across time, even after everyone who was responsible for the original action has died' (Butt 2013: 768–9). This is because, by (2), the original generation can be held collectively responsible for the initial environmental injustice and duty-bound to rectify it. By (1), their failure to rectify this injustice is itself an act of injustice. And because of (3), this unjust failure to rectify is an injustice that will persist through time, despite changes in national membership, with each ensuing generation of citizens implicated in the injustice of the continued refusal to rectify, as time goes on. Thus, though later generations cannot be held responsible for the original unjust *act*, they *can* be held responsible for the ongoing failure to rectify it: 'Insofar as a self-governing community continues to fail to rectify the unjust effects of its polluting acts, it acts unjustly across time. This implicates new entrants into the political community in an ongoing environmental injustice' (Butt 2013: 770).

Now, as Butt acknowledges, this model is not very well suited to considering historical GHG emissions, because 'the extent to which historical emissions can be seen as examples of wrongful pollution is highly debatable, given the claim that our knowledge of the effects of these emissions is a relatively recent development' (2013: 770–1). This relates to the problem I identified in Chapter Nine—of the difficulty of explaining how high consumption of climate sink capacity is wrongful *in itself*. The inadequacy of his model is further exacerbated by the fact that even when emissions *can* be deemed wrongful (say because the excusable ignorance defence does not hold), it may be impossible to link the wrongful emissions of one country to any particular environmental damages in another. This is because the effect of any one country's emissions is filtered through the increase in atmospheric concentration of GHGs that it contributes to, with the climate impacts that result attributable to this overall increase—and not directly to any one country's emissions.

This model *can* be adapted, however, to support a claim of rectificatory duties stemming from colonialism. Imagine, then, that the environmental injustice originally committed against S by E is that of colonial resource exploitation. E colonizes S in order to exploit S's natural resources, using extractive and oppressive institutions to control the land in a way that prevents the people of S from exercising self-determination, ensuring that resource benefits flow out of S and into E. Over this period, the resources of S are subject to overuse and the environment is degraded. When this colonial period formally ends, E withdraws but does not rectify the injustice that it has committed. Years down the line, S continues to suffer from the legacies of colonial practices of resource exploitation. These legacies now make a significant contribution to S's vulnerability to climate change. What should we say about this situation?

If Butt is correct, then the generation of E responsible for these colonial practices owed a duty of rectification to S. The failure to make good on this duty itself constitutes an act of injustice, and this injustice will pass down along each generation of E that fails to rectify. Furthermore, one might add, rather than appearing to be superseded in any way (see Waldron 1992), the injustice of failing to rectify perhaps seems to become exacerbated as time goes on. Not only will S struggle to overcome the original injustice in the absence of any efforts at rectification, but now S is presented with the challenge of adapting to climate change alongside these other legacies. If it were not for these legacies, S would be significantly less vulnerable to climate events; and if these legacies were to be rectified, then we can presume that S's vulnerability would be significantly reduced. If S suffers greater climate disaster because of E's failure to rectify the injustice, it appears that some responsibility for this must fall to E.[13] This alters the moral terrain of the climate change problem in

---

[13] Valentini formulates a similar argument, but focused on *natural* disasters rather than anthropogenic climate disasters. Comparing the assistance offered to Haiti, Japan, and New Zealand in the wake of earthquakes, she argues that: 'while the latter are appropriately seen as recipients of international charity, Haiti is primarily owed justice due to outsiders' contribution to its plight'. The contributions that she cites include French colonialism, interference by international lenders, and US occupation; all of which helped to place Haiti in such a vulnerable position that 'part of the devastating impact of the [Haitian] earthquake is the result of injustice carried out by outsiders, not by nature itself'. Against this background, some of the international

a significant way. It suggests that in various cases, wealthier countries are not just refusing to aid more vulnerable ones; rather, they are withholding rectification that is owed from pre-existing colonial relationships, in a way that grows increasingly harmful for post-independence countries and thus, it might seem, increasingly unjust.[14]

I have used Butt's account of rectificatory duties in order to demonstrate how some duties owed to the climate vulnerable may be rectificatory in nature, owed as a result of past colonial resource exploitation. However, I do not mean to commit myself to this account of rectificatory justice. There have been numerous attempts to show that reparations of some form are owed for colonialism. If Butt's account fails, then one might instead defend duties of rectification by appeal to other grounds.[15] My aim here is not to defend a specific account of rectificatory justice, but rather to show how the reparations question is relevant to the current problem of climate change and therefore demands more consideration in this context.

My hope is that this also provides one way of explaining why the climate debt claim is correct in stating that various wealthy or industrialized parties possess duties to combat climate change that are rectificatory in nature. I have only offered a small part of that picture here, since there are many other injustices that I have not addressed, but which will have contributed to the vulnerability of human communities and thus the disaster risk that they are subject to in a climate-changed world. These injustices will include slavery, war, occupation, political interference, and other forms of domination and exploitation, both historical and ongoing. Such unjust contributions to vulnerability will work in tandem with unjust contributions to exposure and climate events to produce disaster risk. On the exposure side, this will implicate those responsible for practices such as forced containment or displacement of human communities to areas more exposed to weather events.

---

relief offered to Haiti can be viewed not as charity, but as 'a tardy and inevitably suboptimal attempt to give its people what they are owed' (Valentini 2013: 500–1). Clearly, the same could be said when *anthropogenic* climate disasters hit countries that, like Haiti, have been made more vulnerable by the unjust interference of outsiders. The difference is that in this case, duties of rectification will be possessed not only by those who culpably contributed to vulnerability, but also those who culpably contributed to the anthropogenic climate events.

[14] Shue gives the example of France and Haiti to support a claim along these lines (2014: 37): 'we have lots of good reasons to think that the existing international distributions of wealth and resources are morally arbitrary at best and the result of systematic exploitation at worst. Insofar as the existing distribution is unjust toward, say, Haiti, it may turn out that some of Haiti's "own" resources are elsewhere (for example, in France)'. If this is the case, then some of the resources that Haiti should be entitled to use in support of its adaptation to climate change are being unjustly withheld, with Haiti left more vulnerable as a result.

[15] Butt himself presents this overlapping generations account as complementary to a beneficiary pays approach (2013); and has elsewhere defended reparations on grounds of a duty to return misappropriated property (2009a: Ch. 5). For other defences of rectificatory duties see, for example: Fanon 2004: 52–62; Shiffrin 2009; Simmons 1995; Thompson 1990.

On the climate events side, this will implicate individuals, collectives, and corporations that have avoidably continued to exploit fossil fuels, emit GHGs, and engage in deforestation when they knew, or should have known, that they were thereby contributing to a significant environmental problem. A full account of moral responsibility for climate change—and a full accounting of climate debt—will have to attend to these injustices also.

The approach that I am proposing faces some of the same challenges as the historical emissions debt view, in that both accounts must explain how duties to rectify historical injustices can persist through time. HED has an easier task in explaining how historical emissions are causally relevant to the problem of climate change, but a harder time in explaining why consuming a certain amount of climate sink capacity should *on its own* be deemed a historical injustice in the first place. My broader approach to climate debt instead focuses on historical acts that are irrefutably unjust, but faces a more challenging task in explaining precisely how they have causally contributed to climate risk. In addition, whilst HED promises to provide a measure of historical responsibility for climate change that can be relatively easily attributed to different countries, quantified, and then used to divide up climate costs; the picture that I am trying to paint suggests that moral responsibility for climate change is far more diffuse and difficult to apportion.

Thus, even where we can conclude that certain historical injustices have causally contributed to disaster risk, it will likely be difficult to use this conclusion to determine exactly who should bear which costs of responding to that risk. Though I have highlighted an important means of identifying parties who bear a special responsibility to address the climate vulnerability of certain others (namely, those who bear duties of rectification towards the climate vulnerable due to prior colonial relationships), this does not resolve the question of precisely what is owed by those parties. A fully principled allocation of costs appears to depend on difficult determinations of causal responsibility and moral culpability from multiple sources. Furthermore, the content of any rectificatory duties is not something that can be determined in the abstract, but is rather an issue that must be addressed on a case-by-case basis, crucially involving input from those to whom rectification is owed.

It is also important to be clear about what this link between climate change and historical injustice does not show. I certainly do not intend to imply that the legacies of historical injustices should only be rectified if they are now contributing to the problem of climate change, nor do I intend to suggest that factors rendering communities vulnerable should only be addressed if they are the result of historical injustice. The climate problem demands urgent action, and given that identifying and acting on climate debts could take time, the best that we may be able to do in the interim is assign the costs of adaptation and loss and damage roughly on the basis of ability to pay. Ability to pay is a good pragmatic option, but also an option for which my account provides some support, since it suggests that the wealth of many presently advantaged parties both derives from and instantiates injustice. As Simon Caney suggests, 'past histories of the overuse of the natural world' are relevant in part because they prevent 'the advantaged (whose current holdings came about in an unjust way)' from claiming that they are justly entitled to their superior resources (2006a: 478). Instead, these resources should be redistributed to help the poorer and more vulnerable, who are likely to be the very same communities that are burdened by the legacies of our world's many historical injustices.

10.4.3 *Lessons for the future*

The third reason for thinking that histories of colonial resource exploitation have present normative significance can again be illustrated using a two-country model like Butt's. Without assuming any specific theory of rectificatory justice, let us suppose that E does indeed owe reparations to S but is refusing to make good on this duty. This leaves S in a more vulnerable position than it otherwise would be, since the rectification owed would help to alleviate the legacies of colonial resource exploitation that S continues to be burdened with.

Now imagine that in addition to this, E exploits S's position of disadvantage and weaker bargaining power to press for a climate change agreement that benefits E at the expense of S. As Shue suggests, we might describe this as a case of *compound injustice*: 'when an initial injustice paves the way for a second' (2014: 4). One form of such injustice takes place, Shue thinks, when some parties 'press for the acceptance of internally unjust agreements using bargaining strength that results from background injustice against the very other parties now being pressed' (2014: 38). He gives the explicit example of 'when colonial exploitation weakens the colonized nation to such an extent that the colonizer can impose unequal treaties upon it even after it gains independence' (Shue 2014: 4). The ability to inflict such compound injustice clearly creates a further incentive for E to refuse to rectify the original injustice committed against S, so that E can retain its position of dominance in their interactions.

One might also imagine a case in which an actor—E or another party—exploits S's position of disadvantage in order to promote climate policies that threaten to engender, or enhance, injustice in control over and access to the natural world. Imagine, for example, that a state or corporation exploits S's position to push for climate policies that undermine S's control over its land and resources, perhaps by facilitating and incentivizing arbitrary outside interference in decisions regarding their use. In such cases, it might appear that we have a situation in which climate policies are being used to *perpetuate* patterns of injustice concerning the world's natural resources.

This is a pertinent worry because, as W. Neil Adger states, though 'climate change is a significant challenge to structures of governance at all temporal and spatial scales', this is particularly so 'in the area of managing natural resources' (2001: 921). One thing that the international climate negotiations will do, in effect, is create new patterns of control over the world's resources: most obviously the global climate sink, but also fossil fuels, land, water, and various other natural resources that might be used in carbon trading schemes or the production of renewable energy. The worry I am getting at, then, is that if the legacies of historical injustice concerning natural resources are not addressed, the climate regime threatens to become a way by which problematic patterns of control over resources can be perpetuated or enhanced, with parties that occupy a position of dominance in virtue of past injustices further expanding their control over the Earth's resources at the expense of the vulnerable.

The potential for natural resource injustices to be perpetuated should create concerns about what Matthew Paterson has described as 'the marketization of climate governance' (2011: 617). Paterson gestures here to Peter Newell's discussion of the marketization of environmental governance more generally (see Newell 2008), what Newell refers to as 'an ensemble of strategies of market governance including practices of privatisation and commodification of natural resources which derive from a common belief in the ability of markets to provide the public good of environmental protection in the most efficient way' (Newell 2005: 189). In the climate change case, Paterson suggests, such marketization can be observed in the 'major trend in the international climate regime . . . towards the organization of climate governance through the creation of markets in rights to emit GHGs' (2011: 615) and can be explained by the ability of such markets to 'create concentrated, immediate benefits for powerful actors' (2011: 619).

There are several reasons for concern here. Firstly, some might worry that such marketization constitutes increasing commodification of nature and a victory for those who want to privilege an economic understanding of the value of natural resources at the expense of reasonable alternative worldviews.[16] Secondly, one might worry that market solutions are likely to favour parties that are already unjustly advantaged unless designed and regulated

---

[16] See The Hague Declaration (2000: II.9), where indigenous peoples express great concern that 'the measures to mitigate climate change currently being negotiated are based on a worldview of territory that reduces forests, lands, seas and sacred sites to only their carbon absorption capacity. This world view and its practices adversely affect the lives of Indigenous Peoples and violate our fundamental rights and liberties, particularly, our right to recuperate, maintain, control and administer our territories'.

with great care. As Simon Caney and Cameron Hepburn note: 'In general, market systems have a tendency at best to perpetuate existing distributions of wealth, and at worst to exacerbate wealth differences between rich and poor' (Caney & Hepburn 2011: 223). Global carbon pricing, for example, threatens to exacerbate existing inequalities of control over the global climate sink, creating a system of governance in which 'Rich and poor states could not possibly participate on fair and equal terms since the former could draw on their superior financial resources to emit far more greenhouse gas than the latter' (Page 2013: 243).

Thirdly, and relatedly, marketization may have significant negative effects for local communities. Creating new, economic value in the natural resources on which communities depend will not necessarily benefit those communities in a world where access to natural resources tends to be determined by wealth and power, and where many poorer communities still struggle to ensure that their resource claims are given adequate respect due, for example, to insecure land tenure arrangements and exclusion from environmental decision-making. Here, the creation of economic value threatens to create new vulnerabilities: to exploitation by outside agents—or agents of the state—who may seek to seize those resources and thereby acquire the economic benefits for themselves.

Such concerns are indeed raised by market measures like the Clean Development Mechanism and the UN's REDD+ (Reducing Emissions from Deforestation and Forest Degradation) mitigation scheme, which 'act on the principle of industrialized countries (or those who can pay) offsetting their effluents by investing in the developing world' (Marino & Ribot 2012: 324). These measures are designed to place climate mitigation projects in some of the poorest and most marginalized regions globally, and thus threaten to expose already vulnerable communities to any harmful side effects of such developments. REDD+, for instance, threatens to create a conflict of interest between forest peoples and market actors since, 'To carbon traders . . . an uninhabited forest greatly simplifies the logistical tasks of monitoring and paying for ecosystem services' (Beymer-Farris & Bassett 2012: 340). As explained in Chapter One, some worry that this programme may restrict local access to resources, impinge on traditional resource use, dispossess resident communities, or lead to a problematic recentralization of governance whereby forests are brought under state control, undermining the participation of local communities in decision-making about their environment (see Cotula & Mayers 2009; Phelps et al. 2010). In recognition of these threats, the International Forum of Indigenous Peoples on Climate Change released a statement expressing concerns that (IFIPCC 2007):

REDD will not benefit Indigenous Peoples, but in fact, it will result in more violations of Indigenous Peoples' Rights. It will increase the violation of our

Human Rights, our rights to our lands, territories and resources, steal our land, cause forced evictions, prevent access and threaten indigenous agriculture practices, destroy biodiversity and culture diversity and cause social conflicts. Under REDD, States and Carbon Traders will take more control over our forests.

Similarly, roll out of renewable energy technologies will create new or increased demands for extractive resources. As noted in §8.4, these may include: 'aluminum (including its key constituent, bauxite), cobalt, copper, iron ore, lead, lithium, nickel, manganese, the platinum group of metals, rare earth metals including cadmium, molybdenum, neodymium, and indium— silver, steel, titanium and zinc' (Arrobas et al. 2017: xii). These demands can have severe knock-on effects for those living near such resources, whose interests may be ignored by parties that wish to extract. The spectre of the resource curse also arises here, given that the international resource privilege remains a structuring principle of international trade in natural resources. And on top of this, many renewable energy options require large tracts of land (for, say, hydroelectric dams, bio-energy plantations or solar arrays), creating competition with other land-uses and threatening to displace communities whose land tenure is insecure due to pre-existing injustice.

Again, such worries have already been raised by indigenous writers and activists. Whyte notes that the indigenous climate justice movement has worked to highlight how 'it is hard to claim that "at least" Indigenous peoples would be harmed less if rich, industrialised countries lowered their emissions without dealing with colonialism. For many strategies for lowering emissions impose harms themselves on Indigenous peoples if colonialism is not addressed' (2017a: 97). Whyte gives the example of REDD+, which has displaced indigenous peoples' cultivation of rice in forests in Kenya. Victoria Tauli Corpuz similarly expresses the worry that 'if our rights are not recognized, then we have the potential of being evicted, displaced, suffering more from the impacts not only of climate change but also the solutions like if they are going to build more dams, if they are going to build more biofuels plantations, we are at very great risk from the solutions' (quoted in Ciplet et al. 2015: 192).

Historical injustices concerning natural resources thus also have present normative significance in the sense that they can be compounded, perpetuated, or replicated by contemporary climate policies. If we do not pay attention to history, then we risk overlooking these patterns of injustice. To avoid this problem, the international community must ensure that climate governance is designed to support the self-determination of vulnerable political communities, strengthen their powers of environmental decision-making, and protect their rights over the land and natural resources on which they depend.

10.5 Conclusion

In Chapter Nine, I argued that the core climate debt claim—that many wealthy or industrialized parties possess duties to address the unavoided impacts of climate change that are rectificatory in nature, owed because of historical injustices—cannot be vindicated by the Historical Emissions Debt approach. In this chapter I have suggested that a theory of natural resource justice can yet be deployed in support of the climate debt claim, by showing how clear historical violations of natural resource entitlements have contributed to present-day climate vulnerability. Focusing on the example of past colonial resource exploitation in countries that have since gained formal independence, I gave reason to think that such injustice has indeed contributed to vulnerability; and that insofar as this is the case, this situation should be rectified by those responsible for repairing this injustice. I also outlined the importance of recognizing when climate vulnerability results from injustice: both to avoid misunderstanding and misattribution of the drivers of vulnerability; and to identify cases where such injustice is at risk of being perpetuated or compounded by future climate policies.

In theorizing about climate justice, considerations of background injustice—and the current normative significance of historical violations of natural resource entitlements—are thus, in Shue's words, 'unavoidable'; in the sense that they are considerations 'intrinsic, not extrinsic, to any [climate] negotiations that are not simply going to create new injustices, in some cases compounding old ones' (2014: 44). The problem of historical injustice in the use and control of the Earth's resources is much bigger than the problem of climate change; it has unavoidable relevance insofar as it causally contributes to present-day vulnerability; and acknowledging and addressing this background is vital if we are to ensure that climate policies do not perpetuate such injustice in the future.

11

Conclusion: Natural Resource Justice and Climate Change

Climate change is commonly recognized as a global environmental problem that prompts questions concerning the fair use, sharing, and protection of various natural resources. In this work, I have argued that it is important and productive to consider climate change from the perspective of natural resource justice, but that in adopting this approach we should ensure that our judgments about climate change are drawn carefully, from a defensible background theory of resource rights.

In Chapter Two, I argued that the most prominent natural resources argument within the field of climate justice—the atmospheric commons argument for the equal per capita emissions view (EPC)—fails on this front. Theorists putting forward this argument misidentify the global common resource responsible for assimilating anthropogenic greenhouse gas (GHG) emissions; it is the global climate sink (encompassing the atmosphere, ocean, soils and vegetation) that assimilates our emissions, not the atmosphere alone. Proponents of this argument also fail to provide an adequate defence of the principle of equal shares that they apply to this resource.

Some claim it is simply obvious that each human being has an equal right, or claim, to the atmosphere. Even if this were the case, the principle that EPC theorists actually need to defend—that each human being has an equal claim, or use-right, to the *global climate sink*—is too controversial for such a minimal defence to suffice. The global climate sink is partly constituted by natural resources that fall within existing state borders (forests and soils, for example) and equal use-rights to this resource thus conflict with the principle of resource sovereignty, which some have also claimed to be obviously correct. If EPC theorists intend to assert that resource sovereignty does not apply to the resources constituting the global climate sink, then they need to offer a better defence—and a clarification—of their position (explaining, for example, whether they reject the principle of resource sovereignty outright, or just in this particular instance).

A more principled (but nevertheless flawed) defence of EPC is offered by Steve Vanderheiden (2008a). Although Vanderheiden does draw on a broader theory of natural resource justice to support his position—invoking a principle of equal division for natural resources—he applies this principle in a problematic way. The principle of equal division states that the world's natural resources *taken as a whole* should be distributed on an equal per capita basis, but Vanderheiden restricts the application of this principle to the global climate sink in isolation. If EPC is to be successfully defended using the principle of equal division, then we are owed an explanation of why global climate sink capacity *in particular* must be shared on an equal per capita basis. This defence must hold even though some communities appear to possess territorial claims to more of this resource than others and even though individuals currently enjoy very unequal shares of other natural resources. We are also owed a satisfactory defence of the principle of equal division itself.

Vanderheiden draws his principle of equal division from Charles Beitz's account of natural resource justice (see Beitz 1979). It is not clear, however, that Beitz intended his resource redistribution principle (RRP) to be interpreted as a principle of equal division: his relatively brief discussion of the RRP also appears consistent with a more loosely egalitarian or even sufficientarian reading. Furthermore, the distinctive *method* by which Beitz justifies the RRP—namely, his original position device—is flawed due to Beitz's characterization of the parties as representatives of self-sufficient nations. These complications mean that Vanderheiden cannot straightforwardly derive a principle of equal division from Beitz's work. They also, however, prove that David Miller is wrong to class Beitz along with Hillel Steiner, as a proponent of the global equality of resources view that appears to be undermined by the metric problem (Miller 1999: 319, fn.5).

According to the metric problem, the principle of equal division for natural resources cannot be rendered coherent because there is no defensible measure with which to make natural resource shares commensurate. In Chapter Four I argued that the metric problem does indeed undermine the Equal Division conception of original ownership—according to which the world's resources are originally subject to a principle of equal division—because no metric can be shown to be sufficiently impartial, given reasonable global variation in many factors relevant to determining the value of natural resources. Whilst Miller takes the metric problem to refute global egalitarianism for natural resources, however, I take it to show that Equal Division is simply the wrong way to construe such egalitarianism.

The world's natural resources *are* appropriate objects of egalitarian justice due to their possession of two distinguishing features: natural resources are of fundamental value to everybody, but they exist independently of human beings. Each individual thus has a claim to the world's resources that is—originally—equal to that of everyone else. In Chapter Three I used this premise of Equal Original Claims to assess four conceptions of original world ownership that are commonly identified in Western political philosophy—Joint Ownership, No Ownership, Equal Division, and Common Ownership—and rejected the first two conceptions. If Equal Division is not sufficiently impartial to satisfy Equal Original Claims (as I argue in Chapter Four), this simply suggests that natural resource egalitarianism must be formulated on a Common Ownership basis.

In Chapter Five, I proposed to develop a Common Ownership conception of natural resource egalitarianism by rehabilitating Beitz's original account of natural resource justice. Original position reasoning is an appropriate means by which to elaborate on the Common Ownership view, because it is designed to provide an impartial justification of principles for the acquisition of exclusive rights to natural resources. Although the specific original position used by Beitz should be rejected due to certain problematic assumptions that he incorporated, these features can be fixed—by dropping Beitz's assumption of national self-sufficiency and characterizing the parties as representatives of individuals rather than societies. Once these corrections are made, we end up with a global original position where representatives of *all* human beings debate the assignment of rights to the natural resources of a world like our own. I termed this approach 'Contractualist Common Ownership'.

I used Contractualist Common Ownership's cosmopolitan original position to consider three principles for the assignment of rights to natural resources. In Chapter Five, I started by reconsidering the principle of equal division. Although the Equal Division conception of original ownership had been rejected in Chapter Four (on the basis of the metric problem), my contractualist proposal appeared to open up the possibility that a principle of equal division could be defended on the basis of Common Ownership instead—as an object of agreement for parties in the original position. I argued that the parties would reject the principle of equal division and thus that a cosmopolitan original position cannot be used to provide the impartial defence that this principle requires. In its place, I defended a principle of basic needs. Thus, in this chapter a natural resource principle favoured by many global egalitarians was rejected, and a sufficientarian principle proposed in its place.

I also argued, however, that the basic needs principle in isolation constituted an unacceptably minimal conception of natural resource justice, and that the parties would therefore seek agreement on additional principles for the assignment of natural resource rights. In Chapter Six, I examined the candidate principle of resource sovereignty and showed that it cannot be defended on grounds of responsible stewardship or collective self-determination. The importance of collective self-determination *would* be accepted from a cosmopolitan original position, because this capacity—when properly understood and exercised—is an important means by which to protect individuals from domination. However, when self-determination is given this non-domination defence, it does not appear to support resource sovereignty. The value of collective self-determination instead tells in favour of a merely *presumptive* right of exclusive territorial jurisdiction over natural resources, subject to significant limits. Thus, in this chapter the natural resource principle favoured by statists was rejected, and an alternative principle of collective self-determination was proposed in its place.

I concluded that parties representing equal claimants of natural resources in a hypothetical global contract would choose two principles for the assignment of natural resource rights. In descending lexical priority—reflecting the importance with which parties in the original position would endow them—these are:

1. The Basic Needs Principle (BN): The system of natural resource rights must grant every human being the entitlements over natural resources that are necessary for satisfying their basic needs.

2. The Principle of Collective Self-Determination (SD): The system of natural resource rights must grant every political community the entitlements over natural resources that are necessary for engaging in the legitimate exercise of collective self-determination.

Where the political communities in question are understood in terms of Margaret Moore's non-statist, political conception of a people (see Moore 2015) and the *legitimate* exercise of self-determination does not serve to dominate community members, outsiders, or future generations.

In Chapter Seven, I discussed how the two principles will work in tandem to underwrite a system of *limited territorial jurisdiction* over natural resources. Whilst each people must be granted a *presumptive* right of exclusive territorial jurisdiction over the land and surface resources of a region where they can engage in the legitimate exercise of self-determination, this right will be *limited* in various respects. Though the exact limits of this right will have to be assessed on a case-by-case basis, it is predictable that a people's right of jurisdiction will be: bound to a site of just occupation; supplanted by systems of shared or even global jurisdiction for resources that are also significant to the self-determination of other political communities; restricted by a sustainability requirement; and subject to a sufficientarian and gap-reducing tax on any income extracted from the region's natural resources.

With this conception of natural resource justice in hand, I returned to address the problem of climate change in Chapters Eight to Ten. I first revisited the topic of sharing the global emissions budget and showed how the two principles enable us to take a less atomist approach to this problem, being applicable not only to the question of sharing the budget, but also to the prior matter of setting the atmospheric target—and to other issues of mitigation. With regards to the atmospheric target we should aim, first and foremost, to set the emissions budget at a level that protects the basic needs of current and future individuals; and we must therefore seek to calculate each country's subsistence emissions, and how far and how fast they can be reduced.

If a budget that protects the basic needs of existing individuals does not appear to be compatible with protecting the natural resources that future people will require for their basic needs, then rapid reductions to subsistence emissions will have to be combined with greater efforts to increase carbon sequestration, and implement strong pre-emptive adaptation measures designed to secure basic needs in the future. If respect for basic needs instead leaves us with more than one budget to choose between, the principle of collective self-determination suggests that we should favour mitigation over adaptation (because such measures are easier to implement in a controlled manner) and seek to protect political communities from unpredictable climate impacts—which threaten to displace them from the sites where they engage in the legitimate exercise of self-determination—by adopting a more restricted budget. The estimation and allocation of permissible secondary emissions must be determined by fair international agreement, via negotiations that effectively place use rights to the Earth's climate sink capacity under global jurisdiction. These negotiations must be designed to ensure that disadvantaged collectives are protected from domination—crucially including strong representation for communities with insecure land tenure that live on or near resources that act as climate sinks (such as forest peoples).

In the final two chapters I turned to examine the topic of unavoided impacts, via a discussion of historical responsibility for climate change and the concept of climate debt. A common interpretation of this concept proposes to calculate climate debts based on an historical application of the principle of equal per capita emissions, and thus should be rejected along with EPC. In fact, I argued, the idea that climate debts can be calculated using an historical principle of fair shares for climate sink capacity should be abandoned, because we cannot determine what a fair share of this resource would have been considered in isolation—or what a fair share of its benefits would be now.

I suggested that we instead take a broader perspective on the historical use of natural resources more generally, and that when we do so, we can identify many clear injustices that appear to be implicated in the problem of climate change. Natural resources have been used unjustly throughout history (in ways, that is, which undermine basic needs satisfaction and the practice of self-determination): for example, through imperialism, dispossession, and destruction. Focusing in particular on the example of colonial resource exploitation in countries that have since gained formal independence,

I argued that such historical injustice is likely to have lasting legacies of environmental degradation, poverty, inequality, self-determination struggles, institutional weakness, and disadvantage in global wealth and power structures. These legacies will now form part of the reason why some communities are particularly vulnerable in the face of climate impacts. Insofar as this is the case, those responsible for repairing the original injustice—who are likely to be among the wealthy or industrialized—have duties of rectification towards the vulnerable, thus vindicating a climate debt claim. Recognition that historical injustices will have contributed to climate vulnerability is important: both for understanding vulnerability, and because the international climate negotiations are one avenue via which natural resource injustice may be perpetuated or enhanced in the future.

The theory of natural resource justice formulated in this work is designed to pay adequate consideration to both general and particular claims to the Earth's resources. To this end, the (egalitarian) principle of equal division and the (statist) principle of resource sovereignty were each rejected, and an alternative conception of justice—lying somewhere in between these two extremes—proposed in their place. The principles constituting this conception were given a contractualist justification, designed to respect the Equal Original Claims of all human beings; thus offering a new, relational interpretation of what global egalitarianism amounts to with respect to natural resources.

It is a strength of this relational understanding of natural resource egalitarianism that it offers a way around what Chris Armstrong identifies as three of the most common objections to global egalitarianism. These objections are: first, that global egalitarianism is incompatible with collective self-determination; second, 'that it cannot be achieved without endangering cultural diversity'; and third, 'that articulating and/or implementing principles of equality at the global level simply cannot be done', i.e. the metric problem (Armstrong 2011: 51). I avoid the third objection because I reject the principle of equal division for natural resources. I circumvent the first objection by acknowledging the value of collective self-determination and defending a principle designed to sustain it. This enables me to support the more principled claims to natural resources that statists seek to protect (namely, the claims of political communities to jurisdiction over the land where they engage in the legitimate exercise of self-determination). The principle of self-determination is also designed to protect spheres of collective decision-making in which different cultures—and diverse understandings of the value of natural resources—can be given expression (thus dealing with the second objection). The theory here proposed thus defuses these objections to global egalitarianism for natural resources.

I have offered a (partially) integrated and relatively holist approach to climate justice, in contrast to the atomist-isolationism exemplified by EPC.

225

It is sometimes argued that climate change should be treated as an isolated problem of justice for reasons of simplicity and political feasibility. However, I have shown that by taking a more integrated approach, we can address climate change using a theory of natural resource justice that is applicable to several key challenges: that of setting the atmospheric target, assigning mitigation duties, and determining what is owed to those at risk of unavoided impacts. I have also argued that by taking a broader perspective we can better comprehend how our current circumstances have emerged from a history of injustice in natural resource use; acknowledge that the problem of climate change is enhanced by the persisting effects of these historical wrongs; and recognize that we should take care to ensure that international agreements reached against this problematic background do not serve to compound such injustice.

One of the most important tasks remaining is that of integrating this conception of natural resource justice with a more general theory of global justice, encompassing other important goods, institutions, practices, and relations. Because their application is limited to natural resources, the two principles here defended do not provide a complete picture of a fair world. I maintain, however, that they are an important start—and that it is informative to see how far one can get in reasoning about justice concerning natural resources alone.

Bibliography

Abizadeh, Arash. 2007. 'Cooperation, Pervasive Impact, and Coercion: On the Scope (not Site) of Distributive Justice'. *Philosophy & Public Affairs* 35 (4): 318–58.

Acemoglu, Daron. 2003. 'Root Causes: A historical approach to assessing the role of institutions in economic development'. *Finance & Development*: 40 (2): 27–30.

Acemoglu, Daron, Simon Johnson, & James A. Robinson. 2001. 'The Colonial Origins of Comparative Development: An Empirical Investigation'. *The American Economic Review* 91 (5): 1369–401.

Acemoglu, Daron, Simon Johnson, & James A. Robinson. 2002. 'Reversal of Fortune: Geography and Institutions in the Making of the Modern World Income Distribution'. *The Quarterly Journal of Economics* 117 (4): 1231–94.

Acemoglu, Daron, Simon Johnson, & James Robinson. 2006. 'Understanding Prosperity and Poverty: Geography, Institutions, and the Reversal of Fortune'. In *Understanding Poverty*, edited by Abhijit Vinayak Banerjee, Roland Bénabou, and Dilip Mookherjee, 19–36. Oxford: Oxford University Press.

Acemoglu, Daron, & James A. Robinson. 2012. *Why Nations Fail: the Origins of Power, Prosperity and Poverty*.London: Profile.

Adger, W. Neil. 2001. 'Scales of governance and environmental justice for adaptation and mitigation of climate change'. *Journal of International Development* 13 (7): 921–31.

Agarwal, Anil. 2002. 'A Southern Perspective on Curbing Global Climate Change'. In *Climate Change Policy: A Survey*, edited by Stephen H. Schneider, Armin Rosencranz, & John O. Niles, 375–91. Washington, DC: Island Press.

Agarwal, Anil, & Sunita Narain. 1991. *Global Warming in an Unequal World: A Case of Environmental Colonialism*. New Delhi: Centre for Science and Environment.

Altman, Andrew, & Christopher Heath Wellman. 2009. *A Liberal Theory of International Justice*. Oxford Scholarship Online: Oxford University Press.

Anchorage Declaration. 2009. Indigenous Peoples' Global Summit on Climate Change, April 24. Accessed 27 April 2018. http://unfccc.int/resource/docs/2009/smsn/ngo/168.pdf

Anderson, Elizabeth. 1999. 'What Is the Point of Equality?' *Ethics* 109 (2): 287–337.

Angeli, Oliviero. 2015. *Cosmopolitanism, Self-Determination and Territory*. Palgrave Macmillan.

AOSIS. 2008. Proposal to the AWG-LCA: Multi-Window Mechanism to Address Loss and Damage from Climate Change Impacts. Accessed 27 March 2018. http://unfccc.int/files/kyoto_protocol/application/pdf/aosisinsurance061208.pdf

AOSIS. 2012. Statement by Nauru on behalf of the Alliance of Small Island States At the Opening of the Ad Hoc Working Group on the Durban Platform for Enhanced

Action, November 12, Warsaw. Accessed 3 June 2018. http://aosis.org/wp-content/uploads/2013/11/UNFCCC-Openening-Statement-ADP-Warsaw.pdf

Armstrong, Chris. 2009. 'Coercion, Reciprocity, and Equality Beyond the State'. *Journal of Social Philosophy* 40 (3): 297–316.

Armstrong, Chris. 2010. 'National Self-Determination, Global Equality and Moral Arbitrariness'. *Journal of Political Philosophy* 18 (3): 313–34.

Armstrong, Chris. 2011. 'Shared understandings, collective autonomy, and global equality'. *Ethics & Global Politics* 4 (1): 51–69.

Armstrong, Chris. 2012. *Global Distributive Justice: An Introduction*. Cambridge University Press.

Armstrong, Chris. 2013a. 'Justice and Attachment to Natural Resources'. *Journal of Political Philosophy* 22 (1): 48–65.

Armstrong, Chris. 2013b. 'Sovereign Wealth Funds and Global Justice'. *Ethics & International Affairs* 27 (4): 413–28.

Armstrong, Chris. 2015. 'Against "permanent sovereignty" over natural resources'. *Politics, Philosophy & Economics* 14 (2): 129–51.

Armstrong, Chris. 2016. 'Fairness, Free-Riding and Rainforest Protection'. *Political Theory* 44 (1): 106–30.

Armstrong, Chris. 2017. *Justice and Natural Resources: An Egalitarian Theory*. Oxford: Oxford University Press.

Arneson, Richard. 1989a. 'Liberal egalitarianism and world resources distribution: Two views'. *The Journal of Value Inquiry* 23 (3): 171–90.

Arneson, Richard. 1989b. 'Equality and Equal Opportunity for Welfare'. *Philosophical Studies* 56 (1): 77–93.

Arneson, Richard. 2006. 'Distributive justice and basic capability equality: "good enough" is not good enough'. In *Capabilities Equality: Basic Issues and Problems*, edited by Alexander Kaufman, 17–43. New York: Routledge.

Arrobas, Daniele La Porta, Kirsten Lori Hund, Michael Stephen Mccormick, Jagabanta Ningthoujam, & John Richard Drexhage. 2017. *The Growing Role of Minerals and Metals for a Low Carbon Future*. Washington, D.C.: World Bank Group. Accessed 3 June 2018. http://documents.worldbank.org/curated/en/207371500386458722/The-Growing-Role-of-Minerals-and-Metals-for-a-Low-Carbon-Future

Athanasiou, Tom, & Paul Baer. 2002. *Dead Heat: Global Justice and Global Warming*. New York: Seven Stories Press.

Baatz, Christian, & Konrad Ott. 2017. 'In Defense of Emissions Egalitarianism?' In *Climate Justice and Historical Emissions*, edited by Lukas H Meyer & Pranay Sanklecha, 165–97. Cambridge University Press.

Baer, Paul. 2002. 'Equity, Greenhouse Gas Emissions, and Global Common Resources'. In *Climate Change Policy: A Survey*, edited by Stephen H. Schneider, Armin Rosencranz, & John O. Niles, 393–408. Washington, DC: Island Press.

Baer, Paul. 2010. 'Adaptation to Climate Change: *Who Pays Whom?*' In *Climate Ethics: Essential Readings*, edited by Stephen M. Gardiner, Simon Caney, Dale Jamieson, & Henry Shue, 247–62. New York: Oxford University Press.

Baer, Paul. 2011. 'International Justice'. In *The Oxford Handbook of Climate Change and Society*, edited by John S. Dryzek, Richard B. Norgaard, & David Schlosberg, 323–37. Oxford: Oxford University Press.

Baer, Paul, Tom Athanasiou, Sivan Kartha, & Eric Kemp-Benedict. 2010. 'Greenhouse Development Rights: *A Framework for Climate Protection That Is "More Fair" Than Equal Per Capita Emissions Rights'*. In *Climate Ethics: Essential Readings*, edited by Stephen M. Gardiner, Simon Caney, Dale Jamieson, & Henry Shue, 215–30. New York: Oxford University Press.

Banai, Ayelet. 2013. 'Political Self-Determination and Global Egalitarianism: Towards an Intermediate Position'. *Social Theory & Practice* 39 (1): 45–69.

Banai, Ayelet. 2016. 'Sovereignty over natural resources and its implications for climate justice'. *WIREs Climate Change* 7 (2): 238–50.

Barletti, Juan Pablo Sarmiento, & Anne M Larson. 2017. 'Rights abuse allegations in the context of REDD+ readiness and implementation; A preliminary review and proposal for moving forward'. CIFOR infobrief no. 190. Accessed 12 May 2018. http://www.cifor.org/publications/pdf_files/infobrief/6630-infobrief.pdf

Barnett, Jon, & John Campbell. 2010. *Climate Change and Small Island States: Power, Knowledge and the South Pacific*. London: Earthscan.

Barnett, Jon, & Suraje Dessai. 2002. 'Articles 4.8 and 4.9 of the UNFCCC: adverse effects and the impacts of response measures'. *Climate Policy* 2: 231–9.

Barry, Brian. 1973. *The Liberal Theory of Justice: A critical examination of the principal doctrines in 'A theory of justice' by John Rawls*. Oxford: Clarendon Press.

Barry, Brian. 1980. 'Do Countries Have Moral Obligations? The Case of World Poverty'. *The Tanner Lectures on Human Values*. Delivered at Harvard University, October 27: 27–44.

Barry, Brian. 1989. *Democracy, Power and Justice: Essays in Political Theory*. Oxford: Clarendon Press.

Barry, Brian. 2005. *Why Social Justice Matters*. Cambridge: Polity Press.

Barry, Christian, & Laura Valentini. 2009. 'Egalitarian challenges to global egalitarianism: a critique'. *Review of International Studies* 35 (3): 485–512.

Barry, John. 2008. 'Foreword'. In *Political Theory and Global Climate Change*, edited by Steve Vanderheiden, vii–x. MIT Press Scholarship Online.

Baumert, Kevin A., Timothy Herzog, & Jonathan Pershing. 2005. *Navigating the Numbers: Greenhouse Gas Data and International Climate Policy*. World Resources Institute. Accessed 27 March 2018. http://pdf.wri.org/navigating_numbers.pdf

Beckerman, Wilfred. 1992. 'Economic Growth and the Environment: Whose Growth? Whose Environment?' *World Development* 20 (4): 481–96.

Beckerman, Wilfred, & Joanna Pasek. 1995. 'The equitable international allocation of tradable carbon emission permits'. *Global Environmental Change* 5 (5): 405–13.

Beitz, Charles R. 1979. *Political Theory and International Relations*. Princeton: Princeton University Press.

Beitz, Charles R. 1983. 'Cosmopolitan Ideals and National Sentiment'. *The Journal of Philosophy* 80 (10): 591–600.

Beitz, Charles R. 1999. 'International Liberalism and Distributive Justice: A Survey of Recent Thought'. *World Politics* 51 (2): 269–96.

Beitz, Charles R. 2001. 'Does Global Inequality Matter?' *Metaphilosophy* 32 (1/2): 95–112.

Beitz, Charles R. 2005. 'Reflections'. *Review of International Studies* 31 (2): 409–23.

Bell, Derek. 2010. 'Justice and the politics of climate change'. In *Routledge Handbook of Climate Change and Society*, edited by Constance Lever-Tracy, 423–41. London: Routledge.

Bell, Derek. 2011a. 'Does anthropogenic climate change violate human rights?' *Critical Review of International Social & Political Philosophy* 14 (2): 99–124.

Bell, Derek. 2011b. 'Global Climate Justice, Historic Emissions, and Excusable Ignorance'. *The Monist* 94 (3): 391–411.

Bell, Derek. 2013a. 'Climate change and human rights'. *WIREs Climate Change* 4 (3): 159–70.

Bell, Derek. 2013b. 'How Should We Think about Climate Justice?' *Environmental Ethics* 35 (2): 189–208.

Bertram, Christopher. 2018. *Do States Have the Right to Exclude Immigrants?* Cambridge: Polity Press.

Beymer-Farris, Betsy A., & Thomas J. Bassett. 2012. 'The REDD menace: Resurgent protectionism in Tanzania's mangrove forests'. *Global Environmental Change* 22 (2): 332–41.

Blake, Michael. 2001. 'Distributive Justice, State Coercion, and Autonomy'. *Philosophy & Public Affairs* 30 (3): 257–96.

Blake, Michael, & Mathias Risse. 2007. 'Migration, Territoriality and Culture'. In *New Waves in Applied Ethics*, edited by Jesper Ryberg, Thomas S. Petersen & Clark Wolf, 153–81. Basingstoke: Palgrave Macmillan.

Blake, Michael, & Patrick Taylor Smith. 2015. 'International Distributive Justice'. In *The Stanford Encyclopedia of Philosophy* (Spring Edn.), edited by Edward N. Zalta. Accessed 28 April 2018. https://plato.stanford.edu/archives/spr2015/entries/international-justice/

Blomfield, Megan. 2013. 'Global Common Resources and the Just Distribution of Emission Shares'. *The Journal of Political Philosophy* 21 (3): 283–304.

Blomfield, Megan. 2015. 'Geoengineering in a climate of uncertainty'. In *Climate Change and Justice*, edited by Jeremy Moss, 39–58. Cambridge: Cambridge University Press.

Bookchin, Murray. 1994. 'What Is Communalism? The Democratic Dimension of Anarchism', *Left Green Perspectives* 31. Accessed 6 February 2018. http://social-ecology.org/wp/1994/10/left-green-perspectives-31/

Bovens, Luc. 2011. 'A Lockean defense of grandfathering emission rights'. In *The Ethics of Global Climate Change*, edited by Denis G. Arnold, 124–44. Cambridge: Cambridge University Press.

Brandt, Adam R., Jacob Englander, & Sharad Bharadwaj. 2013. 'The energy efficiency of oil sands extraction: Energy return ratios from 1970 to 2010'. *Energy* 55: 693–702.

Brock, Gillian. 1998. 'Introduction'. In *Necessary Goods: Our Responsibilities to Meet Others' Needs*, edited by Gillian Brock, 1–18. Lanham: Rowman & Littlefield.

Brock, Gillian. 2009. *Global Justice: A Cosmopolitan Account*. Oxford: Oxford University Press.

Brooks, Thom. 2012. 'Climate Change and Negative Duties'. *Politics* 32 (1): 1–9.

Broome, John. 2012. *Climate Matters: Ethics in a warming world*. New York: W W Norton & Company.

Brown, Donald A. 2002. *American Heat: Ethical Problems with the United States' Response to Global Warming*. Maryland: Rowman & Littlefield Publishers.

Brysse, Keynyn, Naomi Oreskes, Jessica O'Reilly, & Michael Oppenheimer. 2013. 'Climate change prediction: Erring on the side of least drama?' *Global Environmental Change* 23 (1): 327–37.

Buchanan, Allen. 2004. *Justice, Legitimacy, and Self-Determination: Moral Foundations for International Law*. Oxford: Oxford University Press.

Buck, Susan J. 1998. *The Global Commons: An Introduction*. London: Earthscan.

Butt, Daniel. 2009a. *Rectifying International Injustice: Principles of Compensation and Restitution Between Nations*. Oxford: Oxford University Press.

Butt, Daniel. 2009b. ' "Victors' justice"? Historic injustice and the legitimacy of international law'. In *Legitimacy, Justice and Public International Law*, edited by Lukas H. Meyer, 163–85. Cambridge: Cambridge University Press.

Butt, Daniel. 2012. 'Repairing Historical Wrongs and the End of Empire'. *Social & Legal Studies* 21 (2): 227–42.

Butt, Daniel. 2013. 'The Polluter Pays? Backward-looking Principles of Intergenerational Justice and the Environment'. In *Spheres of Global Justice*, edited by Jean-Christophe Merle, 757–74. Dordrecht: Springer.

California Public Utilities Commission. 2012. *Decision Adopting Cap-And-Trade Greenhouse Gas Allowance Revenue Allocation Methodology for the Investor-Owned Electric Utilities*. Accessed 13 February 2018. http://docs.cpuc.ca.gov/publisheddocs/pub lished/g000/m040/k631/40631611.pdf

Cameron, Emilie S. 2012. 'Securing Indigenous politics: A critique of the vulnerability and adaptation approach to the human dimensions of climate change in the Canadian Arctic'. *Global Environmental Change* 22: 103–14.

Caney, Simon. 2005a. *Justice Beyond Borders: A Global Political Theory*. Oxford Scholarship Online: Oxford University Press.

Caney, Simon. 2005b. 'Global interdependence and distributive justice'. *Review of International Studies* 31 (2): 389–99.

Caney, Simon. 2005c. 'Cosmopolitan Justice, Responsibility, and Global Climate Change'. *Leiden Journal of International Law* 18 (4): 747–75.

Caney, Simon. 2006a. 'Environmental Degradation, Reparations, and the Moral Significance of History'. *Journal of Social Philosophy* 37 (3): 464–82.

Caney, Simon. 2006b. 'Cosmopolitan Justice and Institutional Design: An Egalitarian Liberal Conception of Global Governance'. *Social Theory & Practice* 32 (4): 725–56.

Caney, Simon. 2008. 'Global Distributive Justice and the State'. *Political Studies* 56 (3): 487–518.

Caney, Simon. 2009. 'Justice and the distribution of greenhouse gas emissions'. *Journal of Global Ethics* 5 (2): 125–46.

Caney, Simon. 2010. 'Climate Change, Human Rights, and Moral Thresholds'. In *Climate Ethics: Essential Readings*, edited by Stephen M. Gardiner, Simon Caney, Dale Jamieson, & Henry Shue, 163–77. New York: Oxford University Press.

Caney, Simon. 2012. 'Just Emissions'. *Philosophy & Public Affairs* 40 (4): 255–300.

Caney, Simon. 2018. 'Climate Change'. In *The Oxford Handbook of Distributive Justice*, edited by Serena Olsaretti, 664–88. Oxford: Oxford University Press.

Caney, Simon, & Cameron Hepburn. 2011. 'Carbon Trading: Unethical, Unjust and Ineffective?' *Royal Institute of Philosophy Supplement* 69: 201–34.

Carbon Tracker. 2013. 'Unburnable Carbon 2013: Wasted capital and stranded assets'. Accessed 11 February 2018. http://carbontracker.live.kiln.it/Unburnable-Carbon-2-Web-Version.pdf

Carens, Joseph H. 1987. 'Aliens and Citizens: The Case for Open Borders'. *The Review of Politics* 49 (2): 251–73.

Casal, Paula. 2007. 'Why Sufficiency Is Not Enough'. *Ethics* 117 (2): 296–326.

Casal, Paula. 2011. 'Global Taxes on Natural Resources'. *Journal of Moral Philosophy* 8 (3): 307–27.

Cassese, Antonio. 1995. *The Self-Determination of Peoples: A Legal Appraisal.* Cambridge: Cambridge University Press.

Césaire, Aimé. 2000. *Discourse on Colonialism.* Trans. Joan Pinkham. New York: NYU Press.

Chile. 1952. Commission on Human Rights, Draft resolution submitted by Chile, April 16. Accessed 6 February 2018. http://www.un.org/ga/search/view_doc.asp?symbol=E/CN.4/L.24

Christman, John. 1994. *The Myth of Property: Toward an Egalitarian Theory of Ownership.* New York: Oxford University Press.

Chung, Ryoa, & Alex Sager. 2005. 'Domination and Destitution in an Unjust World'. *Canadian Journal of Philosophy* 35, Supplementary Volume 31: 311–34.

Ciplet, David, J. Timmons Roberts, & Mizan R. Khan. 2015. *Power in a Warming World: The New Global Politics of Climate Change and the Remaking of Environmental Inequality.* Cambridge, MA: MIT Press.

Cohen, Gerald A. 1989. 'On the Currency of Egalitarian Justice'. *Ethics* 99 (4): 906–44.

Cohen, Gerald A. 1995. *Self-ownership, freedom, and equality.* Cambridge: Cambridge University Press.

Cohen, Gerald A. 2009. *Why Not Socialism?* Princeton: Princeton University Press.

Cohen, Joshua. 1993. 'Moral Pluralism and Political Consensus'. In *The Idea of Democracy*, edited by David Copp, Jean Hampton, & John Roemer, 270–91. Cambridge: Cambridge University Press.

Cohen, Joshua, & Charles Sabel. 2006. 'Extra Rempublicam Nulla Justitia?' *Philosophy & Public Affairs* 34 (2): 147–75.

COICA. 1989. 'Two Agendas on Amazon Development'. *Cultural Survival Quarterly* 13 (4). Accessed 30 January 2018. https://www.culturalsurvival.org/publications/cultural-survival-quarterly/two-agendas-amazon-development

Cotula, Lorenzo, Nat Dyer, & Sonja Vermeulen. 2008. *Fuelling exclusion? The biofuels boom and poor people's access to land.* London: International Institute for Environment & Development.

Cotula, Lorenzo, & James Mayers. 2009. *Tenure in REDD—Start-point or afterthought?* Natural Resource Issues 15. London: International Institute for Environment and Development.

Cripps, Elizabeth. 2011a. 'Where we are now: Climate ethics and future challenges'. *Climate Law* 2 (1): 117–33.

Cripps, Elizabeth. 2011b. 'Climate change, collective harm and legitimate coercion'. *Critical Review of International Social and Political Philosophy* 14 (2): 171–93.

Cultural Survival. 2013. 'Munduruku Leaders Voice Opposition to Belo Monte Dam in Letter', June 18. Accessed 29 April 2018. http://www.culturalsurvival.org/news/munduruku-leaders-voice-opposition-belo-monte-dam-letter#sthash.HFopu5ZF.dpuf

Cunliffe, John. 2000. 'Introduction: Left-libertarianism—Historical Origins'. In *The Origins of Left-Libertarianism: An Anthology of Historical Writings*, edited by Peter Vallentyne & Hillel Steiner, 1–19. Basingstoke: Palgrave.

Daes, Erica-Irene A. 2004. *Final report of the Special Rapporteur on Indigenous peoples' permanent sovereignty over natural resources*. Accessed 6 February 2018. http://ap.ohchr.org/documents/alldocs.aspx?doc_id=9700

DARA. 2012. *Climate Vulnerability Monitor* 2nd Edn. Accessed 29 April 2018. https://daraint.org/wp-content/uploads/2012/09/CVM2ndEd-FrontMatter.pdf

De Bres, Helena. 2012. 'The Many, Not the Few: Pluralism About Global Distributive Justice'. *Journal of Political Philosophy* 20 (3): 314–40.

De-Shalit, Avner. 1996. 'National Self-determination: Political, not Cultural'. *Political Studies* 44 (5): 906–20.

De-Shalit, Avner. 2011. 'Climate Change Refugees, Compensation, and Rectification'. *The Monist* 94 (3): 310–28.

Dolšak, Nives, & Elinor Ostrom. 2003. 'The Challenges of the Commons'. In *The Commons in the New Millennium: Challenges and Adaptations*, edited by Nives Dolšak & Elinor Ostrom, 3–34. Cambridge, MA: MIT Press.

Dow, Kirstin, Frans Berkhout, Benjamin L. Preston, Richard J. T. Klein, Guy Midgley, & M. Rebecca Shaw. 2013. 'Limits to adaptation'. *Nature Climate Change* 3: 305–7.

Doyal, Len, & Ian Gough. 1991. *A Theory of Human Need*. London: Macmillan.

Duus-Otterström, Göran. 2014. 'The problem of past emissions and intergenerational debts'. *Critical Review of International Social & Political Philosophy* 17 (4): 448–69.

Dworkin, Ronald. 1973. 'The Original Position'. *The University of Chicago Law Review* 40 (3): 500–33.

Dworkin, Ronald. 1981a. 'What is Equality? Part 1: Equality of Welfare'. *Philosophy & Public Affairs* 10 (3): 185–246.

Dworkin, Ronald. 1981b. 'What is Equality? Part 2: Equality of Resources'. *Philosophy & Public Affairs* 10 (4): 283–345.

Dworkin, Ronald. 2000. *Sovereign Virtue: The Theory and Practice of Equality*. Cambridge, MA: Harvard University Press.

Earth System Research Laboratory. 2018. 'Trends in Atmospheric Carbon Dioxide'. Accessed 13 February 2018. http://www.esrl.noaa.gov/gmd/ccgg/trends/

Eckersley, Robyn. 2012. 'Moving Forward in the Climate Negotiations: Multilateralism or Minilateralism?' *Global Environmental Politics* 12 (2): 24–42.

EJOLT. 2013. 'Ecological debt'. Accessed 27 March 2018. http://www.ejolt.org/2013/05/ecological-debt/

Fabre, Cécile. 2002. 'Justice, Fairness, and World Ownership'. *Law & Philosophy* 21 (3): 249–73.

Fabre, Cécile. 2005. 'Global Distributive Justice: An Egalitarian Perspective'. *Canadian Journal of Philosophy* 35, Supplementary Volume 31: 139–64.

Fanon, Frantz. 2004. *The Wretched of the Earth*. Trans. Richard Philcox. New York: Grove Press.

Figueroa, Robert Melchior. 2011. 'Indigenous Peoples and Cultural Losses'. In *The Oxford Handbook of Climate Change and Society*, edited by John S. Dryzek, Richard B. Norgaard, & David Schlosberg, 232–47. Oxford: Oxford University Press.

Freeman, Samuel. 2007. *Justice and the Social Contract: Essays on Rawlsian Political Philosophy*. Oxford: Oxford University Press.

Gardiner, Stephen M. 2011a. *A Perfect Moral Storm: The Ethical Tragedy of Climate Change*. Oxford: Oxford University Press.

Gardiner, Stephen M. 2011b. 'Climate Justice'. In *The Oxford Handbook of Climate Change and Society*, edited by John S. Dryzek, Richard B. Norgaard, & David Schlosberg, 309–22. Oxford: Oxford University Press.

Gardiner, Stephen M. & David A. Weisbach. 2016. *Debating Climate Ethics*. Oxford Scholarship Online: Oxford University Press.

Garvey, James. 2008. *The Ethics of Climate Change: Right and Wrong in a Warming World*. London: Continuum.

Gaus, Gerald. 2012. 'Property'. In *The Oxford Handbook of Political Philosophy*, edited by David Estlund, 93–112. Oxford Handbooks Online: Oxford University Press.

George, Henry. 2009. *Progress and Poverty: An Inquiry into the Cause of Industrial Depressions and of Increase of Want with Increase of Wealth; The Remedy*. Cambridge Books Online: Cambridge University Press.

Gilabert, Pablo & Holly Lawford-Smith. 2012. 'Political Feasibility: A Conceptual Exploration'. *Political Studies* 60 (4): 809–25.

Gilbert, Jérémie. 2007. 'Nomadic Territories: A Human Rights Approach to Nomadic Peoples' Land Rights'. *Human Rights Law Review* 7 (4): 681–716.

Glennon, Michael J. 1990. 'Has International Law Failed the Elephant?' *The American Journal of International Law* 84 (1): 1–43.

Global Footprint Network. 2012a. 'Glossary'. Accessed 20 September 2013. http://www.footprintnetwork.org/en/index.php/gfn/page/glossary/

Global Footprint Network. 2012b. 'Ecological Creditors and Debtors'. Accessed 28 February 2014. http://www.footprintnetwork.org/en/index.php/GFN/page/ecological_debtors_and_creditors/

Global Footprint Network. 2017. 'Compare Countries'. Accessed 13 February 2018. http://data.footprintnetwork.org/#/compareCountries?type=BCpc&cn=all&yr=2013

Global Footprint Network. n.d. 'FAQs'. Accessed 3 June 2018. http://www.footprintnetwork.org/faq/

Goeminne, Gert, & Erik Paredis. 2010. 'The concept of ecological debt: some steps towards an enriched sustainability paradigm'. *Environment, Development & Sustainability* 12 (5): 691–712.

Goldtooth, Tom B. K. 2004. 'Stolen Resources: Continuing threats to Indigenous people's sovereignty and survival'. *Race, Poverty & the Environment* 11 (1): 9–12.

Goodman, Amy. 2011. 'On climate change, the message is simple: get it done'. *The Guardian*, 14 December. Accessed 3 June 2018. http://www.theguardian.com/commentisfree/cifamerica/2011/dec/14/durban-climate-change-conference-2011

Gosseries, Axel. 2004. 'Historical Emissions and Free-Riding'. *Ethical Perspectives* 11 (1): 36–60.

Gosseries, Axel. 2005. 'Cosmopolitan Luck Egalitarianism and the Greenhouse Effect'. *Canadian Journal of Philosophy* 35, Supplementary Volume 31: 279–309.

Gosseries, Axel. 2014. 'Nations, Generations and Climate Justice'. *Global Policy* 5 (1): 96–102.

Graeber, David. 2014. 'Why is the world ignoring the revolutionary Kurds in Syria?' *The Guardian*, 8 October. Accessed 11 February 2018. https://www.theguardian.com/commentisfree/2014/oct/08/why-world-ignoring-revolutionary-kurds-syria-isis

Greenpeace. 2016. 'Tar sands'. Accessed 29 April 2018. http://www.greenpeace.org/canada/en/campaigns/Energy/tarsands/

Grubb, Michael. 1990. 'The Greenhouse Effect: Negotiating Targets'. *International Affairs* 66 (1): 67–89.

Grubb, Michael, James Sebenius, Antonio Magalhaes, & Susan Subak. 1992. 'Sharing the Burden'. In *Confronting Climate Change: Risks, Implications and Responses*, edited by Irving M. Mintzer, 305–22. Cambridge: Cambridge University Press.

Hague Declaration. 2000. *The Hague Declaration of the Second International Forum of Indigenous Peoples and Local Communities on Climate Change*. The Hague, November 11–12. Accessed 4 April 2018. www.tebtebba.org/index.php/all-resources/category/80-ipfccc-meetings-2000-2004?download=370:hague-declaration-of-the-second-international-forum-of-indigenous-peoples

Halme, Pia. 2007. 'Carbon debt and the (in)significance of history'. *Trames* 4: 346–65.

Hamlin, Alan, & Zofia Stemplowska. 2012. 'Theory, Ideal Theory and the Theory of Ideals'. *Political Studies Review* 10 (1): 48–62.

Hayward, Tim. 2005a. 'Thomas Pogge's Global Resources Dividend: A Critique and an Alternative'. *Journal of Moral Philosophy* 2 (3): 317–32.

Hayward, Tim. 2005b. *Constitutional Environmental Rights*. Oxford Scholarship Online: Oxford University Press.

Hayward, Tim. 2006. 'Global Justice and the Distribution of Natural Resources'. *Political Studies* 54 (2): 349–69.

Hayward, Tim. 2007. 'Human Rights Versus Emissions Rights: Climate Justice and the Equitable Distribution of Ecological Space'. *Ethics & International Affairs* 21 (4): 431–50.

Hayward, Tim. 2008. 'On the Nature of Our Debt to the Global Poor'. *Journal of Social Philosophy* 39 (1): 1–19.

Hayward, Tim. 2013. 'Ecological space: the concept and its ethical significance'. *JWI Working Paper* 2013/02. Accessed 3 June 2018. http://www.sps.ed.ac.uk/jwi/research/working_papers/tim_hayward,_ecological_space_the_concept_and_its_ethical_significance

Hayward, Tim. 2014. 'Equality and Ecological Space'. *JWI Working Paper* 2014/02. Accessed 3 June 2018. http://www.sps.ed.ac.uk/jwi/research/working_papers/tim_hayward,_equality_and_ecological_space

Heath, Joseph. 2005. 'Rawls on Global Distributive Justice: A Defence'. *Canadian Journal of Philosophy* 35, Supplementary Volume 31: 193–226.

Herzog, Lisa. 2012. 'Ideal and Non-ideal Theory and the Problem of Knowledge'. *Journal of Applied Philosophy* 29 (4): 271–88.

Heyward, Clare. 2014. 'Climate Change as Cultural Injustice'. In *New Waves in Global Justice*, edited by Thom Brooks, 149–69. Basingstoke: Palgrave Macmillan.

HLPE. 2013. *Biofuels and food security*. A report by the High Level Panel of Experts on Food Security and Nutrition of the Committee on World Food Security, Rome. Accessed 31 May 2018. http://www.fao.org/fileadmin/user_upload/hlpe/hlpe_documents/HLPE_Reports/HLPE-Report-5_Biofuels_and_food_security.pdf

Honoré, A. M. 1968. 'Ownership'. In *Oxford Essays in Jurisprudence*, edited by A. G. Guest, 107–47. Oxford: Oxford University Press.

Howitt, Richard, Olga Havnen & Siri Veland. 2012. 'Natural and Unnatural Disasters: Responding with Respect for Indigenous Rights and Knowledges'. *Geographical Research* 50 (1): 47–59.

Humphreys, Stephen (ed.). 2010. *Human Rights and Climate Change*. Cambridge: Cambridge University Press.

Hurrell, Andrew. 2001. 'Global Inequality and International Institutions'. *Metaphilosophy* 32 (1/2): 34–57.

IFIPCC. 2007. 'Statement on reduced emissions from deforestation and forest degradation'. Accessed 12 April 2018. https://www.forestpeoples.org/en/topics/un-framework-convention-climate-change-unfccc/news/2011/05/statement-international-forum-indi

Indigenous Environmental Network. 2015. 'UN promoting potentially genocidal policy at World Climate Summit'. Accessed 28 April 2018. http://www.ienearth.org/un-promoting-potentially-genocidal-policy-at-world-climate-summit/

Indigenous Environmental Network. n.d. 'Tar Sands'. Accessed 29 April 2018. http://www.ienearth.org/what-we-do/tar-sands/

Indigenous Network on Economies and Trade. 2017. *Standing Rock of the North: The Kinder Morgan Trans Mountain Pipeline Expansion Secwepemc Risk Assessment*. Accessed 5 June 2018. https://www.secwepemculecw.org/

Ingram, Attracta. 1994. *A Political Theory of Rights*. Oxford: Clarendon Press.

IPCC. 2007a. *Climate Change 2007: The Physical Science Basis*. Contribution of Working Group I to the Fourth Assessment Report of the Intergovernmental Panel on Climate Change. Edited by S. Solomon, D. Qin, M. Manning, Z. Chen, M. Marquis, K. B. Averyt, M. Tignor, & H. L. Miller. Cambridge, UK & New York, NY: Cambridge University Press.

IPCC. 2007b. *Climate Change 2007: Impacts, Adaptation and Vulnerability*. Contribution of Working Group II to the Fourth Assessment Report of the Intergovernmental Panel on Climate Change. Edited by M. L. Parry, O. F. Canziani, J. P. Palutikof, P. J. van der Linden, & C. E. Hanson. Cambridge, UK & New York, NY: Cambridge University Press.

IPCC. 2007c. *Climate Change 2007: Mitigation*. Contribution of Working Group III to the Fourth Assessment Report of the Intergovernmental Panel on Climate Change. Edited by B. Metz, O. R. Davidson, P. R. Bosch, R. Dave, & L. A. Meyer. Cambridge, UK & New York, NY: Cambridge University Press.

IPCC. 2007d. *Climate Change 2007: Synthesis Report*. Contribution of Working Groups I, II and III to the Fourth Assessment Report of the Intergovernmental Panel on Climate Change. Edited by R. K Pachauri and A. Reisinger. Geneva, Switzerland: IPCC.

IPCC. 2012. *Managing the Risks of Extreme Events and Disasters to Advance Climate Change Adaptation*. A Special Report of Working Groups I and II of the Intergovernmental Panel on Climate Change. Edited by C. B. Field, V. Barros, T. F. Stocker, D. Qin, D. J. Dokken, K. L. Ebi, M. D. Mastrandrea, K. J. Mach, G.-K. Plattner, S. K. Allen, M. Tignor, & P.M. Midgley. Cambridge, UK & New York, NY: Cambridge University Press.

IPCC. 2013. *Climate Change 2013: The Physical Science Basis*. Contribution of Working Group I to the Fifth Assessment Report of the Intergovernmental Panel on Climate Change. Edited by T. F. Stocker, D. Qin, G.-K. Plattner, M. Tignor, S. K. Allen, J. Boschung, A. Nauels, Y. Xia, V. Bex, & P. M. Midgley. Cambridge, UK & New York, NY: Cambridge University Press.

IPCC. 2014a. *Climate Change 2014: Impacts, Adaptation, and Vulnerability. Part A: Global and Sectoral Aspects*. Contribution of Working Group II to the Fifth Assessment Report of the Intergovernmental Panel on Climate Change. Edited by C. B Field, V.R. Barros, D.J. Dokken, K.J. Mach, M.D. Mastrandrea, T.E. Bilir, M. Chatterjee, K.L. Ebi, Y. O. Estrada, R.C. Genova, B. Girma, E.S. Kissel, A.N. Levy, S. MacCracken, P. R. Mastrandrea, & L.L. White. Cambridge, UK & New York, NY: Cambridge University Press.

IPCC. 2014b. *Climate Change 2014: Impacts, Adaptation, and Vulnerability. Part B: Regional Aspects*. Contribution of Working Group II to the Fifth Assessment Report of the Intergovernmental Panel on Climate Change. Edited by V.R. Barros, C. B. Field, D.J. Dokken, M.D. Mastrandrea, K.J. Mach, T.E. Bilir, M. Chatterjee, K.L. Ebi, Y.O. Estrada, R.C. Genova, B. Girma, E.S. Kissel, A.N. Levy, S. MacCracken, P.R. Mastrandrea, & L.L. White. Cambridge, UK & New York, NY: Cambridge University Press.

IPCC. 2014c. *Climate Change 2014: Mitigation of Climate Change*. Contribution of Working Group III to the Fifth Assessment Report of the Intergovernmental Panel on Climate Change. Edited by O. Edenhofer, R. Pichs-Madruga, Y. Sokona, E. Farahani, S. Kadner, K. Seyboth, A. Adler, I. Baum, S. Brunner, P. Eickemeier, B. Kriemann, J. Savolainen, S. Schlömer, C. von Stechow, T. Zwickel, & J.C. Minx. Cambridge, UK & New York, NY: Cambridge University Press.

IPCC. 2014d. *Climate Change 2014: Synthesis Report. Contribution of Working Groups I, II and III to the Fifth Assessment Report of the Intergovernmental Panel on Climate Change*. Core Writing Team, R.K. Pachauri, & L.A. Meyer (eds.). Geneva, Switzerland: IPCC.

James, Aaron. 2005. 'Constructing Justice for Existing Practice: Rawls and the Status Quo'. *Philosophy & Public Affairs* 33 (3): 281–316.

James, Aaron. 2014. 'Political Constructivism'. In *A Companion to Rawls*, edited by Jon Mandle & David A. Reidy, 251–64. Wiley-Blackwell.

Jones, Tim, & Sarah Edwards. 2009. *The Climate Debt Crisis: Why Paying Our Dues is Essential for Tackling Climate Change*. Report by the World Development Movement and Jubilee Debt Campaign. Accessed 3 March 2014. http://wdm.org.uk/sites/default/files/climatedebtcrisis06112009_0.pdf

Kant, Immanuel. 1797. 'The Metaphysics of Morals'. In *Practical Philosophy*, translated and edited by Mary J. Gregor, 353–603. Cambridge: Cambridge University Press, 1996.

Kari-Oca Declaration. 1992. The World Conference of Indigenous Peoples on Territory, Environment and Development, 30 May. Accessed 23 March 2014. http://www. uncsd2012.org/index.php?page=view&nr=892&type=230&menu=39

Kari-Oca 2 Declaration. 2012. Indigenous Peoples Global Conference on Rio+20 and Mother Earth. Accessed 6 February 2018. http://www.ienearth.org/kari-oca-2-declaration/

Kartha, Sivan. 2011. 'Discourses of the Global South'. In *The Oxford Handbook of Climate Change and Society*, edited by John S. Dryzek, Richard B. Norgaard, & David Schlosberg, 504–19. Oxford Scholarship Online: Oxford University Press.

Klein, Naomi. 2009. 'Climate Rage'. *Rolling Stone*, 12 November. Accessed 27 March 2018. http://www.rollingstone.com/politics/news/climate-rage-20091112

Knight, Carl. 2011. 'Climate change and the duties of the disadvantaged: reply to Caney'. *Critical Review of International Social & Political Philosophy* 14 (4): 531–42.

Knight, Carl. 2013. 'What is grandfathering?' *Environmental Politics* 22 (3): 410–27.

Kolers, Avery. 2002. 'The Territorial State in Cosmopolitan Justice'. *Social Theory & Practice* 28 (1): 29–50.

Kolers, Avery. 2009. *Land, Conflict, and Justice: A Political Theory of Territory*. Cambridge: Cambridge University Press.

Kolers, Avery. 2012. 'Justice, Territory and Natural Resources'. *Political Studies* 60 (2): 269–86.

Kolers, Avery. 2017. 'Latin America in Theories of Territorial Rights'. *Revista de Ciencia Política* 37 (3): 737–53.

Laborde, Cécile. 2010. 'Republicanism and Global Justice: A Sketch'. *European Journal of Political Theory* 9 (1): 48–69.

Laborde, Cécile, & Miriam Ronzoni. 2016. 'What is a Free State? Republican Internationalism and Globalisation'. *Political Studies* 64 (2): 279–96.

LaDuke, Winona. 1994. 'Traditional Ecological Knowledge and Environmental Futures'. *Colorado Journal of International Environmental Law and Policy* 5 (1): 127–48.

Lawford-Smith, Holly. 2013. 'Understanding Political Feasibility'. *Journal of Political Philosophy* 21 (3): 243–59.

Lawrence, Bonita. 2010. 'Legislating Identity: Colonialism, Land and Indigenous Legacies'. In *The SAGE Handbook of Identities*, edited by Margaret Wetherell & Chandra Talpade Mohanty, 508–25. SAGE.

Locke, John. 1690. *The Second Treatise of Government*. In *Two Treatises of Government: A Critical Edition with an Introduction and Apparatus Criticus by Peter Laslett*. Revised Edn. Cambridge: Cambridge University Press.

Lovett, Frank. 2010. *A General Theory of Domination and Justice*. Oxford Scholarship Online: Oxford University Press.

Luper-Foy, Steven. 1992. 'Justice and Natural Resources'. *Environmental Values* 1: 47–64.

Mancilla, Alejandra. 2016a. 'Shared Sovereignty over Migratory Natural Resources'. *Res Publica* 22 (1): 21–35.

Mancilla, Alejandra. 2016b. 'Rethinking Land and Natural Resources, and Rights over Them'. *Philosophy & Public Issues* 6 (2): 125–41.

Mandle, Jon. 2006. 'Coercion, Legitimacy, and Equality'. *Social Theory & Practice* 32 (4): 617–25.

Margalit, Avishai, & Joseph Raz. 1990. 'National Self-Determination'. *Journal of Philosophy* 87 (9): 439–61.

Marino, Elizabeth, & Jesse Ribot. 2012. 'Special Issue Introduction: Adding insult to injury: Climate change and the inequities of climate intervention'. *Global Environmental Change* 22 (2): 323–8.

Marshall, Liz, & Zachary Sugg. 2009. *Corn Stover for Ethanol Production: Potential and Pitfalls*. WRI Policy Note 4. Accessed 3 June 2018. http://www.wri.org/sites/default/files/pdf/corn_stover_for_ethanol_production.pdf

Martinez-Alier, Joan. 1993. 'Distributional Obstacles to International Environmental Policy: The Failures at Rio and Prospects after Rio'. *Environmental Values* 2 (2): 97–124.

Martinez-Alier, Joan. 2002. *The Environmentalism of the Poor: A Study of Ecological Conflicts and Valuation*. Cheltenham: Edward Elgar Publishing.

Martinez-Alier, Joan, & Stephen Naron. 2004. 'Ecological Distribution Conflicts and Indicators of Sustainability'. *International Journal of Political Economy*, 34 (1): 13–30.

Matthews, H. Damon. 2016. 'Quantifying historical carbon and climate debts among nations'. *Nature Climate Change* 6: 60–4.

Maúre, G., I. Pinto, M. Ndebele-Murisa, M. Muthige, C. Lennard, G. Nikulin, A. Dosio, & A. Meque. 2018. 'The southern African climate under 1.5°C and 2°C of global warming as simulated by CORDEX regional climate models'. *Environmental Research Letters* 13 (6): 1–9.

Mazor, Joseph. 2010. 'Liberal Justice, Future People, and Natural Resource Conservation'. *Philosophy & Public Affairs* 38 (4): 380–408.

McCarthy, Shawn. 2013. 'Transcanada fires back at U.S. environment regulator'. *The Globe & Mail*, 23 April. Accessed 6 February 2018. http://www.theglobeandmail.com/report-on-business/industry-news/energy-and-resources/transcanada-fires-back-at-us-environment-regulator/article11505541/

McKibben, Bill. 2017. 'Stop swooning over Justin Trudeau. The man is a disaster for the planet'. *The Guardian*, 17 April. Accessed 6 February 2018. https://www.theguardian.com/commentisfree/2017/apr/17/stop-swooning-justin-trudeau-man-disaster-planet

Meckled-Garcia, Saladin. 2008. 'On the Very Idea of Cosmopolitan Justice: Constructivism and International Agency'. *Journal of Political Philosophy* 16 (3): 245–71.

Meyer, Aubrey. 2000. *Contraction & Convergence: The Global Solution to Climate Change*. Totnes: Green Books for the Schumacher Society.

Meyer, Lukas, Pranay Sanklecha, & Alexa Zellentin. 2015. 'Symposium: Intergenerational Justice and Natural Resources: Introduction'. *Moral Philosophy and Politics* 2 (1): 1–5.

Meyer, Lukas H. 2013. 'Why Historical Emissions Should Count'. *Chicago Journal of International Law* 13 (2): 597–614.

Meyer, Lukas H., & Dominic Roser. 2006. 'Distributive Justice and Climate Change. The Allocation of Emission Rights'. *Analyse & Kritik* 28: 223–49.

Meyer, Lukas H., & Dominic Roser. 2010. 'Climate justice and historical emissions'. *Critical Review of International Social & Political Philosophy* 13 (1): 229–53.

Miller, David. 1997. *On Nationality*. Oxford Scholarship Online: Clarendon.

Miller, David. 1999. 'Justice and Global Inequality'. In *Inequality, Globalization, and World Politics*, edited by Andrew Hurrell & Ngaire Woods, 187–210. Oxford Scholarship Online: Oxford University Press.

Miller, David. 2000. *Citizenship and National Identity*. Cambridge: Polity Press.

Miller, David. 2005. 'Defending political autonomy: a discussion of Charles Beitz'. *Review of International Studies* 31 (2): 381–8.

Miller, David. 2007. *National Responsibility and Global Justice*. Oxford Scholarship Online: Oxford University Press.

Miller, David. 2008. 'Global Justice and Climate Change: How Should Responsibilities Be Distributed?' *The Tanner Lectures on Human Values*. Delivered at Tsinghua University, Beijing, 24–5 March: 119–56.

Miller, David. 2011. 'Property and Territory: Locke, Kant, and Steiner'. *Journal of Political Philosophy* 19 (1): 90–109.

Miller, David. 2012. 'Territorial Rights: Concept and Justification'. *Political Studies* 60 (2): 252–68.

Mills, Charles W. 2005. '"Ideal Theory" as Ideology'. *Hypatia* 20 (3): 165–84.

Mills, Charles W. 2015. 'Decolonizing Western Political Philosophy'. *New Political Science* 37 (1): 1–24.

Moellendorf, Darrel. 2002. *Cosmopolitan Justice*. Boulder: Westview Press.

Moellendorf, Darrel. 2006. 'Equal Respect and Global Egalitarianism'. *Social Theory & Practice* 32 (4): 601–16.

Moellendorf, Darrel. 2009. 'World-ownership, self-ownership, and equality in Georgist philosophy'. *International Journal of Social Economics* 36 (4): 473–88.

Moellendorf, Darrel. 2011. 'Common atmospheric ownership and equal emissions entitlements'. In *The Ethics of Global Climate Change*, edited by Denis G. Arnold, 104–23. Cambridge: Cambridge University Press.

Moellendorf, Darrel. 2012. 'Climate change and global justice'. *WIREs Climate Change* 3 (2): 131–43.

Moellendorf, Darrel. 2014. *The Moral Challenge of Dangerous Climate Change: Values, Poverty, and Policy*. Cambridge: Cambridge University Press.

Moore, Margaret. 2006. 'Cosmopolitanism and Political Communities'. *Social Theory & Practice* 32 (4): 627–58.

Moore, Margaret. 2012. 'Natural Resources, Territorial Right, and Global Distributive Justice'. *Political Theory* 40 (1): 84–107.

Moore, Margaret. 2015. *A Political Theory of Territory*. Oxford Scholarship Online: Oxford University Press.

Moss, Jeremy, & Robyn Kath. 2018. 'Historical Emissions and the Carbon Budget'. *Journal of Applied Philosophy*. doi:10.1111/japp.12307

Müller, Benito. 1999. *Justice in Global Warming Negotiations: How to Obtain a Procedurally Fair Compromise*. Oxford Institute for Energy Studies.

Narain, Sunita. 2011. 'From forestry to productive forestry'. *Down to Earth*, 15 June. Accessed 3 June 2018. http://www.downtoearth.org.in/content/forestry-productive-forestry

Navarro, Angelica. 2009. 'Climate debt: The basis of a fair and effective solution for climate change'. Presentation for the AWG-LCA Technical Briefing on Historical Responsibility as a Guide to Future Action to Address Climate Change, 4 June. Accessed 13 February 2018. http://unfccc.int/files/meetings/ad_hoc_working_groups/lca/application/pdf/4_bolivia.pdf

Neumayer, Eric. 2000. 'In defence of historical accountability for greenhouse gas emissions'. *Ecological Economics* 33 (2): 185–92.

Newell, Peter. 2005. 'Towards a political economy of global environmental governance'. In *Handbook of Global Environmental Politics*, edited by P. Dauvergne, 187–201. Edward Elgar.

Newell, Peter. 2008. 'The marketization of global environmental governance: Manifestations and implications'. In *The Crisis of Global Environmental Governance: Towards a New Political Economy of Sustainability*, edited by J. Park, K. Conca, & M. Finger, 77–95. London: Routledge.

Nine, Cara. 2008. 'The Moral Arbitrariness of State Borders: Against Beitz'. *Contemporary Political Theory* 7 (3): 259–79.

Nine, Cara. 2010. 'Ecological Refugees, States Borders, and the Lockean Proviso'. *Journal of Applied Philosophy* 27(4): 359–75.

Nine, Cara. 2012. *Global Justice and Territory*. Oxford Scholarship Online: Oxford University Press.

Nine, Cara. 2013. 'Resource Rights'. *Political Studies* 61 (2): 232–49.

Nine, Cara. 2014. 'When affected interests demand joint self-determination: learning from rivers'. *International Theory* 6 (1): 157–74.

Nkrumah, Kwame. 1965. *Neo-colonialism: the last stage of imperialism*. London: Panaf.

Nozick, Robert. 1974. *Anarchy, State, and Utopia*. Oxford: Blackwell Publishing.

Nussbaum, Martha C. 1992. 'Human Functioning and Social Justice: In Defense of Aristotelian Essentialism'. *Political Theory* 20 (2): 202–46.

O'Neill, John. 1992. 'The Varieties of Intrinsic Value'. *The Monist* 75 (2): 119–37.

O'Neill, Onora. 2000. *Bounds of Justice*. Cambridge Books Online: Cambridge University Press.

Oliver, Joe. 2012. 'An Open Letter from Natural Resources Minister Joe Oliver'. *The Globe & Mail*, 9 January. Accessed 30 January 2018. http://www.theglobeandmail.com/news/national/an-open-letter-from-natural-resources-minister-joe-oliver/article2295599/

OPEC. 1998. OPEC Statement to the 4th Conference of the Parties to the UN Framework Convention on Climate Change by Dr Rilwanu Lukman, OPEC Secretary General. Buenos Aires, November. Accessed 6 February 2018. http://www.opec.org/opec_web/en/press_room/1741.htm

Ostrom, Elinor. 1990. *Governing the Commons: The Evolution of Institutions for Collective Action*. Cambridge: Cambridge University Press.

Ostrom, Elinor, & Edella Schlager. 1992. 'Property-Rights Regimes and Natural Resources: A Conceptual Analysis'. *Land Economics* 68 (3): 249–62.

Otsuka, Michael. 2003. *Libertarianism without Inequality*. Oxford Scholarship Online: Oxford University Press.

Page, Edward A. 2007. 'Intergenerational Justice of What: Welfare, Resources or Capabilities?' *Environmental Politics* 16 (3): 453–69.

Page, Edward A. 2011. 'Climate Justice and the Fair Distribution of Atmospheric Burdens: A Conjunctive Account'. *The Monist* 94 (3): 412–32.

Page, Edward A. 2012. 'Give it up for climate change: a defence of the beneficiary pays principle'. *International Theory* 4 (2): 300–30.

Page, Edward A. 2013. 'Climate Change Justice'. In *The Handbook of Global Climate and Environment Policy*, edited by Robert Falkner, 231–47. Chichester: Wiley-Blackwell.

Page, Edward A. 2016. 'Qui bono? Justice in the Distribution of the Benefits and Burdens of Avoided Deforestation'. *Res Publica* 22 (1): 83–97.

Parks, Bradley C. & J. Timmons Roberts. 2006. 'Globalization, Vulnerability to Climate Change, and Perceived Injustice'. *Society & Natural Resources: An International Journal* 19 (4): 337–55.

Pateman, Carole, & Charles W. Mills. 2007. *Contract and Domination*. Polity Press.

Paterson, Matthew. 2011. 'Selling Carbon: From International Climate Regime to Global Carbon Market'. In *The Oxford Handbook of Climate Change and Society*, edited by John S. Dryzek, Richard B. Norgaard, & David Schlosberg, 611–24. Oxford: Oxford University Press.

People's Agreement of Cochabamba. 2010. World People's Conference on Climate Change and the Rights of Mother Earth, 22 April, Cochabamba, Bolivia. Accessed 27 March 2018. http://pwccc.wordpress.com/2010/04/24/peoples-agreement/

Pettit, Philip. 1997. *Republicanism: A Theory of Freedom and Government*. Oxford Scholarship Online: Oxford University Press.

Pettit, Philip. 2010. 'A Republican Law of Peoples'. *European Journal of Political Theory* 9 (1): 70–94.

Phelps, Jacob, Edward L. Webb, & Arun Agarwal. 2010. 'Does REDD+ Threaten to Recentralize Forest Governance?' *Science* 328: 312–13.

Philpott, Daniel. 1995. 'In Defense of Self-determination'. *Ethics* 105 (2): 352–85.

Philpott, Daniel. 2011. 'Sovereignty'. In *The Oxford Handbook of the History of Political Philosophy*, edited by George Klosko, 561–72. Oxford: Oxford University Press.

Pickering, Jonathan, & Christian Barry. 2012. 'On the concept of climate debt: its moral and political value'. *Critical Review of International Social & Political Philosophy* 15 (5): 667–85.

Pogge, Thomas W. 1989. *Realizing Rawls*. Ithaca, NY: Cornell University Press.

Pogge, Thomas W. 2008. *World Poverty and Human Rights: Cosmopolitan Responsibilities and Reforms*. 2nd Edn. Cambridge: Polity Press.

Pogge, Thomas W. 2011. 'Allowing the Poor to Share the Earth'. *Journal of Moral Philosophy* 8 (3): 335–52.

Posner, Eric A., & Cass R. Sunstein. 2009. 'Should Greenhouse Gas Permits Be Allocated on a Per Capita Basis?' *California Law Review* 97 (1): 51–94.

Posner, Eric A., & David Weisbach. 2010. *Climate Change Justice*. Princeton: Princeton University Press.

Price, Tom. 2002. 'The Canary is Drowning: Tiny Tuvalu'. *Global Policy Forum*, 3 December. Accessed 30 January 2018. http://www.globalpolicy.org/component/content/article/172-general/30312.html

Rao, Narasimha D., & Paul Baer. 2012. '"Decent Living" Emissions: A Conceptual Framework'. *Sustainability* 4 (4): 656–81.

Rawls, John. 1993a. 'The Law of Peoples'. *Critical Inquiry* 20 (1): 36–68.

Rawls, John. 1993b. *Political Liberalism*. New York: Columbia University Press.

Rawls, John. 1999a. *A Theory of Justice*. Revised Edition. Cambridge, MA: Belknap Press of Harvard University Press.

Rawls, John. 1999b. *The Law of Peoples*; with 'The Idea of Public Reason Revisited'. Cambridge, MA: Harvard University Press.

Rawls, John. 2001. *Justice as Fairness: A Restatement*. Cambridge, MA: Harvard University Press.

Raymond, Leigh. 2006. 'Cutting the "Gordian knot" in climate change policy'. *Energy Policy* 34 (6): 655–8.

Reitberger, Magnus. 2017. 'Targeting rents: Global taxes on natural resources'. *European Journal of Political Theory* 0 (0): 1–20.

Risse, Mathias. 2005. 'How Does the Global Order Harm the Poor?' *Philosophy & Public Affairs* 33 (4): 349–76.

Risse, Mathias. 2009. 'The Right to Relocation: Disappearing Island Nations and Common Ownership of the Earth'. *Ethics & International Affairs* 23 (3): 281–300.

Risse, Mathias. 2012. *On Global Justice*. Princeton Scholarship Online: Princeton University Press.

Roberts, J. Timmons, & Bradley C. Parks. 2007. *A Climate of Injustice: Global Inequality, North-South Politics, and Climate Policy*. Cambridge MA: MIT Press.

Roemer, John E. 2003. 'Defending Equality of Opportunity'. *The Monist* 86 (2): 261–82.

Roser, Dominic & Christian Seidel. 2017. *Climate Justice: An Introduction*. London: Routledge.

Rousseau, Jean-Jacques. 1755. 'Discourse on the Origin and Foundations of Inequality Among Men'. In *Rousseau: The* Discourses *and other early political writings*, edited and translated by Victor Gourevitch, 111–88. Cambridge: Cambridge University Press.

Sangiovanni, Andrea. 2007. 'Global Justice, Reciprocity, and the State'. *Philosophy & Public Affairs* 35 (1): 3–39.

Satz, Debra. 1999. 'Equality of What among Whom? Thoughts on Cosmopolitanism, Statism, and Nationalism'. *Nomos* 41: 67–85.

Scanlon, T. M. 1998. *What We Owe to Each Other*. Cambridge, MA: Belknap Press.

Scheffler, Samuel. 2003. 'What is Egalitarianism?'. *Philosophy & Public Affairs* 31 (1): 5–39.

Schrijver, Nico. 1997. *Sovereignty over Natural Resources: Balancing Rights and Duties*. Cambridge Books Online: Cambridge University Press.

Schuessler, Rudolf. 2017. 'A Luck-Based Moral Defense Of Grandfathering'. In *Climate Justice And Historical Emissions*, edited by Lukas H. Meyer & Pranay Sanklecha, 141–64. Cambridge University Press.

Schuppert, Fabian. 2012. 'Reconsidering resource rights: the case for a basic right to the benefits of life-sustaining ecosystem services'. *Journal of Global Ethics* 8 (2–3): 215–25.

Schuppert, Fabian. 2013. 'Collective Agency and Global Non-Domination'. In *Cosmopolitanism versus Non-Cosmopolitanism: Critiques, Defenses, Reconceptualizations*, edited by Gillian Brock, 255–71. Oxford Scholarship Online: Oxford University Press.

Schuppert, Fabian. 2014. 'Beyond the national resource privilege: towards an International Court of the Environment'. *International Theory* 6 (1): 68–97.

Schuppert, Fabian. 2016. 'Carbon Sink Conservation and Global Justice: Benefitting, Free Riding and Non-compliance'. *Res Publica* 22 (1): 99–116.

Sealey-Huggins, Leon. 2017. '"1.5°C to stay alive": climate change, imperialism and justice for the Caribbean'. *Third World Quarterly* 38 (11): 2444–63.

Sen, Amartya. 2009. *The Idea of Justice*. London: Penguin Books.

Shiffrin, Seana Valentine. 2009. 'Reparations for U.S. Slavery and Justice Over Time'. In *Harming Future Persons*, edited by Melinda A. Roberts & David T. Wasserman, 333–9. Dordrecht: Springer.

Shue, Henry. 1992. 'The Unavoidability of Justice'. In *The International Politics of the Environment*, edited by Andrew Hurrell & Benedict Kingsbury, 373–97. Oxford: Clarendon.

Shue, Henry. 1993. 'Subsistence Emissions and Luxury Emissions'. *Law & Policy* 15 (1): 39–59.

Shue, Henry. 1994. 'After You: May Action by the Rich be Contingent Upon Action by the Poor?' *Indiana Journal of Global Legal Studies* 1 (2): 343–66.

Shue, Henry. 1999. 'Global Environment and International Inequality'. *International Affairs* 75 (3): 531–45.

Shue, Henry. 2013. 'Climate Hope: Implementing the Exit Strategy'. *Chicago Journal of International Law* 13 (2): 381–402.

Shue, Henry. 2014. *Climate Justice: Vulnerability and protection*. Oxford: Oxford University Press.

Sidgwick, Henry. 1908. *The Elements of Politics*. 3rd Edn. London: Macmillan.

Simmons, A. John. 1992. *The Lockean Theory of Rights*. Princeton, NJ: Princeton University Press.

Simmons, A. John. 1994. 'Original-Acquisition Justifications of Private Property'. *Social Philosophy and Policy* 11 (2): 63–84.

Simmons, A. John. 1995. 'Historical Rights and Fair Shares'. *Law & Philosophy* 14: 149–84.

Simmons, A. John. 2001. 'On the Territorial Rights of States'. *Noûs* 35 (s1): 300–26.

Simmons, A. John. 2016. *Boundaries of Authority*. Oxford Scholarship Online: Oxford University Press.

Sinden, Amy. 2010. 'Allocating the Costs of the Climate Crisis: Efficiency Versus Justice'. *Washington Law Review* 85: 293–353.

Singer, Peter. 2010. 'One Atmosphere'. In *Climate Ethics: Essential Readings*, edited by Stephen M. Gardiner, Simon Caney, Dale Jamieson, & Henry Shue, 181–99. New York: Oxford University Press.

Smith, Kirk R. 1991. 'Allocating Responsibility for Global Warming: The Natural Debt Index'. *Ambio* 20 (2): 95–6.

Steiner, Hillel. 1977. 'The Natural Right to the Means of Production'. *The Philosophical Quarterly* 27 (106): 41–9.

Steiner, Hillel. 1980. 'Slavery, Socialism, and Private Property'. *Nomos* 22: 244–65.

Steiner, Hillel. 1981. 'Liberty and Equality'. *Political Studies* 29 (4): 555–69.

Steiner, Hillel. 1987. 'Capitalism, Justice and Equal Starts'. *Social Philosophy & Policy* 5 (1): 49–71.

Steiner, Hillel. 1994. *An Essay on Rights*. Oxford: Blackwell.

Steiner, Hillel. 1997. 'Choice and Circumstance'. *Ratio* 10 (3): 296–312.

Steiner, Hillel. 1998. 'Territorial Justice'. In *Theories of Secession*, edited by Percy B. Lehning, 61–70. London: Routledge.

Steiner, Hillel. 1999. 'Just Taxation and International Redistribution'. *Nomos* 41: 171–91.

Steiner, Hillel. 2009. 'Left Libertarianism and the Ownership of Natural Resources'. *Public Reason* 1 (1): 1–8.

Steiner, Hillel. 2011a. 'Sharing Mother Nature's Gifts: A Reply to Quong and Miller'. *Journal of Political Philosophy* 19 (1): 110–23.

Steiner, Hillel. 2011b. 'The *Global Fund*: A Reply to Casal'. *Journal of Moral Philosophy* 8 (3): 328–34.

Steiner, Hillel, & Jonathan Wolff. 2006. 'Disputed land claims: a response to Weatherson and to Bou-Habib and Olsaretti'. *Analysis* 66: 248–55.

Stemplowska, Zofia. 2008. 'What's Ideal About Ideal Theory?'. *Social Theory & Practice* 34 (3): 319–40.

Stemplowska, Zofia, & Adam Swift. 2012. 'Ideal and Nonideal Theory'. In *The Oxford Handbook of Political Philosophy*, edited by David Estlund, 373–90. Oxford: Oxford University Press.

Stilz, Anna. 2011. 'Nations, States, and Territory'. *Ethics* 121 (3): 572–601.

Stilz, Anna. 2013. 'Occupancy Rights and the Wrong of Removal'. *Philosophy & Public Affairs* 41 (4): 324–56.

Stilz, Anna. 2015. Decolonization and Self-Determination. *Social Philosophy & Policy* 32 (1): 1–24.

Survival International. 2009. 'Arrested Penan: "Water from the dam will flood our lands"'. Accessed 3 June 2018. http://www.survivalinternational.org/news/4964

Swart, Neil C, & Andrew J. Weaver. 2012. 'The Alberta oil sands and climate'. *Nature Climate Change* 2: 134–6.

Tabuchi, Hiroko. 2010. 'Japan Recycles Minerals from Used Electronics'. *The New York Times*, 4 October. Accessed 30 January 2018. http://www.nytimes.com/2010/10/05/business/global/05recycle.html?_r=0

Tamir, Yael. 1995. *Liberal Nationalism*. Princeton: Princeton University Press.

Tan, Kok-Chor. 2004. *Justice without Borders: Cosmpolitanism, Nationalism, and Patriotism*. Cambridge Books Online: Cambridge University Press.

The Royal Society. 2009. *Geoengineering the climate: Science, governance and uncertainty*. London.

Third World Network. 2009. Sign-On Letter Calling for Repayment of Climate Debt. Accessed 27 March 2018. https://www.twn.my/announcement/sign-on.letter_climate.dept.htm

Thompson, Janna. 1990. 'Land rights and aboriginal sovereignty'. *Australasian Journal of Philosophy* 68 (3): 313–29.

Tideman, Nicolaus, & Peter Vallentyne. 2001. 'Left-Libertarianism and Global Justice'. In *Human Rights in Philosophy and Practice*, edited by Burton M Leiser & Tom D. Campbell, 443–57. Aldershot: Ashgate.

Tsosie, Rebecca. 2007a. 'Indigenous People and Environmental Justice: The Impact of Climate Change'. *University of Colorado Law Review* 78: 1625–77.

Tsosie, Rebecca. 2007b. 'Acknowledging the Past to Heal the Future: The Role of Reparations for Native Nations'. In *Reparations: Interdisciplinary Inquiries*, edited by Jon Miller & Rahul Kumar, pp. 43–68. Oxford: Oxford University Press.

UN. 1948. 'Universal Declaration of Human Rights'. Accessed 3 June 2018. http://www.un.org/en/universal-declaration-human-rights/index.html

UN. 1958. 'Recommendations concerning international respect for the right of peoples and nations to self-determination'. General Assembly Resolution 1314 (XIII), December 12. Accessed 6 February 2018. http://www.un.org/ga/search/view_doc.asp?symbol=A/RES/1314(XIII)

UN. 1960. 'Declaration on the Granting of Independence to Colonial Countries and Peoples'. Accessed 6 February 2018. http://www.un.org/en/decolonization/declaration.shtml

UN. 1962. 'Permanent Sovereignty Over Natural Resources'. General Assembly Resolution 1803 (XVII), December 14. Accessed 6 February 2018. http://www.ohchr.org/EN/ProfessionalInterest/Pages/NaturalResources.aspx

UN. 1966a. International Covenant on Civil and Political Rights. Accessed 6 February 2018. http://www.ohchr.org/en/professionalinterest/pages/ccpr.aspx

UN. 1966b. International Covenant on Economic, Social and Cultural Rights. Accessed 6 February 2018. http://www.ohchr.org/EN/ProfessionalInterest/Pages/CESCR.aspx

UN. 1972. Stockholm Declaration. Accessed 6 February 2018. http://un-documents.net/unchedec.htm

UN. 1992. United Nations Framework Convention on Climate Change. Accessed 13 February 2018. http://www.unfccc.int/resource/docs/convkp/conveng.pdf

UN. 2007. United Nations Declaration on the Rights of Indigenous Peoples. Accessed 6 February 2018. http://www.un.org/esa/socdev/unpfii/documents/DRIPS_en.pdf

UN. 2016. 'About REDD+'. UN-REDD Programme. Accessed 28 April 2018. http://www.unredd.net/about/what-is-redd-plus.html

UN. n.d. 'Special Rapporteur on human rights and the environment'. Accessed 8 August 2017. http://www.ohchr.org/EN/Issues/Environment/SREnvironment/Pages/SRenvironmentIndex.aspx

UNDP. 2013. 'Ecuador Yasuni ITT Trust Fund'. Accessed 28 April 2018. http://mptf.undp.org/yasuni

UNFCCC. 1991. Negotiation of a Framework Convention on Climate Change. Elements relating to mechanisms. Vanuatu: draft annex relating to Article 23 (insurance) for inclusion in the revised single text on elements relating to mechanisms (A/AC.237/WG.II/Misc.13) submitted by the Co-Chairmen of Working Group II. Accessed 27 March 2018. http://unfccc.int/resource/docs/a/wg2crp08.pdf

UNFCCC. 2012. Ad hoc Working Group on Long-Term Cooperative Action under the Convention; Report on the workshop on equitable access to sustainable development. Accessed 13 February 2018. http://unfccc.int/resource/docs/2012/awglca15/eng/inf03r01.pdf

UNFCCC. 2014. Report of the Conference of the Parties on its nineteenth session, held in Warsaw from 11 to 23 November 2013. Addendum. Part two: Action taken by the Conference of the Parties at its nineteenth session. Accessed 22 March 2018. http://unfccc.int/resource/docs/2013/cop19/eng/10a01.pdf

UNFCCC. 2015. Adoption of the Paris Agreement. Accessed 22 March 2018. http://unfccc.int/resource/docs/2015/cop21/eng/l09r01.pdf

Valencia, Alexandra. 2013. 'Ecuador to open Amazon's Yasuni basin to oil drilling'. *Reuters*, August 16. Accessed 28 April 2018. http://uk.reuters.com/article/2013/08/16/uk-ecuador-oil-idUKBRE97F02L20130816

Valentini, Laura. 2012. 'Ideal vs. Non-ideal Theory: A Conceptual Map'. *Philosophy Compass* 7 (9): 654–64.

Valentini, Laura. 2013. 'Justice, Charity, and Disaster Relief: What, If Anything, Is Owed to Haiti, Japan, and New Zealand?' *American Journal of Political Science* 57 (2): 491–503.

Vallentyne, Peter. 2000. 'Introduction: Left-Libertarianism—A Primer'. In *Left-Libertarianism and Its Critics: The Contemporary Debate*, edited by Peter Vallentyne & Hillel Steiner, 1–20. Basingstoke: Palgrave.

Vallentyne, Peter. 2012. 'Left-Libertarianism'. In *The Oxford Handbook of Political Philosophy*, edited by David Estlund, 152–68. Oxford Handbooks Online: Oxford University Press.

Vallentyne, Peter, & Hillel Steiner (eds.). 2000. *The Origins of Left-libertarianism: An Anthology of Historical Writings*. Basingstoke: Palgrave.

Vallentyne, Peter, Hillel Steiner, & Michael Otsuka. 2005. 'Why Left-Libertarianism Is Not Incoherent, Indeterminate, or Irrelevant: A Reply to Fried'. *Philosophy & Public Affairs* 33 (2): 201–15.

Vanderheiden, Steve. 2008a. *Atmospheric Justice: A Political Theory of Climate Change*. Oxford: Oxford University Press.

Vanderheiden, Steve. 2008b. 'Two Conceptions of Sustainability'. *Political Studies* 56 (2): 435–55.

Vanderheiden, Steve. 2009. 'Allocating Ecological Space'. *Journal of Social Philosophy* 40 (2): 257–75.

Vanderheiden, Steve. 2017. 'Territorial Rights and Carbon Sinks'. *Science & Engineering Ethics* 23 (5): 1273–87.

Vidal, John. 2011. 'Ugandan Farmer: "My Land Gave Me Everything. Now I'm One of the Poorest"'. *The Guardian*, 22 September. Accessed 30 January 2018. http://www.guardian.co.uk/environment/2011/sep/22/uganda-farmer-land-gave-me-everything

Vidal, John. 2013. 'Poor countries walk out of UN climate talks as compensation row rumbles on'. *The Guardian*, 20 November. Accessed 27 March 2018. http://www.theguardian.com/global-development/2013/nov/20/climate-talks-walk-out-compensation-un-warsaw

Wackernagel, Mathis, & William Rees. 1996. *Our Ecological Footprint: Reducing Human Impact on the Earth*. Philadelphia, PA: New Society.

Waldron, Jeremy. 1988. *The Right to Private Property*. Oxford Scholarship Online: Clarendon.

Waldron, Jeremy. 1992. 'Superseding Historic Injustice'. *Ethics* 103: 4–28.

Walmsley, Joel & Cara Nine. 2014. 'The Emergence of Borders: Moral Questions Mapped Out'. *Russian Sociological Review* 13 (4): 42–59.

Watene, Krushil. 2016. 'Valuing nature: Māori philosophy and the capability approach'. *Oxford Development Studies* 44 (3): 287–96.

Watt-Cloutier, Sheila. 2004. Plenary Intervention by Elected Chair of Inuit Circumpolar Conference, 10th COP to the UNFCCC, Buenos Aires, Argentina, 17 December. Accessed 3 June 2018. http://unfccc.int/resource/docs/2004/cop10/stmt/ngo/005.pdf

Wenar, Leif. 1998. 'Original Acquisition of Private Property'. *Mind* 107 (428): 799–820.

Wenar, Leif. 2001. 'Contractualism and Global Economic Justice'. *Metaphilosophy* 32 (1–2): 79–94.

Wenar, Leif. 2008. 'Property Rights and the Resource Curse'. *Philosophy & Public Affairs* 36 (1): 2–32.

Wenar, Leif. 2016. *Blood Oil*. Oxford: Oxford University Press.

WHO. 2018. 'Climate change'. Accessed 28 April 2018. who.int/heli/risks/climate/climatechange/en/

Whyte, Kyle. 2017a. 'Is it colonial déjà vu? Indigenous peoples and climate injustice'. In *Humanities for the Environment: Integrating knowledge, forging new constellations of practice*, edited by J. Adamson & M. Davis, 88–105. New York: Routledge.

Whyte, Kyle. 2017b. 'Indigenous Climate Change Studies: Indigenizing Futures, Decolonizing the Anthropocene'. *English Language Notes* 55 (1–2): 153–62.

Whyte, Kyle. 2017c. 'The Dakota Access Pipeline, Environmental Injustice, and U.S. Colonialism'. *Red Ink* 19.1: 154–69.

Wong, Pak-Hang. 2016. 'Consenting to Geoengineering'. *Philosophy & Technology* 29 (2): 173–88.

Young, Crawford. 1994. *The African colonial state in comparative perspective*. New Haven: Yale University Press.

Young, H. P. 1990. 'Sharing the Burden of Global Warming'. *Philosophy & Public Policy Quarterly* 10 (3/4): 6–10.

Young, Iris Marion. 1990. *Justice and the politics of difference*. Princeton: Princeton University Press.

Young, Iris Marion. 2002. *Inclusion and Democracy*. Oxford Scholarship Online: Oxford University Press.

Ypi, Lea. 2008. 'Political Membership in the Contractarian Defense of Cosmopolitanism'. *The Review of Politics* 70 (3): 442–72.

Ypi, Lea. 2013. 'Territorial Rights and Exclusion'. *Philosophy Compass* 8 (3): 241–53.

Zellentin, Alexa. 2015a. 'How to do Climate Justice'. In *Current Controversies in Political Philosophy*, edited by Thom Brooks, 121–37. New York: Routledge.

Zellentin, Alexa. 2015b. 'Compensation for Historical Emissions and Excusable Ignorance'. *Journal of Applied Philosophy* 32 (3): 258–74.

Index